To the Library of The
General Theological Seminary
with warm regards
and happy recollections.

Arthur Reid. Standish II

Robert Greville, Lord Brooke

Robert Greville

LORD BROOKE

By

Robert E. L. Strider, II

HARVARD UNIVERSITY PRESS
Cambridge, Massachusetts

1 9 5 8

*Publication of this book has been aided by
a grant from the Ford Foundation.*

Library of Congress Catalog Card Number 58–5599

TO

R. E. L. S.
(no lordly prelate)

AND

IN MEMORY OF

M. H. S. AND E. G. S.

PREFACE

Lord Brooke has come into a degree of prominence in recent years as a result of the illuminating research that has been undertaken in the area of the seventeenth century, and specifically into the nature of Puritanism, by such authorities as Arthur Barker, Douglas Bush, William Haller, Perry Miller, A. S. P. Woodhouse, and many others. An individual whose life was itself an embodiment of qualities that made Puritanism a driving force in the shaping of the modern western world, Brooke is an arresting study as a political leader, military commander, philosopher, and anti-prelatical pamphleteer. A biographical and critical investigation of Brooke has long been in order.

It is impossible for the student of the seventeenth century to acknowledge even partially his indebtedness to the hosts of scholars who have provided easier access to its portals. I hope that the notes and bibliography will make that indebtedness more evident than a brief prefatory acknowledgment could succeed in doing. For assistance in my own particular studies, however, I want to express my most profound gratitude to Douglas Bush of Harvard University, whose sage advice and generous criticisms have indeed made this book possible, from his first suggesting Brooke as a rewarding subject for study through each step in its growth.

It is a pleasure to be able at last to acknowledge the financial assistance extended to me from time to time over a considerable period by President Rosemary Park of Connecticut College, in her capacity as administrator of the Faculty Research Fund. I would like also to express my thanks for favors and services over a number of years to many cordially helpful staff-members of the Connecticut College Library, the Harvard College Library, the Houghton Library, the Yale University Library, the Union Theological Seminary Library, the Folger Shakespeare Library, and the Library of Congress, and to University Microfilms of Ann Arbor. Officials of the Harvard University Press for a short but decisive interval have been assiduous in giving advice and valuable help, and I acknowledge gratefully and with respect their ministrations of all sorts that have metamorphosed a manuscript into a book.

I wish to thank a number of publishers for permission to quote extensively from works bearing their imprint or for which they control the rights: the Harvard University Press, Cambridge, for quotations from Perry Miller, *The New England Mind* (1939), and from the Loeb Library translation of the *Confessions* of St. Augustine (1931); the Clarendon Press, Oxford, for quotations from *The Cambridge Platonists*, edited by E. T. Campagnac (1901); Methuen and Company, Limited, London, and G. P. Putnam's Sons, New York, for quotations from G. M. Trevelyan, *England Under the Stuarts* (1926); the Columbia University Press, New York, for the use of the facsimile edition of Lord Brooke's *Discourse Opening the Nature of Episcopacy*, in Volume II of William Haller, *Tracts on Liberty in the Puritan Revolution* (1933–34), as the basis for extended discussion of that work; and the University of Missouri, Columbia, Missouri, for quotations from Volume XIX of the *University of Missouri Studies*, namely, *Marsilio Ficino's Commentary on Plato's Symposium*, translated by Sears R. Jayne (1944). I would like to give credit to the Harvard College Library for reproductions of the title pages of Brooke's two treatises, taken from copies of those works in the Houghton Library.

Two of my colleagues at Connecticut College, Dorothy Bethurum and Rosemond Tuve, have generously read the manuscript at various stages in its evolution, and there is no way to thank them adequately for their penetrating suggestions as well as for their constant interest and encouragement. The errors and infelicities of expression that persist are no fault of my mentors and associates. Former professors, colleagues, and friends have been of substantial assistance of many kinds along the way, and I would like particularly to record my gratitude to Hyder Rollins and the late Theodore Spencer of Harvard University; Walter Houghton of Wellesley College; William Haller of the Folger Library; Paul O. Kristeller of Columbia University; James Baird, F. Edward Cranz, Elizabeth Evans, Hazel Johnson, and Marion Monaco of Connecticut College; Edwin L. Minar, Jr., of DePauw

University; Helen and John Kessler of Cambridge; Nancy Morrow of San Francisco; Ralph Graves of New York; and my sister, Sidney S. Bullock of Charlottesville.

Finally, my wife has endured the rigors of this project with notable fortitude and has performed any number of nameless services in its furtherance, even to the extent of reading and criticizing the manuscript with at least an appearance of cheerful approval. And my children, to whom at the moment the subject would prove more tiresome than it will, I trust, to most, have helpfully tiptoed when tiptoeing was in order, and I owe them a special kind of thanks of their own for accepting gracefully a seventeenth-century member of the family for as long as they can remember.

ROBERT STRIDER

Connecticut College
New London, Connecticut
May 29, 1957

Colby College
Waterville, Maine
November 6, 1957

CONTENTS

Robert Greville, Lord Brooke

Part One

The Life of Lord Brooke

Robert Greville, the second Lord Brooke, had reached only his middle thirties when he was killed at Lichfield in March, 1643. Yet by that time he had become one of the most prominent Parliamentarians in all England. He was a commanding officer in the Parliamentary army, appointed lord lieutenant of Warwickshire and commander of the associated counties of Warwick, Stafford, Leicester, and Derby. He was one of the most articulate as well as recalcitrant members of the House of Lords, and as early as 1639 his name and that of William Fiennes, Viscount Saye and Sele, had become almost synonymous with the idea of resistance to the King. One of the most active among those Puritans who sought to promote settlement in America, he devoted energy and supplied financial backing to at least two colonizing enterprises. He was, furthermore, the author of two literary works of notable significance, one an exposition of the nature of truth, the other an argument against episcopacy. These multifarious activities had occupied a mere fifteen years or less, and it is likely that Brooke would have become highly influential in Parliamentary councils during the crucial six years that were to follow. Indeed, there was a possibility that he might have succeeded Essex as commander in chief of the Parliamentary forces.

But whatever his future might have been, Brooke was a leading Puritan at the time of his death. The record of his life reveals a man of intelligence and enthusiasm and of devotion to his cause. In the year following Brooke's death the moderate spirit of his *Discourse on Episcopacy* was praised by Milton. He might also have praised Brooke as a worthy example of the product of the Miltonic ideal of education: "That which fits a man to perform justly, skilfully, and magnanimously all the offices, both private and public, of peace and war." [1]

[1] John Milton, "Areopagitica," *Works*, Columbia ed. (New York, 1931), IV, 346; and "Of Education," IV, 280.

ANTECEDENTS AND ANTICIPATIONS

The Grevilles were an old family of some distinction. A certain
William Grevile, "a citizen of London, and the flower of the wool-
staplers there," is noted as having once loaned the then large sum
of three hundred marks to King Richard II in 1397.[1] During the
next century the family maintained wealth and prominence, and
in the reign of Henry VIII, through the efforts of Sir Edward
Greville of Milcote, Warwickshire, the Grevilles achieved a liaison
with the ancient houses of Warwick, Willoughby, and Brooke.
This union brought them further honors, the eventual culmination
of which was the elevation of Francis, eighth Lord Brooke, to the
Earldom of Warwick in the eighteenth century. Francis had been
created an Earl, with the title Earl Brooke of Warwick Castle, in
1746; but when in 1759 the Warwick line was terminated by the
death of Edward Rich, Earl of Warwick and Holland, George II
conferred the more illustrious title upon the Earl Brooke.

Sir Edward Greville evidently had prestige at court, for in
1522 he obtained the wardship of Elizabeth Willoughby, "one of
the greatest heiresses then in England." [2] This young lady, whose
ancestry through her father, Edward Willoughby, included the
noble families of Brooke and Beauchamp, and whose lineage
through her mother, Elizabeth Nevile, could be traced to Richard
de Beauchamp, Earl of Warwick, had become the sole heiress of
her grandfather Robert Willoughby, Lord Brooke, and heiress

---

[1] For information about the ancestry of the Grevilles I have drawn heavily on
Collins's *Peerage*, ed. Sir Egerton Brydges (London, 1812), IV, 330–361. Collins
accounts apologetically for the origin of the Greville wealth: ". . . whatever be the
antiquity of this name, it stands on authority too notorious to make the mention of
it indelicate, that the present very honourable, and it may be added, illustrious
house, took their rise, like many others, whose wealth and titles have now been for
ages sanctioned by time, from commerce; and in that line which has ever been the
staple commodity of the country, the woollen trade" (IV, 331).

[2] For genealogical chart, see Appendix.

through her maternal grandmother to manors and lands in Warwick, Worcester, Gloucester, Leicester, Lincoln, Somerset, and
other localities.

Sir Edward intended that his ward Elizabeth should marry
John Greville, his eldest son and heir. Tradition holds, however,
that this was the sequel:

> The Knight made a motion to his ward, to be married to John, his eldest
> son; but she refused, saying she did like better of Fulke, his second son.
> He told her, that he had no estate of land to maintain her; and that he
> was in the King's service of warre beyond the seas, and therefore his
> returne was very doubtful. Shee replyed, and said, that shee had an estate
> sufficient both for him, and for herself; and that shee would pray for his
> safeties, and waite for his coming. Upon his returne home, for the worthy
> service he had performed, he was by King Henry honoured with Knighthood;
> and then he married Elizabeth, the daughter of Lord Brooke's son.[3]

The young Sir Fulke Greville and his bride settled at Beauchamp's
Court, Warwick, and reared a family of three boys and four
girls, of whom the two eldest sons were Fulke and Robert.

Fulke Greville, born about 1525, married Anne Nevile,
daughter of the Earl of Westmoreland. Their only son was Fulke,
afterwards Sir Fulke Greville, the Elizabethan poet who was to
have inscribed on his monument:

Fulke Greville,
Servant to Queen Elizabeth,
Councillor to King James,
and Friend to Sir Philip Sidney.
Tropheum Peccati.[4]

It was he who was to be created in 1621 Baron Brooke of Beauchamp's Court, the old Willoughby title brought into the family
by his grandmother, and who was to adopt his young cousin
Robert to be brought up as his heir.[5]

Robert Greville, the second son of Sir Fulke and Elizabeth

---

[3] Collins, IV, 341, quoting a manuscript, purportedly written in 1644, entitled
"The Genealogie, Life, and Death of Robert Lord Brooke." I have been unable to
trace its present location.

[4] William Camden, *Britannia* (1695), col. 512.

[5] Sir Fulke became Lord Brooke on January 29, 1620/21. See *Calendar of State
Papers, Domestic* (hereinafter cited as *C.S.P.Dom.*), James I (1618–1623), p. 217.
On October 6, 1621, he was made Gentleman of the Bedchamber (*C.S.P.Dom.*,
James I [1618–1623], p. 296).

Willoughby, resided at Thorpe Latimer, Lincoln, and married Blanche Whitney of Whitney, Herefordshire. Their only son, Fulke, born probably in 1575, married Mary Copley of Wadsworth County, York, the widow of one Ralph Bosville. It was their second son, Robert, who was to become the heir of Sir Fulke Greville, the first Lord Brooke.[6]

Fulke, the father of Robert, appears to have inherited and continued to live on the estate at Thorpe Latimer, but little is known of his life and occupation. It is said of Fulke's father, Robert Greville of Thorpe Latimer, that he was a servant to Queen Elizabeth, and that it was through his offices that his nephew, Fulke Greville the poet, was first brought to court when very young.[7] But there is no evidence that Robert's own son Fulke took active part in court life. Apart from indications, based on inconclusive and possibly inaccurate evidence,[8] that he may have attended Cambridge, it may be conjectured that Fulke Greville pursued a placid existence as country squire at Thorpe Latimer. It is hardly likely that there is literal truth in the assertion of a later and avowedly Royalist writer that the father of Robert, Lord Brooke, "in his best Preferment, was but Keeper of one of Sir Fulk Grevill's Parks."[9]

The size of the family of Fulke Greville is not clearly established. The first child, Fulke, baptized in October, 1604, died in September, 1605.[10] A daughter, Dorothy, baptized in September, 1605, eventually married Sir Arthur Haselrig of Noxley (or Noseley), Leicester, and the family tie thus established was no doubt strengthened by the similar political views and parallel active parts played by Lord Brooke and his brother-in-law in the two Houses of Parliament during the early months of the Civil War. In addition to these two children and Robert there are

[6] For genealogical chart, see Appendix.

[7] Wood, *Athenae Oxonienses*, II, 429: "After he [Sir Fulke Greville, the poet] had left the university he travelled, and at his return, being well accomplished, was introduced into the court by his uncle, Rob. Grevil a servant to Q. Elizabeth."

[8] See below, pp. 7–9.

[9] Peter Heylyn, *Cyprianus Anglicus* (1668), p. 47. Heylyn wrote, of course, with malice: in defending Laud against Brooke's remark that one of the main objections to bishops was their low birth (*Discourse on Episcopacy*, ch. 2), it was not unnatural for Heylyn to argue that Brooke's own birth was not as exalted as his title might indicate.

[10] *Lincolnshire Pedigrees*, II, 431.

records of others. An Edward was baptized in January, 1613/14, and in October, 1614, a second Fulke, who died in 1616.[11] Whether Edward lived to maturity is not recorded. According to Collins, Robert and Dorothy "were the only issue of Fulke Greville, Esq.," and the generally reliable article by J. M. Rigg in the *Dictionary of National Biography* accepts this statement.[12] Cokayne's *Peerage* describes as follows the letters patent by which Fulke Greville the poet was advanced to the Barony of Brooke: "On 29 Jan. 1620/21 he was cr. Baron Brooke of Beauchamps Court, co. Warwick, with a *spec. rem.*, failing to the heirs male of his body, to Robert Greville and William Greville, in like manner, sons of Fulke Greville of Thorpe Latimer, co. Lincoln . . ." Collins describes the letters patent in very nearly the same words, but without mentioning the existence of William Greville.[13] It is quite possible that he did exist, for there is a record that in November, 1639, certain lands in Thorpe Latimer were leased to one Will. Bradshawe of Kingistone by William Greville, Esq., of Warwick.[14]

Robert Greville was born probably on January 30, 1608. He was about four years old when the first Lord Brooke adopted him and undertook to provide "for his education and breeding, so as to render him worthy of the estate and dignity he intended to confer upon him." [15] The extent of his education and travel is not fully known, but there is a record that he was registered at the University of Leyden in 1624.[16] His status in the University is not recorded, nor is it known what studies he pursued there, but it would not be surprising to learn that Robert Greville first became sympathetic to Puritanism during his sojourn abroad. The militant Puritan leader John Robinson was, after all, pastor of the Separatist church at Leyden from 1609 to 1625, and it was under his direction that the earliest colonizing efforts of the Puritans in the new world

[11] *Lincolnshire Pedigrees*, II, 431.

[12] Collins, IV, 351; *D.N.B.*, XXIII, 163.

[13] G. E. Cokayne, *Complete Peerage* (1887), II, 32; Collins, IV, 348.

[14] *Lincolnshire Notes and Queries*, VIII (1904–05), 208.

[15] Collins, IV, 351. Regarding the date of his birth, it was on January 30, 1628/29, that Greville vacated his seat in Parliament, "having attained majority," in order to succeed to the Barony of Brooke, left vacant in September when the first Lord Brooke died. Cf. *D.N.B.*, XXIII, 163.

[16] Edward Peacock, *Index to English Speaking Students who have graduated at Leyden University* (London, 1883), p. 43.

were made. It was a group of Robinson's parishioners who embarked in the *Mayflower*.[17] One finds, furthermore, in the register of professors at Leyden during the early years of the century some of the great names among the controversialists whose doctrinal differences led up to the Synod of Dort in 1619: Saravia, Junius, Arminius, Vorstius, Episcopius, Molinaeus, Cunaeus.[18] The memory of the Synod was undoubtedly fresh while young Greville was in residence at Leyden, and its theological repercussions must have been still evident in student dinner conversations in that theologically literate age.

When he returned from his travels Robert Greville attended Cambridge and proceeded to an M.A. in 1629.[19] His college at Cambridge is not known for certain, but there is evidence worth noting concerning the careers of other Grevilles who attended the University. Fulke Greville the poet entered Jesus College as a Fellow Commoner in 1568. Tradition has associated him with Trinity, where his arms appear in a window of a hall; but 'if it is true that he was in residence at Jesus, it may be that some other Greville inscribed the family arms on the window at Trinity.[20] There is a supposition that Fulke Greville of Thorpe Latimer, the father of Robert, attended Cambridge, a supposition apparently based on the evidence of an undated letter purporting to have been written by Robert, Earl of Essex, "to Sir Foulke Greville," addressed "cousin Foulke," and signed "Your affectionate cousin and assured friend, E." The first paragraph reads in part:

> You tell me that you are going to Cambridge, and that the ends of your going are to get a scholar to your liking to live with you, and two or three others to remain in the University and gather for you; and you require my opinion what instruction you shall give these gatherers.

He explains that abridgements and notes made by other people are seldom of value, describes the sort of notes that are of greatest

---

[17] *The Works of John Robinson*, ed. Robert Ashton (London, 1851), xl–xli ff.

[18] Martinus Soermans, *Academisch Register* (Leyden, 1704), sig *4v, pp. 26, 33–37, 49, and elsewhere.

[19] J. and J. A. Venn, *Alumni Cantabrigienses* (Cambridge, 1922), part I, vol. II, 265.

[20] Arthur Gray, *Jesus College* (London, 1902), p. 77. George Dyer in his *History of the University and College of Cambridge* (London, 1814), II, 290, lists Fulke Greville the poet as a member of Trinity.

use, observes that history (particularly the works of Tacitus, Livy, and Thucydides) is superior to other writings for the study of humanity, and concludes by advising his "cousin" to do most of the "gathering" for himself and to use his collectors for "gathering arguments and examples to prove or illustrate any particular position or question." [21] On the basis of internal evidence, certain striking similarities in wording and meaning to passages in *The Advancement of Learning* and the *Essays* (especially "Of Studies"), and the fact that Essex and Bacon were at one time intimate friends, Spedding includes the letter among the works of Bacon, tentatively assigning it to the period 1595–96, and suggesting that Bacon may actually have written all but the opening and closing paragraphs.[22]

For the present purpose, however, the identity of the recipient of the letter is of greater interest than the identity of the author. J. B. Mullinger assumes without question that the Fulke Greville favored by the Earl with a letter of advice was the first Lord Brooke's young cousin who, he says, went up to Cambridge about 1595, and that "it was the son of the recipient of this letter whom Brooke adopted as his own son and heir." [23] But there is certainly no proof that Fulke Greville of Thorpe Latimer was the person concerned. Fulke Greville the poet had another first cousin, also a Fulke Greville, who could conceivably qualify as the recipient of the Bacon-Essex letter. This personage is described by Collins as "Sir Fulk Grevile, Knight, one of the Band of Gentleman

---

[21] Francis Bacon, *Works*, ed. Spedding, Ellis, and Heath (London, 1862), IX, 21–26. See also *C.S.P.Dom.*, James I (1603–10), p. 656.

[22] Spedding calls it "such a letter as Bacon would undoubtedly at this time have wished Essex to write and the Queen to know he had written" (IX, 21). The remark loses some of its weight in that the phrase "at this time" implies acceptance of Spedding's tentative assignment of the letter to 1595–96.

[23] Mullinger, *The University of Cambridge*, III, 83. He uses this letter as basis for a theory that the first Lord Brooke was prompted by the Bacon letter, which may have become "an heirloom in the family," to establish in later years a chair of history at the University. The possibility must of course be admitted, but in view of the fact that neither author nor recipient of the letter can be indisputably identified, the theory can hardly be accepted as historical certainty. The first Lord Brooke was sufficiently familiar with Bacon to have absorbed Bacon's enthusiasm for history directly from his writings or perhaps from his conversation, without resorting for inspiration to a family "heirloom" which was ostensibly if not actually written by one of Bacon's friends. So devious a deduction arouses doubt concerning Mullinger's unsupported assertion that the recipient of the letter was the father of the second Lord Brooke.

Pensioners to King James I," the son of Sir Edward Greville of Harrold-Park, Waltham Abbey, Essex, who was younger brother to Robert Greville of Thorpe Latimer and third son of Elizabeth Willoughby and Sir Fulke Greville of Beauchamp's Court.[24] Even from this scant information it appears that the young Sir Fulke in question took a more active part in court affairs than did Fulke Greville of Thorpe Latimer. Furthermore, in that the latter Fulke was, so far as is known, never knighted, the address of the letter to "Sir" Fulke Greville seems to point more probably to the "gentleman pensioner" as recipient. But whatever the truth of the matter, the existence of more than one Fulke Greville is sufficient to call into doubt the assumption that the father of the second Lord Brooke was the recipient of the Bacon-Essex letter and that he was a student at Cambridge.[25]

Robert Greville's residence at Cambridge is a certainty but one knows nothing of his activities there. One might expect him to have followed his cousin and guardian, the poet, to Jesus College. He probably was an apt student, for though his subsequent writings do not reveal genius, they appear to be the product of a thoughtful mind of considerable erudition. Anthony Wood somewhat grudgingly concedes that he was "educated in academical learning, not in this, but in the other university of Cambridge, (as I have been informed) where being tutor'd, became learned, considering his quality." [26]

In 1628 he was returned to Parliament for the borough of Warwick, but he was not to have the opportunity to remain long in the lower House. In September 1628 Fulke Greville the poet died of a stab wound inflicted by a disgruntled former servant. Since he had maintained what a later Greville has called his "obstinate celibacy" [27] to the last of his seventy-five years, the title

---

[24] Collins, IV, 342 (and see genealogical chart in Appendix).

[25] References to other Fulke Grevilles in later years are plentiful. In 1640 Robert Lord Brooke was ordered to pay five thousand pounds to a Sir Fulke Greville and begged that the decree be reviewed (*House of Lords, Calendar; Historical MS. Commission*, 4th Report, p. 31). Another (or the same) Fulke Greville was granted a pass in August, 1643, for his wife and children to go to Holland (*Lord's Journals*, VI, 171a).

[26] Wood, *Athenae Oxonienses*, II, cols. 432–434.

[27] Frances Evelyn Greville, Countess of Warwick, *Warwick Castle and its Earls* (London, 1903), II, 686. There is no call here for exploring the much-discussed question as to why Sir Fulke Greville never married, but a remark made years

passed, as he had long intended, to his young cousin and adopted
son. When Robert Greville reached his majority, on January 30,
1629, he vacated his seat in the House of Commons and became
the second Baron Brooke.

The new peer of the realm took his duties in public life
seriously. From the time at which he advanced to the barony he
moved rapidly toward the position of national prominence that he
was to attain. In less than twelve years a certain commoner, one
Daniel Brinckley, was to refer to Brooke along with two other
noblemen, the Lord Saye and the Earl of Warwick, as "the best
men of the Kingdom." But it should also be noted that these words
of Daniel Brinckley were overheard by a Royalist informer who
interpreted them as seditious and passed them on to his superiors.[28]

---

later by the Viscount Conway and Killultagh to his nephew, Colonel Edward
Harley, which surely must refer to Sir Fulke, is worth quoting: "It is not good for
man to be alone, he is then worse then he is in the worst company. The happynes
which Doctor Donne found out when his wife lay inne, to be a widower and his
wife alive, was but poetike in respect of what my Lord Brooke, that is old Brooke,
did wish for, to have a sonne living and a wife dead" (in a letter of June 10, 1651:
Historical MS. Commission, 14th Report, Portland MSS., II, 195).

[28] *C.S.P.Dom.*, 1640, p. 377.

II

THE PUBLIC MAN EMERGES

Within a year or two after his advancement to the peerage Brooke married Lady Catherine Russell, eldest daughter of Francis Russell, fourth Earl of Bedford. If it is true that Brooke had already developed Puritan sympathies from his education abroad, his marriage into the family of Bedford, one of the wealthiest and most influential Puritans among the nobility, could only have strengthened them. Although Bedford's interests did not lie in the direction of colonization, he probably approved of the efforts of his son-in-law in that and other Puritan enterprises. It is said that the Earl's bent was for "estate management, fen-draining, and water supply," and in this connection it might be noted that Brooke was commissioned in 1636 along with several other peers to survey the Avon and Team rivers as part of a project to render them navigable.[1]

After his marriage Brooke settled in Warwickshire, where he appears to have occupied several establishments. The first Lord Brooke had invested money in improvements for Warwick Castle, and his young successor may have made it at various times his headquarters. There are, for example, letters, containing court gossip and news of general interest, addressed to him at Warwick Castle in the latter part of 1632 from John Pory in London.[2] As for other residences in Warwickshire with which Brooke was associated, a warrant was drafted in 1629, before his marriage, to

[1] See J. H. Hexter, *The Reign of King Pym* (Cambridge, Mass., 1941), p. 84; H. C. Darby, *The Draining of the Fens* (Cambridge, 1940), pp. 32, 40; T. S. Willan, *River Navigation in England, 1600–1750* (Oxford, 1936), p. 57; and Rymer, *Foedera* (London, 1735), XX, 6–8. Furtherance of the river project was checked by the outbreak of the Civil War.

[2] *The Court and Times of Charles I*, ed. Thomas Birch (London, 1848), pp. 184–206. One of Pory's letters, dated December 6, 1632, contains a vivid account of the death of Gustavus Adolphus. For the history of Warwick Castle during this period see the Countess of Warwick, *Warwick Castle and its Earls*, II, 670–684.

grant to Brooke in fee the manor of Knoll,[3] and during the years 1631–1633 certain records indicate that Brooke rented the estate of Ragley from the Conway family. Ragley lay near Alcester in Warwickshire, and the property of the Conways, Grevilles, and Beauchamps in that district was practically continuous. In the summer of 1631 Brooke wrote to Edward, the second Viscount Conway, concerning the terms of rental and asked several favors. He desired Conway to make the writer's stay at Ragley happy "by placing a faithfull minister there," asked for certain privileges relating to the royalties of hawking, hunting, fishing, and fowling, requested that the pictures be left in the gallery and that he have the use of what furniture was left in the house, and begged that Conway pardon the writer's "young zeal" (possibly referring to the request for the "faithfull minister"). Conway replied that the pictures would be left and that the furniture might be freely used, and that Brooke personally would be conceded the stipulation as to the game provided that the herons be as carefully kept as they were in old Lord Conway's time. The agreement for the letting of the house and park was drawn up and prepared for the signatures of Conway and Brooke by July 25, 1631, but evidently a good deal of argument and dickering over the payment of the rent, the question of whether Brooke might hunt the outlying deer, and so on, continued for long after that date. A "final end with Lord Brooke" seems to have been made in August, 1632, but there is still talk of rent as late as April, 1633.[4]

One of the first matters relating to the public good in which Brooke took part concerned the history lectureship founded at Cambridge by his predecessor. The conditions under which this lectureship was to be managed, as appointed in the first Lord

[3] *Historical MS. Commission*, 7th Report, p. 257a.

[4] For the locality of Ragley see *Conway Letters*, ed. Marjorie Nicolson (New Haven, 1930), p. 7. The allusion to "old Lord Conway" probably refers to the first Viscount Conway, who died in 1630. For the Brooke-Conway negotiations see *C.S.P.Dom.*, Charles I, CXCVI, nos. 84–85; CXCVII, no. 32; CCXXII, no. 35 (V, 1631–33, pp. 112, 120, 404); and CCXXXVI, no. 31 (VI, 1633–34, p. 8). Brooke appears not to have taken the best of care of the Ragley property. In 1637 Conway was apprised that some of the walls were down and had to be repaired to keep out wanderers infected with the plague then ravaging England, and he was told also that the park pales required repair, "having been much neglected from the beginning of Lord Brooke's lease" (*ibid.*, CCCLXXVIII, no. 23, in XII, 1637–38, p. 144).

Brooke's will, were unacceptable to the authorities at Cambridge, and on April 30, 1630, an order, which is self-explanatory, was issued by the King:

Whereas his Matie hath bin informed that the late Lo: Brooke did bestow one hundred pound a yeare for euer to the maintenance of a Lecture for Historie in the Universitie of Cambridge, appointing further by his last will, that his heires and executors should hereafter haue the nomination of the Professor and paie the said Penion to him. Which course of establishemt. the heads of the saied Universitie have considered to be soe unfitt as they choose rather to loose the benefitt of the said Lecture then to receive it upon such termes. His Matie being thereupon humbly besought by all parties interested to interpose his authoritie for accomodation of the businesse is gratiously pleased that the Lo: Keeper and the Lo: Archbishipp of Yorke assisted by such Iudges as they shall thinke good to call, shall upon some certaine day to be appointed by them, heare the said cause in the presence as well of the Lo: Brooke that now is, and the Executors of the Lo: Brooke deceased, as of some of the Heades of the said Universitie and indeauor soe to compose the difference, as the Universitie may not be deprived of the honor and benefitt of the said Lecture.[5]

It may be that the Cambridge authorities were originally put on their guard when the lectures were delivered in 1627–28, at the invitation of the first Lord Brooke, by the first incumbent of the lectureship, Dr. Isaac Dorislaus of Leyden. A letter written from Matthew Wren to Laud, then Bishop of Bath and Wells, within ten days of the delivery of Dorislaus's first lecture, alluded to certain exceptionable remarks by Dorislaus to the effect that "he seemed to acknowledge no right of Kingdomes, but whereof the people's voluntary submission had been the Principium Constitutionum." [6] Wren's zeal in calling these seditious utterances to the attention of the ecclesiastical hierarchy resulted in Dorislaus's being forbidden to continue his lectures. The unfortunate doctor returned to Holland, there eventually to be assassinated by a band of Royalists in 1649, and the attempts to "compose the difference," as the royal injunction directed, were unsuccessful. The young Lord Brooke, whose subsequent differences with high Church and Royalist conservatives were to be both more violent and more consequential, was by right of his title involved in the abortive

[5] Quoted by Mullinger, *The University of Cambridge*, III, 678.
[6] The letter was dated December 16, 1627; see Mullinger, III, 86–88; and *C.S.P.Dom.*, Charles I, LXXXVI, no. 87 (II, 1627–28, p. 470).

litigation. It was probably a long-drawn-out affair, for in February, 1631, Dr. Henry Butts of Corpus Christi College, Cambridge, wrote to the principal secretary to the King, Sir John Coke, who was also Sir Fulke Greville's executor and had been a member of the Parliaments of 1626 and 1628 for the University of Cambridge, begging that the matter be settled before the time limited by the will should have expired.[7] It may have dragged on into 1632, if a letter written by Brooke on June 26 of that year to Coke refers, as it appears to do, to the lectureship:

> The tedious and troublesome business with much patience and industry now at length is waded through. If to the sealing and concluding all you can appoint any time before Saturday, in a place convenient where my Lord of Bedford (a party interested) may wait on you, I shall not fail to attend you.[8]

It may be, as Bullough surmises, that the young Brooke had contested the codicil in Sir Fulke's will referring to the lectureship and that he had no desire to follow Dr. Butts' suggestion that he perpetuate the foundation himself.[9] But whatever the outcome of this meeting, the endowment for the lectures lapsed with the passage of years in some uncertain fashion, lost, as one authority put it, "by the iniquity of the times." [10]

The many-sided liberalism that was to be characteristic of Brooke became evident early in his public career. One of its manifestations was his support of the efforts of two reformers, John Dury and John Amos Comenius, who were laboring to achieve some sort of church unification. Dury came from a pastorate on the Continent to England in 1630, hoping to enlist aid for his projects, and during the next few years made several trips to and from the Continent in pursuit of assistance. In 1633 he wrote to Brooke from Heilbronn, recommending the versatile and energetic Samuel Hartlib, who was to make a virtual profession of this sort of thing, as an agent for the furthering of his objectives in England, and saying that his purpose in writing Brooke was partly "to confirm the good motions, which God

[7] *Historical MS. Commission,* 12th Report, Cowper, I, 427; and see Dorothea Coke, *The Last Elizabethan : Sir John Coke* (London, 1937), p. 144.

[8] *Historical MS. Commission,* 12th Report, Cowper, I, 462.

[9] G. Bullough, "Fulk Greville, First Lord Brooke," *Modern Language Review* 28:17 (1933).

[10] Mullinger, III, 89–90.

hath put in your mind towards us and all others which labour faithfully to promote the publique good, of Gods churches." [11] Dury managed in 1634 to interest Laud in his work, and although it was at Laud's suggestion that Dury was subsequently ordained in the Anglican Church, the Archbishop did not appear disposed to rush into unequivocal cooperation. Such was the approbation of Puritan leaders toward Dury's plans that they were apparently not averse to being allied with the Anglicans in support of them, for a number of their most influential spokesmen, including Brooke, John Pym, Sir Nathaniel Rich, and Richard Sibbes, urged Dury to continue to solicit Laud's help.

Dury and Hartlib were both acquainted with Comenius, and, as one might expect, Brooke's name is to be found among those who to a degree financed and sponsored Comenius's visit to England in the year 1641–42.[12] It was probably not only the religious attitudes of Dury and Comenius, but their educational schemes as well, that attracted Brooke. Comenius himself revealed that Brooke was one of the principal supporters of the proposal for a "Baconian College" in England, along with Dr. Williams the Bishop of Lincoln, Archbishop Ussher, John Selden, and Pym, as well as Hartlib, Theodore Haak, John Pell, and others whose interest in such a project has long been known.[13] From this evidence it seems likely that Brooke, if he had lived through the war and survived the Restoration, would have been associated with the men who formed the Royal Society.

In fact, he may indeed have been associated with some of them before the war. He was acquainted, either personally or through a common friend, Henry Darley, with John Wallis, the mathematician and future secretary of the Westminster Assembly, whose estimate that the men who ultimately formed the Royal Society first began to meet together around 1645 is one of the shreds of evidence concerning the Society's origin most frequently

[11] G. H. Turnbull, *Samuel Hartlib, A Sketch of his Life, and his Relations to J. A. Comenius* (Oxford, 1920), pp. 18, 76–77. See also J. Minton Batten, *John Dury, Advocate of Christian Reunion* (Chicago, 1944), pp. 23, 46–47.

[12] R. F. Young, *Comenius in England* (Oxford, 1932), pp. 42–44. Brooke's association with Comenius is discussed here out of chronological order, but it seems more appropriate at this point than later.

[13] Young, pp. 5–6. Young partially translates the autobiographical fragment of Comenius that was discovered in 1913 (pp. 26 ff.).

cited by historians and scholars in later years as authoritative.[14] Wallis, possibly at Darley's request, was to write the only published contemporary criticism of Brooke's *The Nature of Truth,* a volume entitled *Truth Tried: or, Animadversions on a Treatise published by the Right Honourable Robert Lord Brooke, entituled, The Nature of Truth, Its Union and Unity with the Soule.* This book, written as early as April, 1641, had just gone to press in the spring of 1643 when the news came of Brooke's death. Wallis added to the original impression an epistle addressed to Darley and dated March 11, lamenting the event of a week before, and he appended to the text of his critique an elegy as well.[15] If Brooke had known Wallis, then, in the early 1640's, or earlier, or had known friends of Wallis, it is possible that he knew members of the circle of young intellectuals whose conversations led, indirectly if not directly, to the formation of the Royal Society. In fact, a scholar has recently argued convincingly that through Haak there was a link between the Hartlib-Comenius-Dury group who fostered the Baconian "Invisible College" and the group to whom Wallis refers as having begun meeting about 1645.[16] The fact that Brooke is

[14] John Wallis, *A Defence of the Royal Society* (London, 1678), pp. 7–9; and see also Wallis's account of his own life, written about 1696–97, which reveals further evidence as to the origins of the Royal Society, printed in "The Publisher's Appendix to his Preface," *Peter Langtoft's Chronicle,* ed. Thomas Hearne (Oxford, 1725), I, clxi–clxii. The connection between Wallis and Darley may have arisen from the fact that Wallis was chaplain in the house of Sir Richard Darley in Yorkshire from 1640 to 1642 (*ibid.,* clii).

[15] A postscript to the text of the critique, dated April 10, 1641, contains an outline of Brooke's principal points and of Wallis's objections to them (*Truth Tried,* 1643, p. 108). The elegy appears on sigs. S1–S4v. Brooke may have seen the manuscript, for the epistle addressed to Darley, written after the death of Brooke, suggests that Darley had earlier transmitted it to Brooke: "Sir, The Treatise penned long since at your request, had once passed in another Character through Yours to his Lordships Hand, not then intended to be made publique, nor directed to any other then your own eye; what entertainment it then found (such Candour and Noblenesse dwelt in that Breast) You know as well as I: And now, being oft solicited, as well by you as others, It was a second time Advancing, ambitious again to be made happy by the same Hand; (and indeed I had been extreamly injurious to His Candour, if I should have seemed to decline His Eye and present it to another, who taking liberty sometime to dissent from Others, did with the same freedome allow others to dissent from Him, willing to accept of any Assistance in the search of Truth;) but being there prevented, it is fain to Retreat, and fall back to the same hand where it first lodged, as being, next after his Lordship, due to you . . ." (sigs. A1–A1v).

[16] Miss R. H. Syfret, "The Origins of the Royal Society," *Notes and Records of the Royal Society of London* 5:75–137 (1948). F. R. Johnson, it might be noted, maintains that Gresham College may have been a gathering place for men in-

known to have had connections with both groups further supports the possibility that he had this kind of intellectual interest. Certain Baconian overtones and occasional references in *The Nature of Truth*, too, suggest that Brooke's bent followed scientific as well as theological and philosophical lines.

A person of Brooke's breadth of interest and characteristically Puritan energy was doubtless involved in other activities during the early 1630's, an assumption to which occasional fragments of information give evidence. For example, Brooke's name, along with the names of Bedford and Warwick, is mentioned in a letter of 1634 from one of the Bohemian exiles in London to the consistory of the Dutch Church in Austin Friars. Hartlib is also mentioned, and one surmises a relationship between this affair and Brooke's interest in Dury and Comenius, if not perhaps also some connection through Brooke's associations in the Low Countries.[17] Another tantalizing but inconclusive glimpse of Brooke's range during these years is provided by the report of a government informant in 1633 that he had seen the Dutch Ambassador leaving Brooke House in Holborn after a conference of some sort with Brooke and Saye.[18]

There is one enterprise in which Brooke participated during these years that is fully documented. Brooke joined his efforts to those of Saye, many other Puritan noblemen and members of the lower House in Parliament, adventurers, religious refugees, and London merchants in schemes directed toward the colonization of the Western Hemisphere. One would like to think that something of the spirit of John Robinson had survived in the

---

terested in the "new philosophy" long before the generally accepted date 1645, as given by Wallis; see Johnson, "Gresham College: Precursor of the Royal Society," *Journal of the History of Ideas* 1:413–438 (1940). Miss Syfret does not agree, however, that Gresham College was a "precursor," but feels that it was at the most an early influence (Syfret, pp. 84–85). One might refer also to two informative articles by Dorothy Stimson (since then incorporated in large part in chapters 2 and 3 of her *Scientists and Amateurs*, New York, 1948), in which the author demonstrates that the group who formed the Royal Society consisted primarily of young men and maintains that the Puritan temper often found an outlet in scientific investigation: "Comenius and the Invisible College," *Isis* 23:373–388 (1935); and "Amateurs of Science in Seventeenth Century England," *Isis* 31:32–47 (1939).

[17] *Ecclesiae Londino-Batavae Archivum* (Cambridge, 1897), III (2), no. 2311; briefly noted also by Young, p. 44.

[18] *C.S.P.Dom.*, Charles I, CCXLIII, no. 74 (VI, 1633–34, p. 164).

young aristocrat who had perhaps attended his services a few years before in Leyden. The principal projects with which Brooke was associated were the settlements on Providence and Henrietta Islands in the Carribbean, and the founding of Saybrook at the mouth of the Connecticut River, to which he and Saye gave their names.

Of the two small islands off the coast of what is now Nicaragua, Providence appears to have been first suggested as a likely site for colonization, in a letter from Captain Philip Bell, governor of the Somers Islands, to Sir Nathaniel Rich in April, 1629.[19] Robert Rich, the Earl of Warwick, was impressed to the extent that during that summer he aroused interest in Providence Island among his London friends, some of whom were already associated with him in the Somers Islands Company. An expedition was fitted out and sailed in October. Providence (then called Santa Catalina) was reached around Christmas, a fort was established with a garrison and deputy governor, and with glowing reports the expedition returned to England.

During the summer of 1630 Warwick invited subscriptions, and by fall, when the company was complete and the plague then raging had abated sufficiently for the members to assemble together, they were ready for their first meeting on November 19 at Brooke House. After the election of officers the main business was the increase of the "adventure" of each member from two hundred to five hundred pounds.[20] Brooke was present as one of the "adventurers," and at a meeting three days later he and Warwick were assigned the task of providing arms and ammunition for the company's use. The members numbered twenty, including close friends and associates of Warwick, among whom were the Earl of Holland, Sir Nathaniel Rich, John Dyke, Gabriel Barber, and Sir Thomas Harrington; several influential Puritan leaders both in and out of Parliament, such as Brooke,

---

[19] Arthur P. Newton, *The Colonising Activities of the English Puritans* (New Haven, 1914), p. 31. The relevant sections in the early chapters of Newton and documents recorded in *C.S.P. Colonial*, 1574–1660, comprise the principal sources for information on the Caribbean enterprise.

[20] The officers for the first year were the Earl of Holland, Governor (chosen mainly for his political prestige rather than for his interest in the project); John Dyke, Deputy; John Pym, Treasurer; and William Jessopp (not a member), Secretary. *C.S.P. Colonial*, pp. 121–122.

Saye, Sir Benjamin Rudyerd, Sir Gilbert Gerrard, Sir Edward Harwood, Richard Knightley, Christopher Sherland, and John Pym; and a few other interested citizens, involved perhaps through association with Pym, namely, John Robartes, John Graunt, Oliver St. John, Gregory Gawsell, John Gurdon, and Sir Edmund Moundeford. A patent was granted on December 4, incorporating the group as "The Governor and Company of Adventurers for the Plantation of the Islands of Providence, Henrietta, and the adjacent islands, between 10 and 20 degrees of North latitude and 290 and 310 degrees of longitude." [21]

The financial backing of the Providence company was impressive and the enterprise gave every promise of success, yet it was destined to make little mark on American colonization. It has been observed that an expedition setting out from England at about the same time under humbler auspices for a land with a rigorous and even forbidding climate — the expedition to Massachusetts Bay, led by the comparatively obscure Puritans John Winthrop and John White — was to achieve a brilliant and permanent success, while the portion of the Providence exploit, embellished with the prestige of Warwick's name and substantially backed by some of the most powerful Puritans in the realm, was to be total failure. [22]

Early reports from the settlers there, however, were optimistic: "fruits in plenty; hogs and house fowl thrived; three crops of corn in a year; the tobacco not much, if at all, behind the Spanish." [23] Brooke considered it a sufficiently worthwhile investment to warrant his spending money freely to keep it going, contributing generously whenever extra funds were required, and he remained an active member of the company as long as it amounted to anything at all. To be sure, Brooke's interest in Providence was not entirely financial. As measures against the Puritans at home became more severe the motive for colonization as an escape from persecution by Laud and the King became stronger. Brooke was already under suspicion as early as 1633, and in the next year he suffered along with other landed Puritans

[21] *Ibid.*, 121–123 *et passim.*
[22] Cf. Newton, pp. 49–50.
[23] In a letter of about July 1, 1631, from John Hunt to Brooke. *Historical MS. Commission*, 7th Report, p. 589b.

in the enforcement of the forest laws. A third motive, though not a personal one, for continued support of the company was the traditional hatred of the Englishman since Elizabethan times toward Spain. Providence Island in English hands was a threat to Spanish supremacy in the Caribbean, and as such it assumed greater importance to the English than it merited through its potentialities as a colony.

It was actually the Spaniards who drove the first wedge in the destruction of the Providence adventure. In 1635 some Spanish ships attacked the island, and though they were driven off it began to occur to the Puritan sponsors that the locality might not after all be suitable for permanent and peaceful settlement. Yet it was also clear to them, especially the politically astute Pym, that the continued occupation of Providence gave the English an opportunity to harry the Spanish in what were virtually their own waters. The company accordingly petitioned the King for right of reprisal, which was granted.

At a meeting in January, 1636, Pym reviewed the whole matter and computed the cost of paying off past debts and insuring the proper management of the enterprise in the future at ten thousand pounds. Upon a suggestion that one individual might handle the affair more efficiently than could a committee, Brooke offered to undertake it if he could have sole direction. The adventurers, however, reluctant to give any one member so much control, finally decided to raise the funds in an entirely new stock within two years. Brooke promised in return for a voice in the direction to underwrite whatever portion of the ten thousand pounds of stock should fail to be taken up. But this was a promise he did not fulfill, for when the sum reached thirty-nine hundred pounds he added a thousand and no more. The company continued its efforts for some time longer, though apparently not with unmitigated enthusiasm.[24]

One reason for a lessening of vigor on the part of Brooke and some of the others, especially Saye, was the emergence of another colonizing project to which they decided to devote some of their attention. Warwick, who had first aroused sufficient interest in Providence Island to make it possible to form a com-

[24] Newton, pp. 175–211; and *C.S.P. Colonial*, pp. 180–222.

pany, had also been since 1628 the president of the Council for New England. There were, moreover, close relationships between members of the Providence company and some of the settlers in Massachusetts. There had been talk of Warwick's granting a patent for land on the coast of Connecticut, and on March 19, 1632, this design became an actuality. The company of grantees included several members of the Providence group — Saye, Brooke, Holland, Rich, Knightley, and Pym — and five others, namely, Charles Fiennes, Sir Richard Saltonstall, John Hampden, John Humphry, and Herbert Pelham. The grant covered:

all that part of New-England, in America, which lies and extends itself from a river there called Narraganset river, the space of forty leagues upon a straight line near the sea shore towards the southwest, west and by south, or west, as the coast lieth towards Virginia, accounting three English miles to the league.[25]

It was not immediately enforced; but there is evidence that Brooke and Saye, at least, were shortly after that time occupied with some sort of enterprise in the general New England area. In July, 1633, the Providence company agreed to allow those two noblemen five pieces of ordnance "for their use in New England," and in the same year Brooke, Saye, and some others purchased an interest in settlements in Maine, described merely as "Piscataqua" and "Kenebec." [26] This venture involved them in an unpleasantness with the Plymouth colony, who had evidently had a grant giving them the liberty of sole trade in those areas. When a certain Captain Hockin, in the employ of Brooke and Saye, arrived, with the intention of trading there, at "Kenebec" in a pinnace belonging to the two lords, a dispute ensued in which Hockin and one of the Plymouth men were killed. Brooke and Saye wrote in some anger to the Plymouth governor, observing that if they had chosen to do so they might have dispatched a man-of-war to level the settlement in retaliation, but, pointing out that they had refrained from taking this radical step,

[25] Benjamin Trumbull, A Complete History of Connecticut (New Haven, 1818), I, 495–496.
[26] C.S.P. Colonial, p. 169; and John Winthrop, History of New England (1853 ed.), p. 137.

desiring that justice be done in some other way.[27] Nothing of importance came of this diversion to the north, however, and the tract of land forty leagues westward from the Narragansett remained unexploited.

During 1635 Brooke, Saye, and the rest of the company who had received the charter from Warwick three years before finally took action. Young John Winthrop, lately returned from New England, was commissioned by them to proceed once again to the New World with an expedition and to establish a fort at the mouth of the Connecticut River. Winthrop was prompt to execute this assignment, and in October, accompanied by Henry Vane the Younger, he landed in Boston with "men, ordnance, ammunition, and two thousand pounds sterling." A small boat was sent ahead to the mouth of the Connecticut and fortuitously arrived just ahead of a Dutch party who had planned to land at the same spot. In due course a settlement was founded and named Saybrook, and although living conditions were no easier than in other early New England outposts it appeared that the venture would be successful and permanent.[28]

Meanwhile the political status of Puritans at home in England had deteriorated badly. The forest courts, the controversy over ship money, the generally repressive measures of Laud and his hierarchy, the apparently growing strength of Catholicism, all had contributed to the increasing despondency of the Puritan leaders. Matters were so unpleasant, indeed, that Saye and Brooke began to give serious thought to departing for New England themselves. They and "other persons of quality" accordingly composed a list of proposals that were to be regarded as conditions of their removing to New England and sent the proposals

[27] Winthrop, pp. 155-156, 173-174; see also Bradford, *History of the Plymouth Plantation*, ed. Ford (1912), pp. 175-180.

[28] The commission to Winthrop is reprinted in Trumbull, *Connecticut*, I, 497. See also Trumbull, I, 61; and Winthrop, *History of New England*, I, 203. Regarding young Vane a letter of September 18, 1635, from Sir Gilbert Gerrard to Lord Conway is of interest: "Sir Henry Vane has as good as lost his eldest son, who is gone to New England for conscience sake; he likes not the discipline of the Church of England." *C.S.P. Colonial*, p. 214. Vane's subsequent career, both as governor of the Massachusetts Bay colony, from which office he was removed for defending the rights of Anne Hutchinson, and as a Parliamentary leader during the Civil War and Commonwealth, is well known, perhaps largely because of Milton's sonnet in praise of his statesmanship in 1652.

off to Massachusetts for comment. They were answered largely by John Cotton, who had been in the colony since 1633. In effect the proposals and answers were as follows:

1st Demand: That there be in the commonwealth two ranks of men, gentlemen and freeholders.

1st Answer: Two ranks willingly acknowledged. Hereditary dignity and honor allowed to the former, "unless by the scandalous and base conversation of any of them, they become degenerate." Hereditary liberty allowed to the latter, unless they disfranchize themselves by "some unworthy and slavish carriage."

2nd Demand: That the chief power of the commonwealth reside in the gentlemen and freeholders assembled together, for making and repealing laws.

2nd Answer: Agreed.

3rd Demand: That each rank should have a negative vote in public assembles.

3rd Answer: Agreed.

4th Demand: That the gentlemen should attend parliaments or public assemblies and vote personally, the freeholders by deputy.

4th Answer: The freemen do vote by deputy; the gentlemen vote personally, but only those gentlemen who hold public office. Even in England all gentlemen do not meet and vote personally in parliament.

5th Demand: That the two ranks should meet in two distinct houses.

5th Answer: Approve, but it is not yet so practised.

6th Demand: That there shall be set times for meetings or parliaments, yearly or half-yearly.

6th Answer: They have been meeting quarterly, but when things are better settled, yearly or half-yearly probably will suffice.

7th Demand: That the parliament shall have the power to call the governor and all officers to account.

7th Answer: This is already done once a year.

8th Demand: That the governor always be chosen from the ranks of gentlemen.

8th Answer: Never do otherwise, as for instance, this year (1636), Mr. Vane.

9th Demand: That Lord Saye and Sele, Lord Brooke ("who have already been at great disbursements for the public works in New-England"), and such other gentlemen as they shall take into the company, be admitted for them and their heirs, "gentlemen of the country," but afterwards none shall be admitted into the first rank except by consent by both houses of parliament.

9th Answer: Thankfully acknowledges the great disbursements, and is sure that the two great lords will be received in the wilderness with honor, but the criterion for rank and office is membership in one of the churches. Hereditary honors are all very well, but hereditary power cannot be accepted. "Where God blesseth any branch of any noble or generous family, with a spirit and gifts fit for government, it would be a taking of God's name in vain to put such a talent under a bushel. . . But if God should not delight to furnish some of their posterity with gifts fit for magistracy, we should expose them rather to reproach and prejudice, and the commonwealth with them, if we should call them forth, when God doth not, to public authority."

10th Demand: That freeholders shall have a certain personal estate or shall contribute some proportion to the public charge.

10th Answer: The practice is that freemen are those men who are admitted members of one of the churches (lengthy discussion of this point, answering hypothetical objections).[29]

From the tone of the ninth "demand" it may be imagined that the two lords received the reply with some coolness, indeed perhaps with amazement; and even though as late as September, 1635, there is evidence that they seriously contemplated selling their estates and setting out for the New World,[30] one cannot be surprised that the removal was never to take place. It may be

[29] Thomas Hutchinson, *History of Massachusetts Bay*, ed. Lawrence Mayo (1936), Appendix II, pp. 410–413.

[30] Cf. a letter from Philip Nye to Winthrop, dated September 21, 1635 (the year is regarded as questionable by the editor who reprints it, but the evidence certainly suggests that 1635 is correct), in *Massachusetts Historical Society Collections*, 5th series, I, 213.

that the obvious disagreement between the noblemen and the Massachusetts settlers, stubbornly idealistic yet entitled by their brief experience to their strong opinions on practical politics, was too fundamental to be resolved. Or perhaps it was simply, as it has been suggested, that the Puritan leaders in England became more and more deeply immersed in the ever-growing political problems of the stormy thirties and that the auspicious moment passed by.[31]

Even though the two lords did not remove to New England their relations with the colonists remained friendly, as records of correspondence back and forth attest. A letter from Cotton to Saye in 1636 appears to be continuing an argument, or at least a theoretical discussion, which probably had been begun in earlier letters, on the matter of the mixture of church and state.[32] A letter from Brooke to Winthrop, probably written in 1637, requested that satisfaction be given an emissary of Brooke's, a Mr. Woodcock, who had been prevented by some "Dorchester men" from enclosing a bit of ground; and in March, 1638, a letter from Emanuel Downing to Winthrop alludes to discussions the writer has had with Brooke concerning Winthrop's allowance.[33] Brooke must, furthermore, have retained a respect for Cotton as a theologian, for in *The Nature of Truth* he quotes him with obvious esteem, calling him "Reverend, holy, learned." [34] Yet in time some sort of rift began to be discernible in relations between the New Englanders and the Puritans at home, and one may imagine that the trouble stemmed in part from the answers to the "demands." In March, 1640, for example, Governor Winthrop wrote Saye a rather stiff letter alluding to reports that

[31] Newton, p. 184, subscribes to the latter hypothesis. The "democratic" tendencies in Puritan New England, even though Winthrop called the Massachusetts social structure a "mixt Aristocratie," were nevertheless quite pronounced, Professor Parrington to the contrary. Some of these tendencies are suggestively analyzed, with reference to the "ten demands," by B. Katherine Brown, "A Note on the Puritan Concept of Aristocracy," *Mississippi Valley Historical Review* 41:105–112 (1954–55).

[32] Hutchinson, Appendix III, pp. 414–417. This letter is also cited in the article by Miss Brown (see preceding note).

[33] *Massachusetts Historical Society Collections*, 5th series, I, 240–241 and 256. Woodcock may be the individual by that name recommended by Brooke for a position in the Providence Company in 1634; see *C.S.P. Colonial*, p. 176.

[34] Brooke, *The Nature of Truth*, pp. 152–153.

Saye was discouraging colonists from emigrating to New England. Winthrop pointed out "how evident it was, that God had chosen this country to plant his people in, and therefore how displeasing it would be to the Lord, and dangerous to himself, to hinder this work." [35] Saye replied in July, upbraiding Winthrop for drawing a comparison between the New England colonists and the Children of Israel, and tartly insinuating that the New England settlers had not restrained themselves from disparaging the colony at Providence Island. With some justice he maintained that the New England climate was not all it might be. "Is thear any impiety in me," he rumbled, "to move men to live in a warmer climate & in a more frutefull soyle, when it is fre for them to make theyr choyse?" The letter concludes with some invidious comparisons between the governmental structure in Massachusetts and the kind that Saye considered desirable. Winthrop's reply is unfortunately not preserved, but his jottings on Saye's letter are. What good, he asks, has ever come of the Providence enterprise, what happiness have any of the settlers found there, what do they live on? Exactly what has become of the one hundred and twenty thousand pounds the lords of the company have poured into their project?

Brooke's interest, like Saye's, had wandered away from the northern settlement after 1636, back to Providence Island. After the abortive exploratory soundings of the welcome they might expect in New England there are indications of serious intention to remove to Providence. In February, 1638, it was decided at a meeting of the company to dispatch by the end of March an advance party of a hundred and twenty men and their leaders to proceed to the Caribbean and put everything in readiness for the arrival of such members of the company as were expected, among whom were Warwick and Brooke. At a meeting on March 20, a new "adventure" of six thousand pounds was underwritten, to which Brooke, probably in the confidence that some of the company really would be going over, contributed two thousand. [36]

---

[35] A record of the interchange between Winthrop and Saye may be found in *Massachusetts Historical Society Collections*, 5th series, I, 297–303.

[36] *C.S.P. Colonial*, pp. 263–266. Warwick, Saye, Mandeville, and Pym each contributed a thousand pounds to make up the six thousand.

But the lords did not go over, and Brooke's two thousand pounds evidently went the way of the hundred and twenty thousand to which Governor Winthrop had referred so acidly in his memorandum. Meanwhile George Fenwick, who long ago had been left in charge of the settlement at Saybrook, grew weary of awaiting the arrival of the noblemen who had founded the outpost at the mouth of the Connecticut. Burdened by expenses and discouraged by the obvious lack of concern in England for his plight, Fenwick managed in 1644, after considerable bargaining with his hardheaded neighbors up the river, to transfer the title of the Saybrook settlement to the Connecticut colony centered at Hartford.[37]

Although Brooke himself was not to live to hear of this final dissolution of the colony to which he gave his name, it was apparent for a number of years before his death that Saybrook was being abandoned by its principal promoters. It is unlikely, however, that Brooke was giving the matter much thought. Political affairs in England had become more turbulent, and Brooke and Saye were soon involved in matters of greater moment and more permanent significance than the colonization of either Saybrook or Providence Island. The stand that they were to take against the King in the spring of 1639 marked them as figures of consequence in the conflict, both ideological and military, that was soon to erupt.

[37] Trumbull, I, 117–118; and Newton, p. 185.

III

NOISES AND HOARSE DISPUTES

As the decade of the personal rule of Charles I drew toward
a close, public indignation over some of the more overt per-
formances of the regime began to be manifest. The pillorying
of those three heroes of the populace, Prynne, Burton, and Bastwick, in 1637, and the more violent retribution shortly afterward
meted to "Freeborn John" Lilburne only solidified the hostility
that the ship-money edicts had aroused. A more wary and less
egocentric monarch might have taken warning from public
demonstrations of such feeling as to alarm the royal advisers,
but Charles continued in his stubborn course. Consequently,
what had been discontent among Puritan leaders was translated
into active resistance, and the underground opposition that had
taken the form of secret conferences with foreign diplomats or
the quiet encouragement of emigration to the New World became
open defiance.

By 1640, furthermore, the presses were inundated by the
rushing deluge of tracts and pamphlets, some in protest against
the authoritarian excesses of the Erastian officialdom, some in
furious condemnation of episcopacy, some in moderate appeal
to reasonableness. Bastwick's *Letany* (1637) was a best-seller,
and at the other end of the scale Chillingworth's *Religion of
Protestants* (1638) had surely reached an audience. The controversy between Bishop Hall and the Smectymnuans had not
yet burgeoned but the way toward it was being prepared. Milton
had not yet been induced to leave his "calm and pleasing soli-
tariness . . . to embark in a troubled sea of noises and hoarse
disputes," [1] but it was not to be long that he could remain silent.

Brooke was no Milton, certainly. Almost exactly of an age

---

[1] Milton, "The Reason of Church Government," *Works*, III, 241.

with Milton, Brooke was by 1640 a public figure whose activities had already revealed many interests and a capacity for action that Milton had not up to that time demonstrated; and although his erudition is witness to his having read widely, there had been for him no Hortonesque retreat into the quiet and still air of delightful studies during the years following his residence at Cambridge. Nor was he imbued with such a sense of dedication for diviner pursuits that participation in the political melee would represent an irksome interruption. Yet Brooke resembled Milton in the one respect, as did a great many other prominent people, that he felt driven during these violent months to have recourse to print to express his apprehensions and hopes arising from the disparity between things as he thought they should be and things as they were. For Milton such a pursuit meant laying aside the poet's singing robes and descending from the high region of his fancies into the cool element of prose; for Brooke it meant no more than partial withdrawal from the forum of active controversy for a time. But for both it represented an irresistible compulsion to nurture the common good. No Puritan could remain deaf to the calling, and to Brooke it may have seemed that the words of a respected and vigorous leader like himself, prominent enough to have been labeled one of the "best men in the kingdom" on the one hand, one of the two "positive enemies to the whole fabric of the church" on the other,[2] and a person to whom one Puritan theologian already had dedicated a pamphlet,[3] might be heard above the uproar. The first of his treatises was not ostensibly composed for publication, the second was; but both exemplified the views of a "mild and peaceful" proponent of moderation and unity, though these views were uttered with the decision of one whose beliefs were firmly grounded, in a moment of history charged with ominous currents of discord.

It was the insistence of the King to force the Scottish kirks to use the Book of Common Prayer that precipitated the first open rupture between His Majesty and the Puritan noblemen. Al-

---

[2] For the first remark, see p. 10 above; for the second, see Clarendon, *History of the Rebellion* (1826 ed.), I, 409. The other "positive enemy" was Saye.

[3] Thomas Goodwin, *A Childe of Light Walking in Darknesse*. See below, p. 115, n. 64.

though there were no military defeats in the minor conflict of 1639 known as the First Bishops' War, which the King's intransigeance on this matter brought on, the results for Charles were in the long run disastrous. His prestige north of the Tweed was damaged by his powerlessness to force any more decisive a settlement than the inconclusive Treaty of Berwick in June; but the damage to his prestige at home was incalculable, for the obvious disaffection of the nobility toward the Scottish enterprise attested openly to the King's waning strength with those whose support of his policies should have been the most assured. As Gardiner points out, some of the nobility could see that the subjection of the Scottish covenanters would deepen their own subservience to the King, and their interest in the success of the expedition northward was less than lukewarm.[4]

Charles attempted in April of that spring, by proposing a military oath, one of the clauses of which required each nobleman to agree to support the King "to the utmost hazard" of his "life and fortune," to force the hand of those who had shown hesitance in coming to his aid. Even some of the more loyal balked at this requirement, and the phrase was changed to read "to the utmost of my power and hazard of my life." This alteration satisfied those peers who were worried about the likely drain on their personal estates, and the oath was generally taken. There were, however, two notable exceptions. Saye and Brooke refused the oath, just as they had earlier refused to fight under any circumstances for the King in Scotland; and as neither "example nor persuasion" could move them to swear, both were taken into custody.[5]

The defection of Saye and Brooke was hardly unexpected. Their close association in Puritan enterprises, especially their efforts to promote colonization abroad, was well known, and both had long been looked upon warily by the Royalists. Their unfavorable reaction to the King's campaign in Scotland had already been anticipated by observers around the court. On February 20 William Montagu had discussed in a letter to Lord Montagu a request that the King was making of the nobility

[4] S. R. Gardiner, *History of England, 1603–1642*, IX, 11, 29.
[5] *C.S.P.Dom.*, Charles I, CCCCXVIII, no. 99 (XIV, 1639, pp. 96–99).

for horses to be used in the campaign, speculating as to which, if any, of the lords would refuse to contribute the required number: "I think it is hard to certify your Honour what Lords refuse; very few, if any; they talk my Lord Sey and my Lord Brooke, and some of that knott, will not. . ." [6] Another request of the King is described in a letter of February 26 from Edward Reed to Lord Conway:

> The King continues his journey to York. On the 18th March his household moves, and on the 27th himself, where his great army will attend him, and all the Lords upon his commands by letter attend him, but some few not able . . . Lord Brook stands alone, and refuses to attend unless it be adjudged he should by Parliament.[7]

Saye also had objected, but had written on February 20 that he would attend the King; and Reed did not know that on the twenty-fourth Brooke had likewise agreed. Brooke wrote that although he did not feel obliged to attend the King unless Parliament should request him to do so, he would if commanded attend the King in any part of the kingdom of England.[8] Both lords, then, had joined the King at York, but neither had any intention of fighting in Scotland.

Public reaction to the refusal of the pair to take the oath of April 21 was divided according to the Party line. Edward Reed observed that the lords had done amiss,[9] and the attitude of most Royalists was simply that Saye and Brooke were two good men who unfortunately had been under evil influences. The Puritans throughout England generally commended them for the refusal. Robert Woodford, Steward of Northampton, recorded in his diary that "the godly and gracious Lord Sea and Lord Brooke are committed at Yorke for refusing an oath." [10] It was increasingly clear that the two lords were becoming symbols for a cause.

Charles doubtless was nettled at the turn of events but he acted promptly. A set of questions was propounded to the two recalcitrant noblemen:

---

[6] *Historical MS. Commission,* 15th Report (Montagu House Papers), I, 278.

[7] *C.S.P.Dom.,* Charles I, CCCCXIII, no. 92 (XIII, 1638–39, p. 506).

[8] *Ibid.,* CCCCXIII, no. 117 (XIII, 1638–39, p. 516).

[9] *Ibid.,* CCCCXIII, no. 92 (XIII, 1638–39, p. 506).

[10] *Historical MS. Commission,* 9th Report, II, 498b.

(1) Whether will you attend the King's Majesty's person wheresoever he goes, and whether at your own cost or His Majesty's?
(2) Whether do you think the King hath just cause of war?
(3) Whether do you think the taking of castles, crowns, and sceptre be treason or not?

Brooke answered in this vein:

(1) To the first I will attend the King's person wheresoever he goes, but for the charge I leave to His Majesty's pleasure.
(2) I hold rebellion to be a just cause of war, but whether the fact of the Scots be so or no, doth not yet appear to me.
(3) If they have infringed the laws of the land, I hold it high treason, and will in person and fortune hazard myself against them, but if they have not I hope His Majesty will not.

The reply of Saye, though a bit more voluble, was substantially the same:

(1) To the first I conceive as I am a subject and peer of this kingdom, I am at liberty by the laws as being not enforced out of the county where I dwell, except it be an urgent occasion only, as the coming of a foreign enemy unto the land, but yet out of the affection and duty I owe unto His Majesty, I shall be ready to attend His Majesty's person, and as for the charge I refer to His Majesty.
(2) I do not know their government and laws, nor what their proceedings have been, whereby I may be able to give my judgment, but if their intentions and proceedings were to cast off the King's authority and to set up another government, and make religion only a pretence unto this end, I abhor their intentions and proceedings, and think this way a just cause of war.
(3) I do not know what is treason in the kingdom of Scotland, but if they did it with the aforesaid intentions, it were treason in the kingdom of England.[11]

These answers were hardly satisfactory to Charles, but he could do no more than have the lords arrested and their studies searched. The King apparently hoped to find some legal ground for punishment. On the day the oath was first refused he had asked of Secretary Windebank "whether a Lord is not censurable who refuses to serve him in wars out of the kingdom, when offered sufficient pay." The Crown Attorney and Solicitor re-

---

[11] The questions and answers are given here as they appear in the House of Lords Calendar, *Historical MS. Commission*, Appendix to the 4th Report, p. 23.

plied through Windebank that they could not be punished under that indictment, but suggested as an alternative that they might legally be fined if they had arrived at York without proper military equipment. As no further action was taken it may be assumed that the peers had seen fit to comply in every respect with the letter of the law, and after about four days' confinement they were given their liberty.[12]

The Treaty of Berwick ended the abortive hostilities, and for the time being Scotland achieved the nominal abolition of episcopacy, but the uneasy truce had little chance of enduring. The year that followed saw England torn with dissension and the star of Charles decline. The rise of Wentworth, who became Earl of Strafford in January, 1640, served to widen the growing chasm between the King and the liberal minority among the nobility. Charles and his advisers appear generally to have underestimated the power of the opposition to their policies. This error in judgment extended to both civil and ecclesiastical matters, and the seriousness of his miscalculation was revealed to the King only after he had called the Short Parliament, the purpose of which was, in his eyes, to provide money for the coming renewal of hostilities with Scotland.

Parliament met in April and immediately showed an unmistakable indisposition to fight Scotland. Furthermore, the early speeches of this Parliament revealed a strong feeling against bishops, a mood that seemed as pronounced in the Lords as in the Commons. On April 21 Bishop Hall was indiscreet enough to call Saye one who "savoured of a Scottish Covenanter," and was quickly forced to apologize.[13] Three days after that incident twenty-five minority members of the Lords, including, as one might by this time expect, Brooke and Saye, voted that civil and religious grievances should have precedence over matters that concerned the King's supply. The atmosphere did not clear, and when it was finally plain to the King and to Strafford, on whose advice the Parliament had been called, that the money would not be forthcoming, and that furthermore this Parliament under

[12] *Clarendon State Papers, Calendar*, II, 38; and see C. H. Firth, *The House of Lords During the Civil War* (London, 1910), p. 65.
[13] Gardiner, IX, 107.

Pym's leadership was raising the question of the powers of Parliament in opposition to the powers of the sovereign, the King dissolved the Houses. The session had lasted a mere three weeks, until May 5, and the dissolution even so barely forestalled a petition that Pym was preparing against the Scottish war.[14] The very next day a number of the Puritan leaders, including Warwick, Saye, Brooke, Pym, Hampden, and Sir Walter Earl, toward whom Royalist resentment had been growing apace had "all their papers taken from them." Among Brooke's documents were petitions from "silenced ministers" complaining of grievances, and a discourse "between Mr. Cotton, a minister in New England, and Mr. Bull, concerning the English Church Liturgy, one maintaining it against the other." [15]

With all his active participation in Parliamentary controversy, Brooke was not neglecting his intellectual life. Not only was he perusing disputes over the liturgy, but he was also beginning to set some of his own reflections to paper. It is likely that Brooke composed, or at least completed, his first pamphlet, *The Nature of Truth*, during the relative political lull between the Short and Long Parliaments in the summer of 1640. This treatise was a philosophical justification of unity in morals and politics, an appropriate endeavor for a speculative individual in that period of discord. Certain internal evidence suggests 1640 as the time of its composition, and it was ready for publication in November.[16]

[14] *Lords Journals*, IV, 67; and Gardiner, IX, 109, 117.

[15] *C.S.P. Colonial*, p. 312. As for the date on which the seizure took place, the information appears in the Rossingham News Letter for May 12, wherein the event is dated as "Wednesday last." On Gardiner's authority that May 3 was Sunday (Gardiner, IX, 112), May 12 was Tuesday, and "Wednesday last" was May 6, the day following the dissolution. See also *C.S.P.Dom.* Charles I, CCCCLIII, no. 24 (XVI, 1640, pp. 152–153).

[16] An allusion at the end of *The Nature of Truth* concerns a "Great Reader" who "hath Lynx his eyes, yet using overmuch the Septuagenary Spectacles of antiquate Antiquity" (p. 180). This passage would appear to refer to Bishop Hall, whose *Episcopacy by Divine Right Asserted* had been registered in February; who was about seventy years of age at this time; whose "Lyncean eyes" are remarked upon by the Smectymnuan collaborators in *A Vindication* (p. 14), and by Hall himself in *A Short Answer to the Tedious Vindication* (p. 22) in the following year. This evidence is not incontrovertible, of course. But the fact that Brooke quotes Suckling's *Aglaura*, published in 1638, suggests a date at least later than that (see *Nature of Truth*, p. 41); yet even there one must admit that Brooke might have read the play in manuscript before its publication, for he does not quote it as it

If one is to believe a remark by "J. S." (probably John Sadler) in the preface to the reader, Brooke wrote it not for publication but as a "Letter to a private Friend." Indeed, continues Sadler, "since its first writing, and sending, 'twas never so much as perused, much lesse, refined, by its Noble Author."[17] Brooke did move among intellectuals who were concerned not only with specific action and concrete reforms but who, like Hartlib and Comenius, could speculate and theorize on education and the nature of man. In such society and in an age when Sir Kenelm Digby could sit all night penning his observations upon Browne's *Religio Medici* at one breath, letters to private friends of the scope of *The Nature of Truth* were not unheard of.[18]

During the summer months Brooke was also actively concerned in Scottish affairs. As another war appeared more and more imminent an interchange of secret messages between the Scots and some of the English leaders grew to voluminous proportions. One of these messages, from Johnston of Warriston to Lord Savile, written on June 23, became notorious. In it the Scots asked, among other things, for assurance that some of the pro-Scottish lords would help finance, or even join, the invading army then being prepared under Leslie. An answer forwarded on July 8, signed by Savile and six others, Bedford, Essex, Brooke, Warwick, Scrope, and Mandeville, made it clear that the lords did not intend to commit treason, but indicated their continuing support of the Scottish objectives in an honorable manner.[19] As the two countries moved more openly toward war, meetings of the Puritan lords were held at the seat of Saye near Banbury, at Broughton Castle, and elsewhere in that vicinity.[20]

When hostilities finally began, if so farcical a performance as the Second Bishops' War should be dignified by that name,

---

appears in print. That he was acquainted with some of his sources in manuscript is indicated by his quoting Daniel Cawdrey's *Sabbatum Redivivum*, which was not published until 1645 (see *Nature of Truth*, p. 152). As for the publication date of *The Nature of Truth*, the required imprimatur affixed by John Hansley, Prebendary of Holborn, in the name of the Bishop of London, was dated November 19 (*Nature of Truth*, sig. A9v).

[17] *The Nature of Truth*, sigs. A8–A8v.
[18] This treatise will be discussed fully in Part II.
[19] Gardiner, IX, 178–179.
[20] Alfred Beesley, *History of Banbury* (London, 1841), p. 295.

the Parliamentarians were ready with the measure that they had presumably decided upon. On August 20, the summer having worn on with relations worsening daily, the Scots crossed the Tweed with a well-disciplined army in which morale was high. Charles left London the same day and reached York on the twenty-third, where he found his adherents in a state of general demoralization. There was reason, for in military affairs the Royalist cause was going badly; within a week of the arrival of the King they became markedly worse, for the Scots went on to drive the English under Conway from Newburn Ford above Newcastle, and on the thirtieth Newcastle was in Scottish hands. The royal government became confused and distraught, and even Strafford, although he continued to keep up a cheerful front, was discouraged.[21]

It was at this juncture that the King received a petition from twelve lords, including Brooke, signed on the twenty-eighth, which enumerated the grievances of the times and requested that a parliament be summoned to take up such matters and to make a treaty with the Scots.[22] Meanwhile petitions were beginning to be circulated in London among the clergy and the citizens, the burden of which was similar to that of the petition of the peers. When in due course all these came to the attention of the King, it became impossible for him to resist any longer the cry for a parliament. A commission of sixteen peers, among whom were Brooke and several other Puritan leaders, was nominated to treat with the invaders. Deliberations began on October 2, and by the end of the month the Treaty of Ripon had been concluded. Scottish demands were heavy: the payment of a high indemnity, and occupation of the northern counties by a Scottish army maintained daily at English expense, until the terms had been fully met.[23] Yet there was no choice but to accept the proposal, for such troops as Charles and Strafford could muster were themselves on the edge of revolt and were certainly not disposed to fight for a cause that seemed to many of them dubious at

[21] Gardiner, IX, 193–195.

[22] *C.S.P.Dom.*, Charles I, CCCCLXV, no. 16 (XVI, 1640, pp. 639–640). The petition may be found in Rushworth, III, 1260, and in Rymer, *Foedera*, XX, 435.

[23] Gardiner, IX, 207–215. See also *Notes on the Treaty of Ripon*, Camden Society Publications (London, 1869).

best. The Second Bishops' War was settled, and not only was the English Government discredited by the settlement, but the King had had to call upon those Parliamentary leaders who were hostile to his policies to assure any solution at all. Finally, on November 3, Parliament was called once more, in the assembly to be known throughout history as the Long Parliament. As Trevelyan put it, "the Short Parliament had been called to pay for the conquest of the Scots, but its more famous successor was called to buy them out of England." [24]

The mood of the lords at the very outset was hardly one of meekness. On November 10, when the new Parliament was but a week old,

> It was moved, That whereas Two Peers of this High and Honourable Court have had their Studies and Pockets searched for Papers, that it may be considered whether it be not a Breach of the Privileges of a Peer of the Kingdom, especially it being done presently after the Dissolution of the last Parliament, and within the Time of Privilege of Parliament.

Warwick and Brooke were asked to "declare the manner" of the event, and further investigation revealed that the warrants for the searches had been signed by Windebank and Vane, Secretaries of State. The Lords protested to Commons that two of their members had infringed the privileges of the upper House, and one unfortunate lesser official was committed briefly to the Fleet.[25] The matter went no further, but it is interesting as a portent. The Lords were serving notice that there would be no more trifling.

It is understandable that a minor matter like the infringement of privilege should have been relegated quickly to the background in that stormy month. Both Lords and Commons were shortly embroiled in a situation of far greater consequence, the impeachment of Strafford, who was by the twenty-fifth of November a prisoner in the Tower. His speedy arrest showed conclusively that the Long Parliament was conscious of its power to a degree that had not been seen in Westminster before. Not only did this Parliament have popular support, but it was in effect backed up by armed force. The Scottish army encamped

---

[24] Trevelyan, *England Under the Stuarts*, p. 194.
[25] *Lords Journals*, IV, 86b. See also *d'Ewes Journal*, November 10, 1640.

in the north was kept from invading England further only by
payments of eight hundred and fifty pounds per day, in accord-
ance with the terms of the Treaty of Ripon. Charles depended
on the will of Parliament for the money. If Charles lost the mone-
tary support of Parliament the Scottish army would march. Parliament therefore held a whip, in the form of a foreign army, over
the head of its King, a situation probably unprecedented in England or anywhere else.[26] Not only that, the leaders were at the
same time quite aware of this power and certain that there was
no danger this time of sudden dissolution. It is no wonder that
events moved swiftly.

The impeachment of Laud soon followed that of Strafford.
Meanwhile the city of London took a direct hand in governmental affairs; on December 11 a petition signed by fifteen
thousand Londoners urging church reform and the abolition of
episcopacy, "with all its roots and branches," was presented to
the Commons.[27] Agitation by adherents of both sides became
increasingly violent. In January a congregation of Separatists in
Southwark was interrupted during a secret devotional meeting
and some of its members were imprisoned and sent before the
Lords; on the next Sunday several peers, probably including Saye
and Brooke, visited the scene in Southwark and contributed to
collections for the poor.[28] The case against the bishops became
allied with the case against the Book of Common Prayer and
other institutions of prescribed worship, and debate in Parliament for the next few months centered on ecclesiastical affairs,
even as appropriate punishments were being devised for the arch
antagonists.

The part played by Brooke during these debates and during
the trial, passage of the Bill of Attainder, and finally the execution of Strafford in May, cannot be fully charted but it can be
imagined; it is certain that he did not remain silent. For example,
Sir John Coke the Younger reported in a letter to his father dated
March 13–14, in which the principal news concerns the trial of
Strafford, the following episode:

[26] Gardiner, IX, 219.
[27] Gardiner, IX, 247; also Trevelyan, 205–206.
[28] Gardiner, IX, 266–267.

The Lord Brooke was called to the bar yesterday by the Earl of Bath, but excused by the Earl of Essex. The exception that Bath took was that in a speech he mentioned these heads, viz., God, the Parliament and the King, putting the king after the Parliament.

Coke remarks also in the course of the letter that Bath was "a very good friend to the Bishops." [29] The interchange may have come to be regarded as a standing joke. In the following July Edward Nicholas wrote to Sir John Pennington concerning rumors that the King, anxious to regain the confidence of Parliament after the execution of Strafford and desperately casting in every direction, might offer some of the major offices at court to members of the opposition. He wrote that Saye was rumored to be the next Lord Treasurer; Hampden, Chancellor of the Duchy; Pym, Chancellor of the Exchequer; Holles, Principal Secretary of State; and Bath and Brooke members of his Majesty's Privy Council.[30] Gardiner appears to have accepted these rumors soberly at face value,[31] and the possibility that they were genuine must be admitted; but the inclusion of Bath and Brooke in such close conjunction would suggest that Nicholas's letter was at least in part jocular. Whatever it may have meant, it is certain that throughout the debates on episcopacy Brooke was distinctly no "friend to the Bishops."

Indeed, he had undoubtedly been following the furor in the press that spring over episcopacy with the keenest attention. Bishop Hall was already the semiofficial spokesman for the Anglican position, by virtue of his *Episcopacy by Divine Right Asserted* of the previous year, when his *Humble Remonstrance* was printed in January, 1641. The pamphlet was in appearance a slight and rather innocuous publication, but it succeeded in stirring up all sorts of latent sparks, for replies and counterreplies, vindications and animadversions, followed it thick and fast. By the late summer of 1641 the Smectymnuan *Answer*, Hall's *Defence*, the Smectymnuan *Vindication of the Answer*, and Hall's *Short Answer to the Tedious Vindication* had appeared, Archbishop Ussher had published *The Iudgement of Doctor Rainoldes*

---

[29] *Historical MS. Commission*, 12th Report (Cowper), II, 273–274.
[30] *C.S.P.Dom.*, Charles I, CCCCLXXXII, no. 96 (XVIII, 1641–1643, p. 63).
[31] Gardiner, IX, 498–499.

touching the Originall of Episcopacy, and the slumbering giant, Milton himself, had been aroused. *Of Reformation in England* had appeared in May, *Of Prelatical Episcopacy* probably in June, and *Animadversions upon the Remonstrant's Defence* before the end of the summer. Likewise Brooke, whose antagonism to epis- copacy, while it may have arisen from his theoretical convictions regarding Church polity, was daily sharpened by his active participation in Parliamentary debate, felt impelled to unlock his word-hoard. But like most busy men of public affairs, he was finding little opportunity for the retirement that literary com- position demands.

An opportunity was shortly provided. Factionalism within Parliament had obviously been growing as the debates of the spring and summer went on, and it was to reach its full develop- ment between August and November. The King had determined in August upon a curious visit to Scotland, a mission that was to be marked by more than a modicum of double-dealing, and when he set out the two parties were still reasonably united. It is significant that the security measures voted by Parliament at this time were rather clearly directed against the King, evidently in the fear that he might somehow use the Scottish dissidents to strengthen the royal power over Parliament.[32] Yet when it began to look as though Charles had no intention, after all, of enlisting the Scottish army to help him dissolve his own Parliament in London, the Houses took heart, and, weary with the pressure of work, harassed by the plague and an epidemic of smallpox then raging in the city, but confident that immediate dangers to their existence had been allayed, voted adjournment on August 28. That day of the voting of adjournment, says Gardiner, was "the last time when the two parties into which the House of Commons was divided loyally cooperated with one another." [33] During the few days remaining until adjournment actually took place, debate was held on the subject of the state religion; and although both parties were more or less at one in their decision to abolish some of Laud's ritualistic innovations, when it came to a question of tampering with the Book of Common Prayer

[32] Gardiner, X, 5; and Trevelyan, pp. 216–217.
[33] Gardiner, X, 10. The adjournment was to take effect on September 8.

they could not agree. Ominous misunderstanding marked the last few days of the session, and although adjournment finally was reached without unduly passionate outbursts the wedge had been driven. When Parliament reconvened on October 20 the devotees of episcopacy had become Royalists.

It was during this brief interval that Brooke undertook to write the *Discourse Opening the Nature of that Episcopacie, which is Exercised in England,* "the Retirements of Your Humble Servant," as he explained in the Epistle Dedicatory, "in the Last Recesse." [34] It is evident from the breadth and erudition of the argument that here were ideas that had been long germinating; but the violent partisanship in debate that had become more pronounced as the time for the recess drew near no doubt augmented the impetus that drove Brooke to compose his tract with such haste and concentration. It was ready for the press in November, and one imagines that its publication strengthened Brooke's reputation as one of the rising young leaders of the still diffuse Puritan wing. His cogent reasoning illuminated at least one area in the controversy more clearly than the previous pamphleteers had done, and his fine spirit of toleration and reasonableness, while not unique, was a refreshing breath that caught the admiration of Milton. [35] By this time the imminence of civil war was generally recognized, and it was clear that this young intellectual, author of two important treatises, active Puritan leader and fearless antagonist of royal and high Church authority, was certain to figure prominently in the events that were to unfold.

[34] *Discourse,* sig. A3.
[35] This treatise and its relationship to contemporary pamphlets will be fully discussed in Part III.

DISPUTES BECOME DIVISIONS

On the reassembly of Parliament in November the breach between Puritans and Royalists was quickly manifest. Though Pym consented to shelve for a time the Root and Branch Bill, he pressed immediately for the exclusion of the bishops from the upper House. One may be sure that Brooke concurred in this objective, for his tolerant attitude toward unlettered and unlicensed preachers, defended so eloquently in the *Discourse*, which was just appearing, was not extended to the episcopacy. The division became clear and even grew to violent opposition over two serious questions: whether the measures taken to quell the new Irish rebellion should be of Parliament's choosing and direction or of the King's; and whether the Grand Remonstrance, a history of grievances against the King, containing recommendations for church reform, and passed on the night of November 22 in a stormy session by a narrow margin of eleven votes, should be printed and published as the work of the Commons as a whole.[1]

The return of Charles from Scotland a few days later hardly contributed to the restoration of good feeling. In the month following, the actions of Parliament, notably the Impressment Bill and the Militia Bill, a "Root-and-Branch Bill to regulate the Army," now that the Church had for the moment ceased to be the center of attention,[2] served to alienate the King more thoroughly than ever. It is true that a protest made by the bishops on December 30, in which the integrity of both Houses was impugned, cemented for a moment the rival parties.[3] But this brief accord was dissipated once and for all in the furor that followed

---

[1] Gardiner, X, 75–79: "No king, said one party, shall rob us of our religion. No Parliamentary majority, said the other party, shall rob us of our religion."

[2] Gardiner, X, 95.

[3] Gardiner, X, 123.

the impeachment of five members of the Commons by the King on the charge of high treason — Pym, Hampden, Holles, Strode, and Haselrig (Brooke's brother-in-law). The attempted impeachment began on January 3, 1642, and the city of London itself joined forces with Lords and Commons in an alliance for their mutual safety. On the tenth, after a week of frustration for Charles and defiance on the part of the Parliament and the city, the King left London with his Queen. On the eleventh Parliament sat in triumph, with Pym as its actual though not its nominal head.

During the eight months that followed, a majority of the peers and a considerable minority of the Commons left London and joined the King at York. Realizing that the worst was upon him the King behaved, for once, with prudence and practical foresight.[4] He sent the Queen on a money-raising expedition to the continent, summoned Prince Rupert to assist in military preparations, employed Hyde to justify the royal course from a legal point of view, and himself acted with honesty and directness toward the nobility in Yorkshire, where he had taken up his abode. But in one endeavor he encountered solid opposition from Parliament: his attempts to prohibit the mustering of militia except under royal command.

The history of the struggle for the militia is complex, and it is sufficient to note that it culminated in the issuance on June 11 of Commissions of Array to direct the trained bands to adhere only to officers appointed by the King.[5] In May the Royalists who yet remained in London, including all the Lords and Commons who could be induced to join the King, began to stream toward York in the wake of the trusted Hyde. Popular feeling against military preparations was evident as the people began to absorb the shocking realization of the inevitability of war.[6] Charles finally recognized that he could expect no assistance

[4] I have omitted detailed consideration of the abortive attempts Charles made during these months to conciliate Parliament, as they have little direct bearing on the actions of Brooke at this time.

[5] Gardiner, X, 202.

[6] A pamphlet of May 24 (*Thomason Catalogue*, I, 112), was entitled: "Horrible News from Yorke, Hull and Newcastle. Concerning the Kings intent to take up arms against the Parliament."

from Scotland against Parliament and that the possibility of help from Holland was remote. He fell back at last on his loyal peers, persuaded them to accept his declaration professing his horror of conflict, and then proceeded toward enforcement of the Commissions of Array.[7]

On June 16 Henry Hastings, the King's leading commissioner, made the first attempt toward this end in Leicestershire, a locality in which the sympathies of the inhabitants lay predominantly with Parliament. Hastings met with such prohibitive opposition that even though he followed up his initial rebuff by entering the county two weeks later with a Royalist force he was entirely unsuccessful. Pamphlets printed in London proclaimed him a conspirator and a traitor, and the Parliament that now remained at Westminster considered his actions tantamount to a declaration of war.[8] On July 11 both Houses concurred in an opinion that the King had begun hostilities, and on the twelfth Essex was appointed Parliamentary general in command of the army.[9]

Another of the King's maneuvers to carry out the Commissions of Array brought Brooke into prominence, where he was to remain more or less consistently until his dramatic death eight months later. This was the attempt of the Earl of Northampton, acting for the King, to enforce the Commissions in Warwickshire.

In the ordinance published by Parliament on March 5, Brooke had been appointed Lord Lieutenant for Warwickshire, replacing Northampton.[10] He was therefore vitally affected by the withdrawal of the Royalists to York, and during the next few months he garrisoned Warwick Castle and prepared for action. He appears also to have had some connection at this period with his kinsman Robert Rich, Earl of Warwick, in affairs concerning the

---

[7] Gardiner, X, 202–205.

[8] Gardiner, X, 206 ff. A pamphlet dated July 21 (*Thomason Catalogue*, I, 139) was entitled: "Terrible Newes from Leicester, Warwick and Staffordshire . . . Wherein is discovered a great conspiracie against the town of Leicester and the Earl of Stamford plotted by M. Henrie Hastings." Another dated July 22 (*Thomason Catalogue*, I, 139): "The Impeachment and Charge of Mr. Henry Hastings, sonne to the Earle of Huntington, concerning his manifold misdemeanours, the insurrections occasioned by the said Mr. Hastings in the County of Leicester."

[9] *Lords Journals*, V, 201 *et passim*.

[10] *Lords Journals*, IV, 625.

Navy. Warwick, also replacing Northampton, had been appointed Lord High Admiral by Parliament, toward the end of securing the ships for Parliament. Certain orders dated June 4 directed Warwick and "Robert Lord Brooke, all commanders and officers at sea under him," to search ships suspected of carrying supplies and ammunition to the Irish Catholic rebels.[11] But Brooke's principal efforts appear to have gone into strengthening the Warwick area, and when Northampton arrived in that vicinity Brooke was evidently ready for him.

The conflict between the rival peers began around the first of July, at a time when articles of impeachment were being drawn against Northampton and eight other lords for absenting themselves from Parliament — though summoned repeatedly to appear — in order to attend the King at York.[12] It was also at about this time that the King's instructions to Northampton for enforcement of the Commissions in Warwickshire were printed in London.[13] William Montagu reported, for example, to Lord Montagu that on June 27 a letter was read in the Commons from a member in Warwickshire to the effect that "my lord Northampton is come to Coventry with the commission of array for that county, and hath been soliciting the mayor and townsmen of Coventry, but finds no great willingness to obey him nor that commission"; and further, that Brooke had gone "down," presumably to Warwick, on the twenty-fifth.[14] Edward Reed wrote to Sir John Coke on July 5 that "My Lord Brooke I hear is not like to do much in the militia in Warwickshire; but I know he hath a good zeal, he will do as much as he can." [15]

[11] Though Brooke's association with the Navy may seem rather enigmatic the orders are probably authentic; they are corroborated by a number of state documents. See *C.S.P.Dom.*, Charles I, CCCCXCI, no. 3 (XVIII, 1641–43, p. 334); House of Lords Calendar, *Historical MS. Commission*, 5th Report, p. 27; *Lords Journals*, V, 106; *Commons Journals*, II, 607a.

[12] *Articles of Impeachment exhibited in Parliament against Spencer Earle of Northamp. William Earle of Devonsh. Henry Earle of Dover, Henry Earle of Monmouth, Robert Lord Rich, Charles Lord Howard Charlton, Charles L. Grey of Ruthen, Thomas Lord Coventry, Arthur lord Chapell, &c. for severall high Crimes and Misdemeanors* (London, 1642), p. 5.

[13] *Thomason Catalogue*, I, 129.

[14] *Historical MS. Commission*, 15th Report (Montagu House Papers), I, 306.

[15] *Historical MS. Commission*, 12th Report (Cowper), II, 318. This letter also touched on a matter, concerning Saye, that is at least of peripheral interest. Saye had been summoned on June 29 to York to attend the King, who had given him a

He was indeed doing what he could, and it was not inconsiderable. On the sixth the Speaker of the Lords ordered that the
gratitude of the peers for Brooke's care and diligence be conveyed to him, for word had just been received from Brooke "That
he hath put the Ordinance for the Militia into Execution, and the
Trained Bands were full, and that many Voluntiers came in; and
that he hath taken the Magazine into the Castle of Warwicke." [16]
There was also entered in the Lords Journal a copy of the petition from the deputy lieutenants, captains, officers, and soldiers
of the trained bands and volunteers of the Warwick militia. The
petitioners thanked Parliament for appointing Brooke the Lord
Lieutenant of the County of Warwick; signified their readiness
to fight for and adhere to "His Majesty and both Houses of Parliament"; prayed that His Majesty's sacred person be rid of his
evil counsellors, "pestilent Troublers of the Church and State,"
and that those who leaned to the malignant party be punished;
and finally, descending in characteristic Puritan fashion to practical matters, requested that the magazine at Coventry be removed and laid up safely at Warwick Castle.[17]

Some time around the middle of the month this magazine was
duly acquired. A contemporary single-sheet news letter, written
by one J. S. to his "speciall Friend" in London, reported that on
a certain day in July Brooke had read the Commission of Array
to the seventeen hundred or so armed volunteers at Warwick,
"besides many hundreds without Armes," declaring its illegality,
and the same day had gone to Coventry, procured the magazine,
and brought it to Warwick Castle.[18] This ammunition, according
to another Warwickshire informant, was obtained bloodlessly,
and consisted of "two great Cart loades, and a Waggon loaded

"dispensation" to absent himself from Parliament. Saye asked the House of Lords
for its wishes and was ordered to "stay and give attendance upon this House, about
the weighty affairs of the Kingdom now in Agitation" (*Lords Journals*, V, 169).
Reed reported that Saye had "moved the House for leave, but cannot obtain it.
What his next message will be from York is to be expected . . ."

[16] *Lords Journals*, V, 187b.

[17] *The Humble Petition and Resolution of the Deputy Lieutenants, Captains,
Officers, Souldiers and Voluntiers of the Trained Bands of the County of Warwick*
(London, 1642).

[18] *A True Relation of the Lord Brooke's setling of the Militia in Warwickeshire*
(London, 1642).

with Gun-powder bullets and match." The same correspondent went on to remark that Brooke had further fortified the Castle with "foure great peeces of Ordnance." [19]

On the eighteenth it was resolved in Parliament that Brooke should have authority from both Houses "to take such Forces into his Castle at Warwick as he shall think necessary for Defence of the publick Magazine there: And that they shall be paid out of the Subscription Monies of that County: And that he be desired to advance the Subscription Monies there." [20] This final stipulation was probably more easily ordered than accomplished. A letter of July 25 from one Innocent Rashe, a servant employed in the Warwick area, reported that "Lord Brooke has made great preparation for his castle. He has great store of men in it, and they say he gives to divers men 4s. 8d. a week; but how this money is to be paid few do know." [21] Remembering from Brooke's colonizing enterprises in the previous decade that he was never niggardly in using his private resources for what he regarded as the public good, one can at least conjecture the method of payment. In fact, the news sheet from J. S. had included the observation that "The Lord Brooke at his owne cost and charges entertained all the Souldiers, both Trained bands and Volunteers, with Wine and Strong drinke, and other accommodations, to his great credit and honour." [22] But however he managed it, Brooke succeeded within the month in providing Warwick Castle with a sufficient armed garrison.

Any lingering hopes for peace had by this time been dissipated by the King's uncompromising reply to a petition from both Houses, presented to him on July 16, requesting an accommodation. Charles's answer, though "trim'd with the same neat quipps as formerly," [23] demanded dismissal of the Parliamentary troops, surrender of Hull and the fleet, disavowal by Parliament of power to make laws without the King's consent, and adjourn-

---

[19] *Some Speciall Passages from Warwickshire concerning the proceedings of Lord Brooke* (London, 1642).

[20] *Commons Journals*, II, 678b.

[21] *C.S.P.Dom.*, Charles I, CCCCXCI, no. 89 (XVIII, 1641–43, p. 361).

[22] *A True Relation* (see above, n. 18).

[23] Phrase in a letter from Samuel Hinton to Sir Richard Leveson, date uncertain, but ca. July 27. *Historical MS. Commission*, 5th Report, pp. 182–183.

ment of Parliament to some point outside London, before he would consent even to discuss their differences.[24] Matters had obviously gone too far for a retreat of such magnitude on either side.

Tension between the rival parties could scarcely have been more acute anywhere than it was in Warwickshire. A certain Captain Robert Leigh had, for example, preferred an indictment at the Warwick assizes on July 21 against Brooke for opposing the Commission of Array. When the Lords heard about it they took the indictment as a "great Breach of the Privilege of Parliament," and ordered that Leigh be sent for as a delinquent.[25] Nothing came of the indictment or the order, of course, but the tension continued to increase. Brooke went on with his fortifying and strengthening, assured of the general support of the countryside. By the end of the month Brooke and Northampton were engaged in what Richard Baxter called "scuffling" over the militia and armaments in the locality, several weeks of protracted activity that was only technically short of warfare.

The first encounter between them was precipitated by the arrival in Banbury on July 29 of six pieces of ordnance, granted by Parliament to Brooke for the defence of Warwick Castle. Brooke arrived in Banbury the next morning early with about a hundred men, after riding all night, and by nine o'clock had started back toward Warwick with the ordnance. They had gone only a few miles when Northampton, accompanied by some two hundred horse and about the same number of "musketeers and pikes," caught up with them. In the words of a contemporary pamphleteer,

the news thereof being carried backe to Banbury, and townes adjoyning; presently the Lord Brooke was assisted with more men and munition, the Countrey came in very thick to his assistance, and but few to the Earle of North-hamptons; but my Lord Brookes company increasing in a few houres to the number of a thousand at least, women also to his company bringing in Beere and Victuall in aboundance, and six or seven cartload of harrowes

<hr />

[24] Lords Journals, V, 235. See also Gardiner, X, 213–214. Some interesting observations on the reaction of London to the King's answer are to be found in a letter from Sir John Coke the Younger to his father, dated July 25, Historical MS. Commission, 12th Report (Cowper), II, 318.

[25] Lords Journals, V, 256a, 241b–242a.

to welcome their horses: the Earle of North-hampton seeing their forces increase so unexpectedly and the love of the Countrey brought in so fast; He curse and swore bitterly that he was come into the mouth of all the divels and roundheads in the Countrey.[26]

Northampton produced his Commission of Array and — between oaths, the Puritan pamphleteer would apparently have his readers believe — demanded the ordnance, which Brooke, in a properly godly fashion, "affirmed" he should not have. The impasse continued from ten in the morning until five in the afternoon, during which time the troops on both sides were ready to open fire if commanded.[27] Finally the two leaders agreed to a compromise. The ordnance was to be returned to Banbury, and each commander engaged his honor to give three days' notice to the other before attempting to remove it. Brooke is reported to have agreed to this scheme only in order to avoid beginning actual war then and there, before he should have had the opportunity to lay the matter before Parliament. The disputed ordnance was returned to Banbury, where a number of Parliamentarian sympathizers undertook to guard it, and Brooke went on to London to report to his peers.

The abortive engagement seems to have been regarded as a triumph for Brooke by Puritan partisans around the countryside, perhaps because so many had come, if the accounts could be believed, to his aid. One witness described the affair in this manner:

In Warwickshire the Lord Brooke has carried the militia clean against Lord Northampton. . . There was a little scuffling between them, but no harm done; and it was about 5 or 6 pieces of ordnance which Lord Brooke brought here in town to send to Warwick Castle which the Earl of Northampton would have taken from him for the King; but Lord Brooke was too hard for him as you may perceive by a printed paper here inclosed.[28]

[26] *The Proceedings at Banbury since the Ordnance went down for the Lord Brooke to fortifie Warwick Castle* . . . (London, 1642), p. 2. This pamphlet is the principal source for a description of this action, but additional (and corroboratory) information is contained in *The Copie of a Letter sent from a special friend in Coventry* (London, 1642), a single-sheet newsletter.

[27] *The Copie of a Letter*, etc.

[28] *Historical MS. Commission*, 5th Report, p. 161. The "printed paper" was probably *The Copie of a Letter* . . . *from Coventry*. If it had been *The Proceedings at Banbury*, the writer would have known that in the long run Brooke had not been "too hard for him."

But most of the letters and pamphlets describing the events in the area during these weeks are strongly flavored with Parliamentary bias, and it may be that some of them represent in large measure propaganda rather than factual reporting. For example, one specific and quite detailed pamphlet purports to recount a "famous victory" obtained by Brooke over Northampton on August 3. The writer maintains that Brooke, living up to his word, gave Northampton the required three days' notice, set out for Banbury, and was met by Northampton on the way, upon a heath near Keintith in Warwickshire. Though Brooke had set out with only three hundred musketeers, sixty pikes, and two hundred horse, such was the affection in which he was held throughout the area, the writer maintains, that before he had marched three miles his company had increased to three thousand. When Northampton's force was encountered, Brooke's command moved into battle formation so impressive in strength and so skillfully deployed, not to mention so high in spirits and so certain of their rectitude, that the Royalists were demoralized and fled, leaving Northampton "but one of his Gentlemen and two foot-boyes to attend him; which caused the said Earle to try whether he or his foot-boyes could run fastest." [29]

This pamphlet made diverting reading for the anti-Royalists, no doubt, but one questions the degree of its authenticity. For one thing, Brooke was elsewhere reported to have gone up to London after the engagement of July 30 to consult with Parliament, and one letter from Warwickshire dated August 8 complains that "the Parliament forces are too slow; our Lord Brooke is not with us, we think him very long." [30] For another, if Brooke had won such a "famous victory" over Northampton, there would have been no obstacle in the way of his marching on to Banbury with his force "three thousand" strong to obtain the ordnance. Yet the fact is that Northampton is the one who eventually removed it, probably around August 8, and used it, furthermore, to

[29] *A Famous Victory obtained by the Right Honorable the Lord Brooks, against the Earle of Northampton, on the third of August, 1642, neere Keintith in Warwickshire* (London, 1642), p. 8.

[30] "The Copie of a Letter out of Warwickshire," dated August 8, and appended to *The Proceedings at Banbury,* on the last page, which is unnumbered but should be p. 8.

besiege Warwick Castle within a few days thereafter, during the absence of Brooke. *The Proceedings at Banbury*, the author of which is of indisputably Puritan sympathy, describes North-ampton's arrival at Banbury, pointedly observing that "the Lord Brooke had noe notice from the Earle of three dayes warning, as was agreed between them," and gives a long account of the stratagem by which Northampton outwitted the guardians of the ordnance and made off with it.[31] This achievement is also witnessed in a letter from one of the guardians, "Mr. Fines" [Fiennes], one of the sons of Lord Saye, to John Pym. Fiennes said he had been resolved "to lose his dearest blood" in defend-ing the ordnance and even to "break them in pieces" rather than let Northampton have them, but had delivered them up when Northampton appeared with some fifteen hundred men because "there was no wayes able to make resistance."[32]

Northampton's attack on Warwick Castle, which took place probably between the eighth and fourteenth of August, was un-successful. A "Letter from a Gentleman of Warwicke to his Friend in London," appended to a rather lurid tract, full of ac-counts of God's punishment of the wicked for drunkenness, lewdness, and general ungodliness, entitled *True and New Newes with an Example from Warwick Castle*, describes how Northamp-ton and several other noblemen captured the ordnance at Banbury "this day seavennight in the morning" and proceeded to War-wick, where the town admitted them without resistance. The operation at Banbury, as it has been noted, probably took place on the eighth, and the "Letter from a Gentleman" suggests that the siege of Warwick Castle followed very shortly, perhaps the same day. Northampton evidently expected the castle to fall as readily as the town had been occupied, but a vigorous defence was put up by Sir Edward Peto, whom Brooke had apparently left in command, and the castle remained in Parliamentary hands. Northampton installed some of the Banbury ordnance in the tower of the church, and after some parleying, in which Peto refused to deliver the castle, both sides opened fire. One of Peto's

[31] *The Proceedings at Banbury*, pp. 3–6.
[32] *Exceeding Joyfull Newes from Warwick-Castle and Banburie* (London, 1642) (pages unnumbered).

shots "tooke of a pinacle of the tower & made the Cavaliers stir."
The Royalists countered by firing one of the Banbury guns, "which
broke all in pieces, and some say hurt the L. Comptons sonne,
whereupon they suspect all the ordnance that came from Banbury to be poysoned." [33] Other accounts of the artillery duel
indicate that it was Northampton himself rather than his son who
had been wounded.[34] The number of days' duration of this action
is uncertain, but the fact that the castle remained unsubdued is
clear enough, whether or not there is any truth to the colorful
detail that Peto hung out "his winding sheet and the Bible," [35]
or whether Northampton really did attempt to "beat down the
Walls." [36]

Brooke, meanwhile, had assembled a large force of six thousand or so, at the behest of Parliament, and was soon to be marching down from London to relieve the castle.[37] He arrived no
later than the eighteenth, a date on which the King himself had
planned to come to Warwick in person, though he was to post-
pone this visit until the twentieth and finally was not to come at
all.[38] The shire was in something of an uproar as it became the
focus for the maneuvering that immediately preceded actual
hostilities. A pamphlet entitled *Horrible News from Warwickshire* alludes to the "many troubles and distractions," which Warwick has "groned under these late dayes, being occasioned by

[33] *True and New Newes with an example from Warwick Castle* (London, 1642),
unnumbered final page (should be p. 8).

[34] A letter from Edward Reed to Sir John Coke, dated August 14, reports that
"My Lord of Northampton is at Warwick with the ordnance he brought from
Banbury, and did plant some of them upon the steeple there to batter my Lord
Brook's castle; where at the first shot one of the pieces brake and did strike some
of the cheek away of my Lord Compton's." *Historical MS. Commission*, 12th Report
(Cowper), II, 320. Unidentified pamphlets cited by Frances Evelyn Greville, *Warwick Castle and Its Earls* (London, 1903), II, 694, and by Alfred Beesley, *History
of Banbury* (London, 1841), pp. 302–303, corroborate the fact that it was Northampton who was wounded.

[35] *True and New Newes*, unnumbered final page.

[36] *Exceeding Joyfull Newes from Warwick-Castle and Banburie*, sig. [A?]4.

[37] *His Majesties Proceedings in Northamptonshire, Glocestershire, Wiltshire, and
Warwickshire, from the 16. of August to the 23. Wherein Is Declared His Royall
Intention and Resolution therein concerning the Inhabitants of those Counties.
Likewise the Resolution of these worthy Pillars of the Protestant Religion. Namely,
The Lord Brookes, Colonell Hollis, Colonell Hampden, Colonell Goodwin, Colonell
Fines, Who are now marching towards Warwickshire with 6000. horse and foot*
(London, 1642), p. 5.

[38] *Horrible Newes from Warwickshire* (London, 1642), p. 6.

those broyles between the Lord Brooks and the Earle of Northampton." The writer states that it was the King's intention to
take the castle and Brooke's intention to hold it, and he attributes
to Brooke a willingness to meet the King and if necessary, "the
malignant party offering any violence," to "hazard his life in
the defence of his Majesty and the Parliament, and the preservation of the peace of the Kingdom." [39]

On the eighteenth Brooke and Northampton confronted each
other in a parley of major significance, for its failure to produce
any sort of settlement made the official outbreak of warfare a
few days later inevitable, at least as far as the Warwickshire area
was concerned. A full account of their meeting is recorded in a
pamphlet entitled *Propositions from the Kings most Excellent
Majesty . . . To the Lo: Brooks, and the Gentry and Commonalty assembled at Warwick, on Thursday last, August 18.
With the Lo: Brooks his Answer to the said Propositions*, printed
in London on August 20. Since the King had been obliged because of the pressure of "other affaires" to defer his visit to Warwick in person, the Earls of Newcastle and Northampton, with
a force of some five thousand, were sent instead. Though they
marched from Nottingham during the night, Brooke knew they
were coming and met them with an assembly of some seven
thousand about two miles from Warwick.[40] A parley was held
between the two forces and the following propositions were made
to Brooke:

1. That the Lord Brookes should immediately lay down his Arms and submit to his Majesties mercie, from whom he should receive a gracious
   pardon.
2. That the Lo: Brooks should resigne the castle of Warwick into such
   hands as his Majesty should thinke fit.
3. That the Lord Brooks should disavow the Ordinance of the Militia, and
   endeavour the execution of the Commission of Array.
4. That the Lord Brooks should deliver the Magazine of that County into
   the hands of the Earle of Northampton.
5. That the Lord Brooks should immediately repair to Nottingham, and

[39] *Ibid.*, pp. 3, 5.
[40] *Propositions from the Kings most Excellent Majesty*, p. 2. The manifest Puritan authorship of the pamphlet is revealed in an aside to the effect that when
Brooke met the Royalist force they were "comming from Grove-Parke, from Mr.
Dormers, a great Papist; where it seemes the Lords had been to refresh themselves."

appeale for his Majesties Pardon or upon neglect thereof, to undergo
his Majesties severest censure.
And that if he refused to performe these their honourable demands, they
vowed to make him the subject of their that dayes fury.[41]

These ultimata were delivered by the Earls of Newcastle and
Lindsay, but it is probable that Northampton, as commander in
the field, stood with them.

The writer describes Brooke as being "so farre incensed"
by these threats "that he was about to leave them without reply,
but after a little consideration he wheeld about, and boldly
marcht up to them." It must have made an impressive scene.
Spencer Compton was forty-one and had succeeded his father
as Earl of Northampton in 1630. Brooke was thirty-four and had
become a peer in 1629. Both had attended Cambridge. Both were
outspoken and energetic in defence of their respective political
allegiances. One had replaced the other as Lord Lieutenant of
Warwickshire. Though neither of them could foresee it, both were
destined to be killed in action the following March, Brooke at
Lichfield and Northampton at Hopton Heath.[42] As they faced
each other it is not difficult to imagine Brooke as appearing "incensed." The portrait of him that hangs in Warwick Castle
reveals an aristocratic young man, erect in bearing, haughty in
expression. Brought up to be successor to the title of his distinguished cousin Sir Fulke, he had doubtless grown accustomed
to deference. Furthermore, he was a strong Calvinist, genuine
in his piety but confident, as Calvinists generally were, of his
own rectitude. It was characteristic of Puritans to believe that
the regenerate could usually tell whether they were in a state of
grace,[43] and Brooke had once shown by an inadvertent slip of
the pen in *The Nature of Truth* that he regarded himself as one
of the "best men." [44] An eminently successful young nobleman
who had made a mark in political, intellectual, and military
affairs, who had married into an important family and was well
along in producing one of his own, who enjoyed gentlemanly

[41] *Propositions*, pp. 3–4.
[42] For biographical facts about Northampton see G. E. Cokayne, *Complete Peerage* (London, 1887), VI, 72.
[43] Perry Miller, *The New England Mind* (New York, 1939), p. 49.
[44] *The Nature of Truth*, p. 57.

diversions like hunting and hawking, bowling and playing chess,[45] who was well liked by his politically sympathetic neighbors and revered by the men under his command, Brooke must have thought of himself as urbane, poised, and utterly righteous as he answered the Royalist propositions on his own home ground from what probably seemed to him a position of unassailable virtue.

"My Lords," he is said to have replied,

I much wonder that men of judgement, in whose breasts true honour should remaine, should so much derogate from their Ancestors and noble Predecessors, as to seeke (for private ends) the ruine of that Kingdom they should endeavour to support. Doth fond ambition, or your selfe-will'd pride so much bewitch you, that you cannot see the crown of all your actions? When the great Councel of the Parliament was first assembled, you then were Members; why did you not continue? Was it because your actions were so bad, you were ashamed to own them? Had you done evill in some petty kind, Submission might have quitted you from that, and you have been still honoured, loved, and feared; but by these actions (which tend both to the ruine of King and Kingdome, and your selves too) you cannot make amends for former evils.

As for these Propositions, take this in Answer:

When that His Majesty, His posterity, and the peace of the Kingdome shall be secured from you that seeke the ruine of them all, I gladly shall lay downe my Arms and Power.

As for the Castle, it was delivered to my trust by the High Court of Parliament, who reserve it for the Kings use; and dare boldly say will so imploy it, and not like you imploy it against the King.

As for the Commission of Array, you know it is unlawful, and like your actions, destructive both to the Laws and Religion of the Kingdome.

For the Magazine of the County, it was delivered to him both by the Parliament, and the Countrey; and although he was not an Earle, yet he dares be a truer subject to his King, and a faithfuller servant to his Countrey; and being so, he was resolved to keep it till Northampton could shew him greater authority for his delivery of the same.[46]

As touching His Majesties Pardon, as he was confident that he had not given any occasion of offence to His Majesty, so he needed not pardon; that being a duty belonging to offenders, such as themselves; and he advised them to sue out a pardon with speed, for feare that their offences being once knowne, they prove impardonable; for he doubted not but that in a short time His Majesty would finde who are his best friends. As for their fury, he bade them spit their venome; for he hoped that Northampton should

[45] Recall the stipulations regarding the rental of Ragley, p. 12 above. See also Greville, *Warwick Castle and Its Earls*, II, 717–718.

[46] Shift to indirect discourse as in the printed text of the pamphlet.

be translated to Warwick, and stand centry upon Warwick-castle, to fright crowes, kites, and buzzards.[47]

After this interchange the Royalist noblemen, incensed in their turn, "wheeled about, and marched away, not once so much as taking their leave." Brooke returned to Warwick and read to his men part of the "Resolution of the Lords and Commons," declaring "the true cause for which we raise Armes."

Two days later the King, who had reached Warwickshire as planned, was refused entry into Coventry. On the twenty-second Edward Reed wrote to Sir John Coke, "Strong forces are for the King in Warwick, and so is my Lord Brooke well prepared; this week will say something of that business but as yet they look the one upon the other." [48] Reed's prophecy was fulfilled even as he wrote, for on that day the King issued a proclamation at Nottingham declaring Essex a traitor, and from that moment the war is considered to have begun.[49]

[47] *Propositions*, pp. 4–6.
[48] *Historical MS. Commission*, 12th Report (Cowper), II, 321.
[49] Gardiner, X, 218–220.

V

CIVIL WAR AND PEACE NEGOTIATIONS

During the first month or two of the war Brooke was involved, between trips to London, in a number of minor skirmishes. None of them was especially significant and it is hardly worthwhile to attempt to trace them in detail. But it is interesting, in view of the fact that the war might properly be said to have begun in Warwickshire, that Brooke was engaged in one small affair, perhaps the first true encounter of the civil war, before official hostilities were a day old.

On the night of August 22 Brooke and his command were at Southam, some ten miles from Coventry. Through intelligence from local observers and scouts he heard that Royalists were nearby, possibly a detachment in "retreate" from Coventry, as one account puts it.[1] Rather than rest himself and his "wearyed Troopes, and Regiments after their long march," [2] Brooke ordered his men to advance and prepare for battle in a field adjacent to the town, "where they continued till the morning, their beds being the ground, although it was a sharpe cold night, which nothing daunted them, but rather animated them with courage against the approach of their Adversaries." [3] In the morning when Northampton's men appeared, Brooke, "having set his Army in order, planted his Canon in a place most convenient to annoy the enemy, let flie at them, and made such a lane, that the enemy was so long in re-ordering, that they thought they would not

[1] *The Manner and Good Successe of the Lord Brookes Forces in pursuing the Cavaliers from Coventry* (London, 1642), single-sheet newsletter. This tract is reprinted more or less verbatim as part of *A True and Exact Relation of the present estate of the City of Norwich* (London, 1642). What the Cavaliers in question were believed to be in "retreat" from is not clear.

[2] *Ibid.*

[3] *A True and Perfect Relation of the First and victorious Skirmish between the Army under the conduct of Lord Brooks . . . and the Army under the command of the Earle of Northampton* (London, 1642), p. 4.

have made head againe, but at last they did." [4] According to this Puritan witness, who would have gone on describing the "wonderful courage and shouts of joy" of Brooke's troops in the face of the enemy if "the messenger" had not been in such a hurry to be gone, the Royalists were forced to withdraw, taking their casualties with them. He admits that although no Parliamentarian was killed, "some 12. were wounded by the firing some powder, and one shott himselfe through the foot with a pistoll, and another his fellow through the back." The other pamphleteer who recounted the action, however, claimed "not a man hurt through the Providence of God." Furthermore, he saw clear evidence of divine support of the Parliament in yet one more miraculous circumstance: ". . . in this skirmish a Bullet out of one of the peeces of the adverse party came over the Lord Brookes his head but mist him, which shewes the protection of God is over them in this their just cause." [5] By such reasoning the justice of the cause would within a few months become difficult to maintain.

For the following month or so Brooke was occupied in and around the Warwick area. Various tracts in the Thomason collection suggest a few inconsequential triumphs, including the capture of forty-six Cavaliers near Brackley between the twenty-third and the twenty-eighth, of sixty more by some of Brooke's forces on the twenty-ninth, a "victory" on September eighth over certain Royalists on the way to Nottingham. [6] On a trip to London to report to Parliament, Brooke was honored by the Lords for his accomplishments by being appointed Speaker for the day, September 16. [7]

Early in October Essex and the main force of the Parlia-

---

[4] *The Manner and Good Successe*, etc.

[5] *A True and Perfect Relation*, p. 6.

[6] The following pamphlets may be noted: (a) one dated August 28, *A True Relation of the taking of 46 Cavalliers at Brackly by the Lord Brookes his regiment*, Thomason, I, 162; (b) one dated August 31, a Wednesday, *A True Relation of the manner of taking of the Earl of Northampton, and 60. Cavalliers by Colonell Hampden, and Colonell Goodwin, with some of the Lord Brookes his Forces . . . on Munday last* (London, 1642); (c) one dated early in September, *A Famous Victory obtained by the Earl of Stamfords forces . . . Also another Victory obtained by Lord Brooks, 8 Sept., against divers Kentish Cavaleers that were going to the standard at Nottingham*, Thomason, I, 165.

[7] *Lords Journals*, V, 357a.

mentary army moved into the vicinity of Warwick, where they remained concentrated for the rest of the month. On about October 18, when the King was near Coventry, Essex requested that the King receive a petition from both houses of Parliament, the import of which was that His Majesty would be welcome in Westminster if he came with peaceful purposes. Charles not only denied the petition but also refused to grant a safe convoy for its bearers,[8] eliciting a protest from Bedford, Mandeville, Wharton, Brooke, and some others, who called it a "most high indignity" that the authority of Parliament should be scorned by the rejection of their "submissive, dutiful and earnest" desires for peace.[9] But the King, who was moving toward London, was intent on reaching it in his own way and continued to press forward with his forces toward Oxford.

Essex had marched westward toward Worcester on receipt of intelligence that the royal army was there, but doubled back when he heard that they were moving south through Warwickshire. On the night of October 22 the King, hearing that Essex was on his trail, ordered his troops to occupy the eminence of Edgehill, south of Warwick on the Oxford road. On the next day the first major battle of the civil war was fought. Some fourteen thousand troops were involved, and the outcome was for a considerable time in doubt.[10] Various accounts of the battle agree in the one particular that lack of coordination between Prince Rupert's cavalry and the ground forces was the factor that prevented an undisputed Royalist victory; but the first reports that reached London were conflicting, and even in retrospect it is difficult to name the victor. The "promise of future success," however, as Gardiner puts it, "was undoubtedly on the side of Essex," for his army was revealed not as a motley, raw, undisciplined crowd, but a surprisingly unified and cooperative group.[11]

Brooke himself, though his own regiment had been on the scene and had fought successfully, missed the main engagement. According to one report, Essex had sent him to Warwick for

[8] Gardiner, *History of the Great Civil War* (London, 1893), I, 39 (references to Gardiner henceforth will signify this work unless otherwise designated).

[9] *Historical MS. Commission*, 10th Report, VI, 88.

[10] Gardiner, I, 42.

[11] Gardiner, I, 51.

ammunition, with which he was to join the army on the march. As Brooke proceeded from Warwick toward Edgehill on the twenty-third he met some of the army in retreat from the field, "prevailed with many to return with him; and making what haste he could to join battle, arrived in time to have some share, personally, in the success of the day, and in keeping the field the night following." [12] A letter from Stephen Charlton to Sir Richard Leveson, dated October 25, makes an interesting appraisal:

> The main battle began on Sunday last [the 23rd] about one o'clock p.m. and lasted until 6 at night; and then it was hard to say who should have the better. But on Monday morning Lord Brook's forces and Col. Hampden's and Col. Goodin came up with 600 or 700 fresh men and 10 or 12 pieces of cannon, and fell upon the flank of the King's army and wholly routed them, and this is the general report; and they say that the King's horse had a great advantage over the Earl of Essex, but his foot they say fought like devils; and besides they say that the country came in pel-mell to help the Earl of Essex.[13]

However one interprets the outcome, the King did proceed on to Oxford with an appearance of triumph, whether or not his cause had really suffered as some observers thought.

One result of the battle of Edgehill was an attempt on the part of certain members of Parliament to negotiate for peace, even though it should mean compromise. Efforts were made toward this end between November 4 and 7, but the King's unwillingness to deal straightforwardly with the Parliamentary commission was interpreted as an attitude of refusal to negotiate.[14] Leaders of Parliament held a mass meeting in the Guildhall on November 8 to inform the people of London of the failure of negotiations and to recruit more men for the Parliamentary forces. Brooke appears to have been the chairman of this meeting, and two speeches that he made on the occasion and one by Sir Henry Vane the Younger were published in a pamphlet.

The speeches are scarcely notable as literature, but a glance at them shows, if nothing else, the fervor with which Parliamentary patriots argued their cause and gives some indication

[12] Collins, *Peerage*, IV, 354.
[13] *Historical MS. Commission*, 5th Report, p. 160.
[14] Gardiner, I, 54.

of Brooke's standing among the leaders. Brooke opened the meeting with an apology:

My Lord Maior and Aldermen, and the rest of the Gentlemen all here assembled, I am to deliver a Message to you from the Lords and Commons now assembled in Parliament; but before I shall do that, I shall crave leave to excuse something that hath hapned: There should have been divers Lords, and some Gentlemen of the House of Commons here, far fitter to have done this work, that is now put upon me, if they could possibly have attended the service, that were appointed by the House, as the Lord Generall of the Horse, the Earl of Bedford, and some other Lords, but you will all conceive, that they being all men imployed in the Army, they could not attend this your service, but they are about your service, and the good of the Kingdom, which is giving order for your safety, and theirs; and therefore I hope you will take it in good part, that there is no other appearance here.[15]

After assurance that he would give no "long prefacings," he came to the point of his address:

I doubt not but you have heard some whisperings of an Accommodation, no doubt of that, and no man that is an honest man, a Religious man, a Freeman, that loves Religion, and the Kingdom, but would have an Accommodation, for nothing is more miserable, and nothing is more distracting then War, but that an Accommodation should come upon terms ignoble, and disadvantagious, that never was in the thought of either House; and I hope never will be; And I am to tell you, never shall be.

Brooke went on to describe the attempt the Parliament had recently made to present a petition to the King, reviewing the manner in which His Majesty had responded, notably his having refused to grant a safe conduct to one of the six members of the commission, Sir John Evelyn, on the ground that he had been proclaimed a traitor. But Evelyn had been branded traitor only the day before the denial of the safe conduct, and it was interpreted by Parliament that the King had simply used him as an excuse for refusing to negotiate. Brooke reported that on the seventh both Houses had voted "no" on the question, "Whether a safe Conduct shall be accepted upon these terms." He concluded by pointing out, as the Parliamentary resolution to acquaint the people of London with the failure of the attempt to make peace

[15] *Three Speeches Spoken in Guild-Hall, Concerning His Majesties refusall of a Treaty of Peace, and what is to be done thereupon, two by Lord Brook, and one by Sir Henry Vane* (London, 1642), p. 3.

had provided, that Charles had been willing to receive a petition from the rebels in Ireland but not from the Parliament of his own countrymen: "We are no Rebels, but dutifull in all we do, they are Rebells and Traytours in the judgement of all men, and yet he will receive no Petition from us, but He will receive a Petition from them."

Vane followed Brooke and covered essentially the same ground, first describing the indignity offered Parliament by the King's refusal and then exhorting the Londoners to support the just cause with their purses and to defend themselves against violence and oppression.[16] When Vane had finished Brooke spoke again. First he gave the audience to understand that real danger from Royalist troops was near at hand, but he followed these alarming revelations with the assurance that God was undoubtedly on the side of Parliament. For proof he cited a great victory in which at the very lowest estimate two thousand Royalists had been killed and only about a hundred Roundheads, "unlesse you will take in women and children, Carmen and doggs (for they slew the very dogs and all)." This account is hardly recognizable as a description of Edgehill, the only major battle thus far, but it no doubt served to demonstrate to anyone who might have believed it God's preference for Parliament. Having established this fact Brooke drew toward his peroration: ". . . what is it we fight for? it is for our Religion, for God, for liberty and all, and what is it they fight for? for their lust, their will, for tyrranny, to make us slaves, and to overthrow all." He paid tribute to Essex and exhorted all good Londoners to "affect the cause, and ioyne with him, hand and heart and sword." Though it is likely that "Gideons sword will do the work alone," it is up to every citizen to do his part. "Doubt not to go out to worke and fight couragiously, and this shall be the day of your deliverance."[17]

The meeting produced tangible results in the form of money and recruits, but the danger created by the proximity of Prince Rupert and his cavalry was incentive for another petition for peace. This time Charles seemed to the Parliament to act with

[16] *Three Speeches*, pp. 5-7.
[17] *Ibid.*, p. 8.

bald duplicity; while he professed to be considering the petition he ordered Rupert to attack Brentford, on the outskirts of London, on November 12. Holles's regiment, stationed outside Brentford, was the first to be attacked, whereupon it fell back on the town, where Brooke's regiment was quartered. The fight was bloody but Rupert won a clear victory and occupied the town. Among his prisoners was John Lilburne, who had enlisted in Brooke's regiment; upon his capture the Royalists threatened to hang him, and he was saved only by Parliament's threats to hang Royalist prisoners in reprisal.[18]

The rest of the month of November was marked by accusations of bad faith on the part of the King and of noncooperation on the part of Parliament. Petitions from various groups in London continued to be conveyed to the King at Oxford through December and January. But it was evident in all these negotiations that, on the one hand, Charles was not of a mind to make peace without regaining the royal prerogatives he had lost, and on the other, the more realistic members of Parliament such as Pym had little hope that a satisfactory agreement could be reached without the compromises they refused to make. Although attempts to negotiate were still being made in February, it was apparent by then to almost everyone that such efforts had scarcely a chance of success.

It was during these peace negotiations that Brooke was the victim of a malicious practical joke. On December 19 two speeches were said to have been made in the Lords, the first by the Earl of Pembroke, speaking for an accommodation, the second by Brooke, speaking against it. One passage in the speech purportedly made by Brooke ran as follows:

I know we have many difficulties to wrestle with, and that many fall from us daily; they who have much to lose . . . will be quickly weary of us, and yet some men of good Fortunes will not leave us; they who have a sense of gratitude, or pass'd obligations, or future hopes from His Majesty, will be startled at our Resolution: yet I see many here the most notoriouslie obliged, indeed as much as servants can be to a master, in this good cause, have mastered those vulgar considerations, and had the courage almost to despise him to his face: besides, the wisest men will not think themselves incapable of future favours, if they use their utmost power to reduce him to

[18] Gardiner, I, 57, 73; and Haller, *The Rise of Puritanism*, p. 283.

a necessity of granting: They who are transported with naturall affection to their Fathers and Brothers, kindred, friends, will not keep us companie; yet this troubles me the lesse, whilst I see those Noble Lords in my eye (upon whom I can never look enough) who, banishing those womanish and effeminate fancies, cheerfullie undertook to serve against that Armie, wherein they knew their own fathers were; and on my conscience (I speak it to their honour) had they met them alone, would piouslie have sacrificed them to the commands of both Houses.[19]

The language of this speech was sharper than was Brooke's wont, the sentiments a good deal more bloodthirsty than he was accustomed to express, and the disrespectful attitude toward the King quite out of character for him. The printing of the speeches brought from him a violent reaction. Clarendon's posthumously published *Life* tells the story in these words:

There was at that time a pleasant story upon those speeches. The lord Brooke had met with them in print, and heard that he was much reproached for so unchristian a speech against peace, though the language was such as he used in all opportunities: Whereupon one morning in the house of peers, and before the house sat, he came to the earl of Portland, (who yet remained there with the king's approbation, and knew well enough from whence the speeches came, having himself caused them to be printed,) and shewing them to him, desired he would move the house, that that speech might, by their order, be burned by the hand of the hangman; by which means the kingdom would be informed, that it had never been spoken by him. The earl said, he would willingly do him the service; but he observed, that the speeches were printed in that manner, that where the earl of Pembroke's speech ended on the one side of the leaf, his (the lord Brooke's) speech began on the other side, so that one could not be burned, without burning the other too; which he knew not how the earl of Pembroke would like; and therefore he durst not move it without his consent. Whereupon they both went to the earl, who was then likewise in the house; and Portland told him what the Lord Brooke desired, and asked him whether he wished it should be done. He, who heard he was very well spoken of, for having spoke so honestly for peace, said, he did not desire it. Upon which Brooke, in great anger, asked, if he had ever made that speech; he was very sure he had never made the other; and the other with equal choler replied, that he was always for peace; and though he could not say he had spoken all those things together, he was sure he had spoken them at several times; and that he knew as well that he had always been against peace, and had often used all those expressions which were in the speech, though,

---

[19] *Two Speeches Made in the House of Peers, on Munday the 19 of December, For, and Against Accommodation. The One by the Earl of Pembroke, the other by the Lord Brooke* (London, 1642), p. 6.

it may be, not all together. Upon which they entered into a high combat of reproachful words against each other, to the no small delight of the earl, who had brought them together, and of the rest of the standersby.[20]

The barb of the story lies in the fact that Clarendon had written both speeches as a jest for the King. The King had once boasted that he could recognize the style of anything Clarendon wrote; whereupon Clarendon showed him the speech attributed to Pembroke but actually written by Clarendon himself, and the King was taken in.[21] But the expense of the joke was ultimately borne by Brooke, who never learned the true facts. Years later Horace Walpole, who held Brooke in unusually high regard [22] but whose respect for Clarendon was distinctly qualified,[23] was moved to disgust at the recollection of this performance, particularly at the fact that Clarendon never in his lifetime revealed the truth to the public. In his *Catalogue of the Royal and Noble Authors of England* Walpole included a short sketch and criticism of Brooke. At the time he wrote it, it was still believed that the speech in answer to Pembroke had been delivered by Brooke, and Walpole has this to say:

> As the utmost impartiality is intended in this treatise, it is right to acquaint the reader, that this lord Brooke, with Roman principles, was not without Roman prejudices, and gross ones too. In this speech he declared his approbation of such men in the parliament's army *as would piously have sacrificed their own fathers to the commands of both houses.*[24]

The *Catalogue of the Royal and Noble Authors* first appeared in 1758; but the belated publication of Clarendon's *Life* in 1759

---

[20] Clarendon, *Life* (Oxford, 1827), I, 162–163.

[21] Clarendon, *Life*, I, 161.

[22] For example, see Walpole, *Works* (1798), I, 357: "The Lord Brooke exerted the utmost spirit and gallantry in the war." In his letters and throughout his writings Walpole from time to time expresses his admiration of Brooke, usually in conjunction with expressions of his lack of admiration for Sir Fulke, the first Lord Brooke. A representative example is the following excerpt from a letter of June 10, 1777, to the Countess of Upper Ossory concerning her stay at Warwick Castle: "I beg the possessor's pardon, but I set very little store by Sir Fulke Greville. Oh, but in the castle is a portrait of my hero, Lord Brook of the Civil War. . ." (Walpole, *Letters*, ed. Mrs. Paget Toynbee, 1914, X, 56).

[23] Walpole says of Clarendon that "No man ever delivered so much truth with so little sincerity. . . One may pronounce on my lord Clarendon in his double capacity of statesman and historian, that he acted for liberty but wrote for prerogative" (Walpole, *Works*, 1798, I, 387–388).

[24] Walpole, *Works*, I, 358 (italics Walpole's).

revealed that the speech was not Brooke's at all. In the final revision of his works, therefore, as represented in the edition published in 1798 after his death, Walpole appends the following note after the paragraph quoted above:

> I leave this passage as it stood in the former editions, because the justice due to the character of this patriot lord will appear in the stronger colours, when the censure extorted from me by the appearance of truth is contrasted with the real truth. In fact, his lordship never made the speech in question. From the private history of the earl of Clarendon it at last comes out, that that speech was coined by the chancellor, who seems struck with his own art, not with the lengths to which party carried men in order to blacken their antagonists. One might excuse what he did in the turbulence of factions; one wonders that he could coolly recollect such an imposition so many years afterwards, without paying one repentant syllable of apology to an injured foe! — At least let it be my part to observe, that this speech, which he did *not* make, is the worst act I can find recorded of lord Brooke.[25]

Whatever opprobrium may have attached to Brooke's name as a result of Clarendon's pleasantry, his reputation among the Parliamentary leaders was not damaged. As peace negotiations began to appear less and less hopeful, Essex and his staff determined to form military associations of counties, "so as to combine into active resistance the scattered elements of the Parliamentary party over a considerable extent of country." [26] In addition to a Midland Association and an Eastern Association, the counties of Warwickshire and Staffordshire were consolidated under one command, which was assigned on December 31 to Brooke.[27]

For the first few weeks of 1643 there were no active military engagements of consequence in this locality, but Brooke was undoubtedly busy with administrative matters. There is also evidence that early in the year he contributed two hundred pounds to the Parliamentary treasury,[28] and during January Lady Brilliana Harley was considering asking Brooke to use his influence to help a certain Mr. Yates, visiting preacher at Hereford, who had been accused by the congregation of being a Roundhead and thus kept from preaching.[29] An appeal to Brooke's authority

[25] Walpole, *Works*, I, 359.
[26] Gardiner, I, 77.
[27] *Lords Journals*, V, 520.
[28] *Historical MS. Commission*, 13th Report (Portland), I, 86.
[29] *Historical MS. Commission*, 13th Report (Portland), III, 103, in a letter to

in his new administrative capacity occurs in a letter from Sir William Brereton to Captain Francis Rowe, dated February 10 from Nantwich in Cheshire, which Brereton had taken late in January. Sir William requested that Parliamentary troops be ordered to his locality and prayed that Brooke be acquainted with the fact "that if he do not come down speedily he loseth a brave opportunity and loseth the hearts of Staffordshire." [30] But whatever Brooke had been doing in these weeks, the time for decisive action on his part was near at hand.

her husband, Sir Robert Harley, dated January 24, 1642/3. Lady Harley had occasionally appealed to Brooke on other matters, and she mentioned him more than once in her correspondence. See *Letters of the Lady Brilliana Harley*, ed. Thomas T. Lewis, Camden Society Publications (London, 1845), pp. 49, 170, *et passim*.

[30] *Historical MS. Commission*, 13th Report (Portland), I, 96.

VI

"LAST WEEKS PROCEEDINGS"

Toward the end of February Brooke had gathered his forces
together in preparation for action in Warwickshire and Staffordshire. On the occasion of the election of his captains and commanders, probably around February twentieth and no later than
the twenty-sixth, Brooke delivered a speech subsequently printed
in London. Unlike the harangue in November in the Guildhall
it is a well-constructed oration, not without literary merit. Brooke
began with a salute to England, describing "the flourishing and
beauteous face of this Kingdom, overspread with the leprosie of
a Civill War," and summarized the reasons that impelled him,
and which he felt should impel others, to join the Parliamentary
cause:

> No man is born for his own use only, saith that great Common-wealths-
> man of the Romans, Cicero, his friends and Countrey-men claim an ample
> share in his abilities, as your friends, your Countrey, nay your Religion and
> God himself demands in yours. And surely it would be both unnaturall and
> impious to denie such powerfull suitors your assistance. I need not remon-
> strate what it is you are to fight for, the Cause is so open and obvious to
> every understanding. It is for your wives, your children, and your substance,
> your lives and liberties, nay that which is more powerfull to move mens
> affections, the testimony of good consciences, and what ever can be to
> humaine frailty deare and precious; all these, as if they sought the way to
> new mischiefes through the old ones, are pointed at by the Popish malig-
> nants now in arms against us.[1]

After enumerating atrocities perpetrated by the "Popish" enemy,
a conventional technique, he returns to the free conscience as
the strongest motive for joining actively in the struggle. He also
disposes of one of the most common objections:

[1] *A Worthy Speech made by the Right Honourable the Lord Brooke, at the
election of his Captaines and Commanders at Warwick Castle* (London, 1643)
(dated by Thomason February 26), pp. 3–4.

. . . whereas the going against the King may stagger some resolutions, I shall easily disabuse you from those vaine surmises and incertain imaginations, 'tis for the King wee fight, to keep a Crown for our King, a Kingdom for our Soveraign and his posterity, to maintain his known rights and priviledges; which are relative with the peoples liberties . . . (and long may he live and reign over us).[2]

Brooke explains his refusal of the proffered assistance of German mercenaries, arguing that men who fight for a cause, whose "hearts goe with their hands," are more likely to bring the war to a swift conclusion than those who fight for pay and "covet to spin out the warres to a prodigious length." He attacks with some violence the able and wealthy men who look to the Parliamentary army for defense yet contribute nothing to its maintenance. And he concludes with a prayer:

That God Almighty will arise and maintaine his own cause, scattering and confounding the devices of his enemies, not suffering the ungodly to prevaile over his poore innocent flocke. Lord, we are but a handfull in consideration of thine and our enemies, therefore O Lord fight thou our battailes, goe out as thou didst in the time of King David before the Hosts of thy servants, and strengthen and give us hearts, that we shew our selves men for the defence of thy true Religion, and our owne and the King and Kingdomes safety.[3]

Military operations were shortly to be resumed, if they were not already under way. A pamphlet entitled *The Last Weeks Proceedings of the Lord Brooke*, printed March 1, indicates that Brooke had been in Northampton on Tuesday, February 21, raising recruits and ammunition though "countermanding all plunder, which accordingly was performed, except a little parcell of Money which Captaine Browne's cornet took from a Woman, for which since he is cashiered." [4] On Wednesday Brooke moved to Coventry to do more recruiting, but hearing that some three hundred Royalists were in Stratford advanced to that area on Friday, with a brief stop at Warwick for reinforcements. On Friday night the enemy was engaged:

My Lord sent Horse to prevent intelligence, yet a countryman and friend of theirs, espying us 2. miles on this side, crossed the Fields, and gave the

[2] *A Worthy Speech*, pp. 5–6.
[3] *Ibid.*, p. 8.
[4] *The Last Weeks Proceedings*, p. 2.

enemy advertisement, upon which they drew out themselves under a hill, where they could view us in our march, we drew the greatest part of our Artillery to the Vanne, they having the greatest part of our Horse, and we expediting the first charge there, but withall suspecting their wheeling about, we drew up our reere, so that we stood tryangle upon three hils in full view each of other; from the reer division we let flie a drake, which ran through the midst of them, and forced them to wheele off towards the Town, and we hasted after them so fast as our Carriages and the plowd Lands well softened with the raine, would permit us. But our enemies hast was such, that we could not come within musquet shot of them.[5]

Shortly after the entry into Stratford some powder exploded in the town house, "no doubt designed to have surprised my Lord and all his chiefe, presuming they would have sate in councell there," but no one was killed. The correspondent concludes:

We returned to Warwicke last night, and this morning we are following another designe, and my Lords Forces left at Coventry, joyne issue with us. The country comes in to Coventry: And so [to?] my Lords service in great multitudes, whereupon the Committee have sent for his Lordship, but I trust his Lordship will first dispatch the designe.[6]

The "designe," now that Warwickshire was fairly well under control, was the subjugation of Straffordshire, and toward that end the first task was the relief of Lichfield, which had been occupied by Lord Chesterfield and a small Royalist detachment. Brooke proceeded to Lichfield with a force of about twelve hundred,[7] arriving Wednesday, March 1, and began an assault on the cavaliers, who had fortified themselves in the cathedral close. It was scarcely an engagement of such importance as to require the presence of the commander of the associated counties. But Brooke was on the scene and personally directed the operation, in the course of which on the following day he unexpectedly met his death. As the author of the prophetically titled *Last Weeks Proceedings* had hoped, Brooke did first attempt to "dispatch the designe," but he was never to respond to the call of the Committee in London.

[5] *The Last Weeks Proceedings*, pp. 3–4.
[6] *Ibid.*, p. 5.
[7] Collins, *Peerage*, IV, 355. This must have been the advance alluded to in a letter dated February 27 from the Earl of Lindsay to the Earl of Manchester, that Lord Brooke had marched with his forces at night "but it was not known whither" (*Historical MS. Commission*, 8th Report, II, 55a; the letter is incorrectly assigned to the year 1639 in that collection, but clearly refers to 1643).

According to Clarendon the Royalists who had occupied Lichfield did not constitute a formidable garrison:

. . . some gentlemen of that county [Staffordshire], rather well affected than experienced, before they were well enough provided to go through their work, seized on the Close in Lichfield for the king; a place naturally strong, and defended with a moat, and a very high and thick wall; which in the infancy of war was thought a good fortification.

Clarendon's account of the brief action is succinct and probably as accurate as any:

To suppress this growing force, within the limits of his association, the lord Brook advanced with a formed body of horse, foot, and cannon, part drawn from the Earl of Essex's army, and the rest out of the garrisons of Coventry and Warwick; and, without any resistance, entered the city of Lichfield; which being unfortified, was open to all comers. The number in the Close was not great, nor their provisions such as should have been, and very well might have been, made; so that he made no doubt of being speedily master of it; sir John Gell having brought up a good addition of strength to him from Derby. He was so far from apprehending any danger from the besieged, that himself lodged in a house within musket-shot of the Close; where, the very day he meant to assault it, sitting in his chamber, and the window open, he was, from the wall of the Close, by a common soldier, shot with a musket in the eye; of which he instantly died without speaking a word.[8]

Details in various accounts of the event differ; one report was that Brooke was standing in a doorway to which he had come to ascertain the occasion of a sudden shout; another that he was standing in the street to watch the effect of a cannon shot.[9] There is no question, however, but that he was killed outright. Brooke's soldiers were reported as "almost distracted" and "ready to disband,"[10] had not Gell led them successfully to the capture of the close and the taking of its garrison as prisoners. Gell's completion of the action did not alter the fact that the Parliamentary party had received a telling blow. The leaders knew that Brooke was virtually irreplaceable; indeed, he was already being con-

[8] Clarendon, *History of the Rebellion* (London, 1826), III, 454–455.

[9] Anthony Wood, *Athenae Oxonienses*, ed. Bliss (1815), II, cols. 432–434; and Gardiner, I, 97.

[10] *Historical MS. Commission*, 13th Report (Portland), I, 103; and 9th Report. II, 388a.

sidered as a possible successor to Essex as commander in chief.[11]

If the Parliamentarians were stunned, however, the Royalists were overjoyed, and they claimed to have reason for their joy far beyond the mere fact of the death of one of their most formidable adversaries. It happened that the cathedral at Lichfield was St. Chad's, and that March 2, the day on which the assault began and on which Brooke was killed, was St. Chad's Day. Furthermore, it was reported that on that very morning Brooke, who was accustomed to pray in public, had prayed that "if the cause he were in were not right and just, he might be presently cut off," and that on the way to Lichfield from Coventry he had instructed his chaplain, probably Peter Sterry, to preach a sermon on the text "If I perish, I perish" (Esther 4:16).[12] What more convincing proof of the injustice of their cause and the sinfulness of waging war against the King, asked the Royalists, could the Parliamentarians possibly want? Laud, in the Tower, entered in his diary that Brooke, who had ever been "fierce against bishops and cathedrals," had been killed with "his bever up, and armed to the knee, so that a musket at that distance could have done him but little harm," with the clear implication that St. Chad had intervened to avenge the desecration.[13] Anthony Wood unearthed a story that attributed to Brooke a remark he was supposed to have made in 1640, that he hoped he should live to see not one stone left upon another of St. Paul's, and Wood dwelt with stern satisfaction on the fact that that "church stands yet and that eye is put out which hoped to see the ruins of it." [14] The tradition that the death of Brooke was a manifestation of divine vengeance persisted for years. Horace Walpole sneered at Clarendon for citing, as other Royalists had done, the prayer Brooke was said to have uttered on the morning of his death:

It is lamentable that my lord Clarendon should relate gravely many remarks of the populace on his death, in their language called *judgments*. Lord Brooke it seems had prayed aloud that very morning, "That if the cause he was engaged in were not just and right, he might instantly be cut off." —

[11] Gardiner, I, 98.

[12] Wood, II, cols. 432–434; Clarendon, *Rebellion*, III, 455; and V. de Sola Pinto, *Peter Sterry* (Cambridge, 1934), p. 13.

[13] Wood, *loc. cit.*

[14] *Ibid.*

Had lord Clarendon mentioned this as an instance of lord Brooke's sincerity, it had been commendable: but did the noble historian suppose that the Ruler of the universe inflicts sudden destruction as the way to set right a conscientious man? [15]

But the story was still current in the time of Scott, who alluded to it in *Marmion*:

> . . . Fitz-Eustace' care
> A pierced and mangled body bare
> To moated Lichfield's lofty pile;
> And there, beneath the southern aisle,
> A tomb, with Gothic sculpture fair,
> Did long Lord Marmion's image bear,
> (Now vainly for its site you look;
> 'Twas levell'd, when fanatic Brook
> The fair cathedral storm'd and took;
> But, thanks to Heaven, and good Saint Chad,
> A guerdon meet the spoiler had!) [16]

The triumphant shouts of the Royalists that vengeance had been done and that God had revealed himself to be on the King's side were balanced by expressions of genuine grief among the Parliamentarians. Lady Harley wrote to a friend on March 8 that she would be glad to receive some assurance of his safety "which will some way refresh my thoughts after the sad news of my Lord Brooke's death." [17] An anonymous pamphleteer who described himself as "A loyall Subject to the King, and a lover of the late Lord Brookes, and all his welwishers" published a tribute, in the fulsome style of the worst seventeenth-century funeral sermons, entitled *Englands Losse and Lamentation*. In the course of it, for example, Lichfield is arraigned as "the sinke of iniquity, cage of uncleane and wicked spirits: ungodly, prophane, and most prodigiously wicked: chiefe instrument of the Kingdomes misery!" [18] But certain passages do suggest some of the respects in which Brooke was admired by his contemporaries (if one makes proper allowance for rhetorical distortion and exaggeration):

[15] Walpole, *Works*, I, 357.
[16] Scott, *Marmion*, canto VI, xxxvi.
[17] *Historical MS. Commission*, 14th Report (Portland), III, 106.
[18] *Englands Losse and Lamentation* (London, 1643), sig. A3v.

Is there not a Prince, and a great man fallen in Israel? fallen by uphold-ing thee? and not onely a Prince, and a great man, but a holy just, and righteous, great man: a Pillar of the Church a Supporter of the State, That right Honorable Robert Lord Brooke; rightly to be honoured to lasting pos-terities? He was honest, and just to all men; righteous in all his wayes, and religious in his whole life; learned in all arts: And able in all Sciences: Loyall to his King, faithfull to his Country: And valiant in his undertakings for the defence of both: to his end pittiful to his enemies, in his end happy to himselfe. And by his end terror to his enemies; whose bloud will hasten vengeance upon the actors, and causes of such cruelties.

Who can but commend his parts and honour his vertues, Morall and Divine? What man can staine his life, blemish his practise, tax his fidelity, or gainsay his stoutnesse, courage, and valour, in him as much manifested, in so little a time, as ever in any man? At his first meeting with his great Antagonist E. N. betweene Banbury, and Edge-hill, Heroick, Brooke, offered to deside the contraries quarrell, by a Lordly combat (as is known to those whom it then concerned,) and for his undaunted courage against the face of an Enemy in battell; Let Keinton, and Branford make report; Stratford cannot deny it, and Lichfield must confesse the same. . .

O England. . . That hast lost a Noble refreshing Brooke . . . a pillar of the Kingdome, a staffe of the War, a peere of the Parliament, a Patriarch of his Country, a sincere servant of God: and a loyall Subject to the King, and State.[19]

Henry Harington published *An Elegie upon the Death of the Mirrour of Magnanimity, the right Honourable Robert Lord Brooke* reminiscent in imagery (though hardly in poetic execu-tion) of Donne or Crashaw:

> Back blushing morne, to thine Eternall bed,
> Ruffle for ever the tresses of thine head
> In some thick Cloud, and thou whose raies do burn
> The Center of the Universe, returne . . .
> Brave Brooke is dead, like Lightning, which no part
> O'th body touches, but first strikes the heart,
> This word hath murdred all; it can a shower
> Enforce from every eye, it hath a power
> To alter natures course, how else should all
> Run wilde with mourning, and distracted fall.
> Is't not a grosse untruth to say, thy breath
> Expir'd too soon? or that impartiall Death
> Thy Corps too soon surpriz'd? No, if thy yeares

[19] *Englands Losse and Lamentation*, sig. A2v. There is, incidentally, no record elsewhere that Brooke ever challenged Northampton to single combat.

Be numbered by thy Vertues, or our teares,
Thou didst the old Methuselam outlive;
Though Time not forty yeares account can give
Of thine abode on earth, yet every hower
Of thine unpattern'd life, by Vertues power
A yeare in length surpast, each well-spent day,
The body maketh young, the soule makes gray.
Ah cruell Death! who with one cursed Ball,
Didst make the Atlas of our State to fall,
In one thou all hast slaine, whose Death alone,
A death will be unto a Million.
Could none but his sweet Nectard blood appease
The fire-sprung Bullets heat? Must it needs seaze
His sacred face, it selfe there to enshrine,
Not in an earthly, but a Tombe divine . . .
And is this blessed Brooke (whose Cristall streames
Sweld with such store of Grace, whose blisseful beames
Enlightened all) is it so soone drawne drie,
Leaving its ancient current, to fill each eye
With mournefull teares, surely in Paradise
It selfe it now dischannels, where no vice
Or shade of it appeares, a place most pure,
Where all such Saints for ever must endure.
. . . if yet some vertuous be,
They but weake apparitions are of thee.
Thine actions were most just, thy words mature,
And every scean of life from sin so pure,
That scarce in its whole history we can
Finde Vice enough to say thou wert but man.
'Tis past all mortals power, then much more mine,
To tell what vertues dwelt within this shrine;
Yet if illiterate persons walk this way,
And ask what jewell glorifies this clay,
Say, good Brookes ashes this Tombe hath in keeping,
Then lead them forth, lest they grow blind with weeping.
Tell but his name, no more, that shall suffice,
To draw downe floods of teares from dryest eyes.
Our griefes are infinite, therefore my Muse,
Cast Anchor here; mine eyes cannot effuse
Any more teares; this for thy comfort know:
Fate cannot give us such another blow.

At least two more elegies were printed, an anonymous one entitled
*An Elegie upon the much lamented Death of the Right Honour-
able the Lord Brooke,* and one by Brooke's philosophical op-

ponent, the mathematician John Wallis, who further honored him with an anagram:

GREVILIUS

VERGILIUS

And if VERGILIUS, why not MARO too?
Our AMOR sure he was, we Lov'd him so.[20]

The Parliamentary Chronicle declared that Brooke's name and memory deserved "to remain deeply engraven in letters of gold on high-erected pillars of marble," [21] Baxter praised him in the *Saints Everlasting Rest*,[22] and Milton the following year was to pay tribute in the *Areopagitica* to a fallen compatriot in the fight for freedom of conscience:

What would be best advised then, if it be found so hurtful and so unequal to suppress opinions for the newness, or the unsuitableness to a customary acceptance, will not be my task to say; I only shall repeat what I have learned from one of your own honorable number, a right noble and pious Lord, who had he not sacrificed his life and fortunes to the Church and Commonwealth, we had not now missed and bewailed a worthy and undoubted patron of this argument. Ye know him I am sure; yet I for honour's sake, and may it be eternal to him, shall name him, the Lord Brook.[23]

Gradually the Parliamentary forces recovered from the blow. The war continued without interruption, and in June the Earl of Denbigh was appointed commander of the associated counties that included Warwickshire.[24] There are references from time to time in state documents to sums of money loaned by Brooke and to their repayment by Parliament to the executors of his estate.[25] The maintenance of the garrison at Warwick Castle, an expense formerly borne by Brooke, was referred to the Committee for the Safety of the Kingdom.[26] As late as January, 1648, Parliament ordered payment of five thousand pounds to Lady Brooke for

[20] Wallis, *Truth Tried* (London, 1643), sig. S4v. The elegy is printed on sigs. S2–S2v.

[21] Neal, *History of the Puritans*, I, 447.

[22] Baxter, *Saints Everlasting Rest* (London, 1649), pp. 82–83.

[23] Milton, *Works*, IV, 346.

[24] *Lords Journals*, VI, 92.

[25] *Lords Journals*, V, 640a; *Commons Journals*, II, 990b.

[26] *Commons Journals*, III, 33.

the benefit of her youngest son Fulke, born after the death of his father at Lichfield.[27]

Lady Brooke figures prominently in the records for some time following her husband's death. Little is known of her situation during the period of Brooke's active service in the war, beyond the fact that she was expecting her fifth child when he was killed. But after Brooke's death the King granted the wardship of Brooke's eldest son and heir, Francis, the third Lord Brooke, to Lord Digby, the Earl of Bristol. Lady Brooke petitioned Parliament that her son be discharged from the composition of his wardship to so pronounced a Royalist:

> That whereas the King's Majesty hath granted unto George Lord Digby the Wardship of Francis Lord Brooke her Eldest Son, by colour whereof he hath not only entered into most of her Son's Manors and Lands, but likewise into most of the Lands wherein your Petitioner hath any Jointure, and receiveth the Rents, and hath converted the Stock thereupon to his own Use, and imprisoned many of the Tenants, to their great Loss and almost utter undoing, and to the great Damage of your Petitioner and her said Son: and whereas their hath been much unavoidable Loss and Damage sustained in Warwick Castle, as well as in the Buildings and Gardens, as in the Furniture, Bedding, and Household-stuff, by reason of the continual Residence of the Garrison and many Prisoners there; and whereas your Petitioner's Husband was at great charges as Commander in Chief for the Two associate Counties of Warwicke and Stafford, for which he never received any Recompence or Pay, in which Service he lost his Life, leaving your Petitioner young with child of a Son now living, for whom he had made no Provision:
>
> She humbly prayeth, that her Eldest Son (in regard his Father was slain in the Parliament's Service) may be freely discharged from Composition for his said Wardship; and that his Wardship may be granted to your Petitioner, for his Use.[28]

The petition was granted, along with a further request by Lady Brooke that Bristol's house in Queen Street be settled upon herself and her youngest son.[29]

It was through this posthumous son that Brooke was to become ancestor of the present Warwick line. Francis, third Lord Brooke, died without heirs in 1658; the second son, Robert, fourth

[27] *Lords Journals*, IX, 661.
[28] *Lords Journals*, VI, 692a.
[29] *Lords Journals*, VI, 690b, 692a–693a.

Lord Brooke, a Royalist who was active in the Restoration, died in 1677, also without heirs; the third and fourth sons, Edward and Algernon, had in the meantime died, and the title passed to Fulke, who brought up a family and kept the line alive. In 1746 the Barony was raised to an Earldom, and in 1759 the Earl Brooke was created Earl of Warwick.[30]

It is impossible to speculate with any certainty upon the course that Robert, Lord Brooke, would have pursued had he lived. From some of his utterances it would appear that he could not have countenanced the execution of the King, but in 1643 it would have been difficult to find any public figure who would seem likely to condone such an action. Dugdale believed that Brooke could not have held to his stubborn course for much longer:

> A person he was, who, for the Nobleness of his extraction . . . and many personal endowments, deserv'd a better fate, at least to have fallen in a better cause. Who (had he liv'd, 'tis believ'd by his Friends) would soon have seen through the Pretences of that Faction.[31]

Clarendon, whose sympathies lay with Dugdale's, took a different view:

> They who were acquainted with him believed him to be well natured and just; and rather seduced and corrupted in his understanding, than perverse and malicious. Whether his passions or conscience swayed him, *he was undoubtedly one of those who could have been with most difficulty reconciled to the government of church or state*: and therefore his death was looked upon as no ill omen to peace, and was exceedingly lamented by his party; which had scarce a more absolute confidence in any man than in him.[32]

Walpole, for once, agrees with Clarendon:

> . . . royalist writers condescend to say, that if he had lived a little longer, he would probably have seen through the designs of his party and deserted them. This silly sort of apology had been made for other patriots, and by higher writers than mere genealogists, as if nothing but the probability of a conversion could excuse those heroes who withstood the arbitrary proceedings of Charles and his ministers, and to whose spirit we owe so much of our liberty. . . [T]here is not the least reason to suppose that this Lord

[30] Collins, *Peerage*, IV, 351–361.
[31] Dugdale, *Baronage*, II, 442.
[32] Clarendon, *Rebellion*, III, 455 (italics mine).

Brooke would have abandoned his principles: Lord Clarendon represents him as one of the most determined of the party; and it is not probable that a man who was on the point of seeking *liberty* in the forests of America, would have deserted her banners when victorious in her own Britain.[33]

The position taken by Walpole and Clarendon appears to be more tenable than that of Dugdale, the "mere genealogist." Brooke, who did not hesitate to spend his wealth and risk his life for Parliament and who did not bow blindly to the king he professed to love, demonstrated often enough that he had the courage of his convictions and that those convictions were deeply rooted.

[33] Walpole, *Works*, I, 356–357.

Part Two

"The Nature of Truth"

The search for truth was especially characteristic of the seventeenth century, and it was pursued in many ways and by many different sorts of seekers. Bacon's efforts toward this end involved the discovery of scientific truth, and the impetus he gave to the development of science in the "century of genius" is well recognized. If he was not actually the father of any particular scientific achievement he was at least, in Professor Bush's phrase, the godfather of many. Lord Herbert of Cherbury, on the other hand, devoted himself in *De veritate* to the formulation of principles of religious truth that seemed finally acceptable and consonant with the authority of reason and the testimony of the "common notions" inherent in the mind of man. Boyle and Newton and countless virtuosi followed in Bacon's train, Hobbes and Locke and the eighteenth-century deists followed in Lord Herbert's.

The quest went on in areas other than that of formal philosophy. The metaphysical poets expressed with careful precision, drawing upon terms and images from the new science in order the more exactly to do so, their understanding of the truth of relationships between man and man, man and woman, man and God, man and the universe, relationships that defy rational definition. The truth of human destiny was a matter of grave concern to every thinker, whether he was poet or scientist, philosopher or theologian. Life seemed meaningful to Taylor principally in terms of its being a preparation for death, for Hobbes only as consisting of particles of matter in motion. To Bishop Goodman the world seemed to be running down, to George Hakewill every phenomenon in nature witnessed the providence of God. To Milton ultimate truth rested upon the justification of the ways of God to man through the endowment of man with freedom of choice and the rectification of the inevitable abuses of this freedom by the Christian sacrifice and redemption.

These investigations into the truth of the nature and destiny of man were not in the main carried on by cloistered scholars but by active men of affairs in a world of shifting political and religious currents: noblemen and commoners, Lord Chancellors and Latin Secretaries, bishops and deans. Furthermore, their researches and speculations were not in that century stultified by "areas of specialization"; the scientist concerned himself with theology no less than the theologian with science.

It is less surprising, then, that an energetic young political reformer should have turned his attention to speculative philosophy in that century than it might prove to be in the twentieth. This was Brooke's concern in the summer of 1640, an effort culminating in publication of *The Nature of Truth* in the fall. Brooke had shown even by that time that he was an active Puritan who expressed his calling through a burning drive toward political and religious reform. This first of his two published tracts reveals some of the intellectual and spiritual bases for his beliefs and actions.

VII

RENAISSANCE HERITAGE

In the first book of the *Corpus Hermeticum,* the strange document of the early Christian era attributed to the shadowy Hermes
Trismegistus, a man has a vision of "a Being of vast and boundless magnitude" called Poimandres, who offers to tell him whatever he wishes to hear. The man without hesitation asks, "I would
fain learn the things that are, and understand their nature, and
get knowledge of God." [1] It is more or less on the scale of this
request that Lord Brooke undertook his investigation of the nature of truth. There are few matters of seventeenth-century interest that he does not touch upon in the something under two
hundred pages of this suggestive treatise, which, partly because
it reaches into so many corners of learning, may be considered a
representative product of the later English Renaissance. As it will
appear later, Brooke was to some extent a Baconian; it will become clear as well that he also took, if not all, then a goodly
portion of knowledge for his province.

The seventeenth century was an age of versatility and an age
of many paradoxes, which produced versatile and often paradoxical men, and great men withal. A courtier and statesman
could become a philosopher and the expositor of a new scientific
method. An Olympian poet could achieve distinction as a political
pamphleteer. A country doctor could respect his own reason
above the dictates of the theologians and yet love to lose himself
in a mystery and pursue his reason to an *O altitudo!* A libertine
poet could become Dean of St. Paul's, and an obscure vicar could
anatomize delightfully and compendiously the prevalent psy-
chological disorder of the day.

It was an age, too, when many currents met and crossed. Men
were preoccupied with theology; heaven and hell were living

[1] *Hermetica,* ed. Walter Scott (Oxford, 1924), I, 114–115.

realities, and the best-sellers were religious tracts. Science moved into one of its great periods of growth. During these years Bacon evolved the experimental method; Harvey discovered the circulation of the blood; the new science of Copernicus, Kepler, and Galileo gained increasing acceptance, and the way was paved for Newton. Under the impact of humanism and science philosophy changed its course, and the Platonic and scholastic traditions fused and blended in the era of Descartes, Hobbes, Spinoza, and Locke. The spirit of Christian humanism led some minds to a reconciliation of reason and faith and a broad toleration, though disruptive forces growing out of scientific rationalism began to appear. Then through two revolutions political reform was accomplished in England and constitutional monarchy was eventually established, advancing the cause of public and private liberty.

Brooke was a part of this age, though he died before the political reforms for which he labored were accomplished and before the disintegrating forces in philosophy had shaken the relative security of the humanistic principles in which he put his faith. His versatility in action is more than evident from the record of his life. His range of thought and reading is demonstrated by the frame of reference of *The Nature of Truth.* There one finds evidence of wide theological knowledge, from the Bible and the early Church Fathers to such famous Puritan theologians of his own time as William Ames, Hugh Broughton, and John Cotton. One finds the Renaissance gentleman's acquaintance with classical literature and philosophy; and the synthesis of his classical learning and his religious faith is sufficiently complete to warrant his being called a Christian humanist, like the great poet he may to some degree have influenced. Brooke was acquainted with scholastic as well as classical philosophy, and with the Renaissance thinkers who were descended in one way or another from Plato and Aristotle. In ideas and method he reflects the heritage of Augustine and Aquinas, whether or not he knew their writings directly or through the medium of Puritan theology. Among his favorite writers was very likely the Platonist Ficino, and he was familiar at least by name with the Renaissance defenders of Aristotle, such as Scaliger.

Among secular writers and ideas of his own era Brooke knew something of Bacon, and he was at least aware of the discoveries of Copernicus, Kepler, and Galileo. As evidence of an interest in natural science and the curiosities of learning he read the *History of Memorable Things* by the Italian antiquarian Pancirollus and was probably familiar with the encyclopedia of J. H. Alsted. He illustrates his argument with allusions to tides, to the "trigonall glasse," and to the theory of Gilbert which drew such scorn from Bacon, that the earth is a magnet. Brooke had read in the literature and philosophy of his own contemporaries, for he quotes a play by Sir John Suckling (evidence, perhaps, that his strong Puritanism did not render his taste prudish) and the *Nosce Te Ipsum* of Sir John Davies, and he alludes, though only in passing, to Lord Herbert's *De veritate*. He was evidently acquainted with the *Argenis* of John Barclay, and with a poem in praise of tobacco by Barclay's elegist, Raphael Thorius.

There are paradoxes, too, in the life and work of Brooke. For one thing, it was unusual that a young nobleman of wealth and position should so zealously labor in the cause of reform. One finds even more striking paradox in his writings. In one chapter of *The Nature of Truth*, for example, Brooke disproves a scholastic notion by a scholastic method. In another he calls Copernicus, a scientist, to witness that the senses, the very bases of scientific investigation, are, as Bacon in his "idols" recognized them to be, unreliable as evidence. As one reads through the treatise one becomes clearly aware that Brooke was the relatively rare combination of Puritan and humanist. He believed in freedom of interpretation, liberty of conscience, and toleration, yet believed, as all Calvinists did, in predestination, so that he may be both linked with and distinguished from Milton, his great contemporary.[2]

It is not merely Brooke's versatility, however, nor the paradoxical quality of some of his ideas, nor the combination of these two characteristics, that gives him relevance for the modern in-

[2] Milton was, however, a Calvinist until 1645 or so. See Maurice Kelley, *This Great Argument* (Princeton, 1941), p. 14 and ff. At the time Brooke was writing, then, he and Milton, who were also about the same age, were even more in agreement than they may appear to be to posterity, who have come to think of Milton most characteristically as an Arminian.

vestigator. He is important in other ways, partly for his influence on other thinkers, partly because he stated certain principles of value in his own right, and partly because his thought reflects and illuminates a number of contemporary philosophical and theological trends. He is interesting in a further respect in that his own life can be seen as a translation of his beliefs into action. It is far too much to say, as one authority has said, that Brooke was the founder of English idealism; [3] for, beside the fact that his method is more discursive and less well disciplined than that of the formal philosopher like Locke or Leibniz, one finds on investigation that his idealistic pronouncements were part of his heritage rather than notions original with him. Yet it is manifestly true that some of Brooke's utterances in *The Nature of Truth* are philosophically significant, and his position can profitably be studied as representative of certain phases of the thought of his day.

For example, as the Renaissance was partly a revolt from scholasticism and partly a continuation of its heritage, so one can see in Brooke a partial revolt from scholasticism and a considerable dependence upon it. He objects time and again to scholastic points of view, but fills his argument with scholastic categories, and he often argues, as I have already noted, by the scholastic method. Terms like "form," "substance," "activity," "reasonable soul," are common in this treatise. And yet Brooke's conception of the soul is radically different from the scholastic definitions deriving from Aristotle, and his ecstatic view of all creation as one sublime and unified emanation from God is in the mystical rather than the scholastic tradition. To Brooke all things can be reduced eventually to one radiant unity, an idea that has its roots in Platonism and Neo-Platonism, on both of which bodies of knowledge Brooke appears to have drawn, both directly and indirectly. His parallel of truth with "light" could have been drawn by Plotinus or could have appeared in the Hermetic writings. His inspired monism owes a heavy debt to Ficino. Brooke is an antischolastic and a Platonist, but his debt to scholasticism and Aristotelianism is great.

[3] J. Freudenthal, "Beiträge zur Geschichte der englischen Philosophie," *Archiv für Geschichte der Philosophie* 6:190–207, 380–399, especially 190, 388, and 399 (1892–93).

At the outset of this discussion, in which I shall endeavor to clarify the ideas, trace the main sources, and evaluate the contemporary significance of *The Nature of Truth*, it might be well to quote Brooke's description of his quest, one of his finest passages, to shed light on the path that this investigation is to follow:

Indeed Truth is that golden apple, which though it hath (in some sense) beene offered to the fairest; yet the most refined wits, the most high-raised fancies of the world, have courted her in vaine, these many ages: For whilst they have sought, with a Palsie hand, this Glorious star, through the perspective of thicke reason, they have either mounted too high, and confounding the Creator with the creature, made her God; or descending too low, and deserting the universal nature, have confined their thoughts to some individuall Truth, and restrained her birth to severall parcels within the Chaos.[4]

Brooke is mainly a rationalist; he trusts in right reason to guide man as far as man can guide himself.[5] Yet he does not consider faith to be inferior to reason, nor does he, like Browne, urge his haggard and unreclaimed reason to stoop unto the lure of faith. Indeed, he goes further than Browne and maintains, with the Cambridge Platonists, that faith and reason are the same, differing only in degree. He carries his rationalism to such a point that he considers time and place to exist only as products of the human mind. And yet at the same time he is almost a mystic inspired by an ineffable vision of the unity of all things, a unity so immanent and inclusive that it makes the petty wranglings of mankind, in which Brooke acknowledges himself to be involved, fall away before the face of divine beauty.

[4] *The Nature of Truth*, sigs. A11v–A12.

[5] Professor Barker, *Milton and the Puritan Dilemma* (Toronto, 1942), pp. 57–58, acknowledges that Brooke does not adequately define right reason, but suggests that this fact may in itself show the confidence he put in it.

VIII

THE ARGUMENT

The Nature of Truth continually and persistently maintains one proposition: namely, that man and all his attributes and works — in fact, all creation in all its diversity — are one with God. The point that Brooke is most intent on driving home is the harmony of all things, and the treatise itself can be appropriately described as a harmony of the multifarious philosophical and theological elements that formed the thinking of the author.

The opening chord is sounded in a "Preface to the Reader" by one who signs himself "J. S." If one is to believe John Wallis — and there appears to be no reason why one should not — "J. S." is John Sadler.[1] The substance of the preface is that this "Divine

---

[1] Wallis quotes the "Preface to the Reader" several times in his refutation, *Truth Tried,* each time prefacing his remarks with a phrase such as, "As Mr. Sadler says . . . ," as if it were a well-known fact that "J. S." is Sadler. See *Truth Tried,* pp. 7, 33, 99. John Sadler (1615–1674) was educated at Emmanuel College, Cambridge, where he became eminent for his knowledge of Hebrew and other Oriental languages. For some time he was a fellow of Emmanuel, from which he graduated B.A. in 1633 and M.A. in 1638. He became Master of Magdalene College, Cambridge, in 1650, and was a friend of Cromwell. He held several public offices during the Commonwealth, including two terms as M.P. At the Restoration he lost all his positions and retired to an estate in the country to look after his fourteen children. In 1662 he is reputed to have prophesied the plague and the great fire. At Cambridge he was accounted a man of great piety and scholarship, though, as one acquaintance remarked, "it must be owned he was not always right in his head, especially towards the latter end of his being master of the college." He is said to have written *Masquarade du ciel,* a "Celestiall Map, representing the late commotions between Saturn and Mercury about the Northern Thule," dedicated to the Queen, in 1640; *Rights of the Kingdom,* a discussion of the "duty, power, election, or succession, of our Kings and Parliaments," in 1649; and *Olbia. The New Iland lately discovered,* for Samuel Hartlib in 1660. See the article by Thompson Cooper, "John Sadler," *D.N.B.,* XVII, 593–4. One cannot but feel that the same author could hardly have written the "Preface" to Brooke's treatise at the time that he was composing, or had recently composed, a masque for the Queen. It may well be that two or more Sadlers are involved. But it is quite possible for the Sadler of Brooke's preface to have been the Sadler who wrote *Rights of the Kingdom* in 1649, who was a friend of Cromwell, held offices under the Commonwealth, and composed a tract for Samuel Hartlib in later years.

Discourse of Truth" has come to the writer from a noble hand, and he cannot bear "to stifle such a Beauty" at its birth; furthermore, since no one can resist truth, he has determined to publish it. Sadler explains that the author has "dived deep in those Prophetick Mysteries" of two chapters from the New Testament, Matthew 24 and Revelation 20, and has there perceived a close relationship between the human soul and truth.

Sadler alludes to the fact that the book was first written only as a letter to "a private Friend," and maintains that the author had not even perused, much less "refined," the book before its publication. The "private Friend" may or may not have been Sadler, but in that connection one may mention Brooke's own account of the composition of the treatise. In a postscript he alludes to the friend's "more serious and usefull studies," asking him to lend his "favourable construction in the perusall":

You have here my poore thoughts upon the twenty-fourth Chap. of Matth. that I was forced to, because I quote it, more than once, in sense differing from our Commentators: yea, I was necessitated to run through the whole Chapter. It will appeare in costly robes, adorned with lofty and glorious language, sweetned by many a pleasant and cleare Simile, quickned by divers acute and learned Criticismes: These, none of these are mine: My Cabinet enshrineth no such Treasure. I confesse, to save the labour of contending with Pareus, and others, I delivered to a Friend of Yours, and Mine, onely the *substratum* of the Discourse, desiring him, from those principles to undertake my adversaries. In lieu of this, he returned me the Chapter, imbellished with so much wit and learning, that I durst not call it mine, and so thought to have suppressed it; and Had done so, but that from the Law of friendship, you may challenge a share in what is His; and from that reason it liveth now, and is presented to Your view, hoping (for his sake, not for mine) to finde grace in your eyes.[2]

If this statement is to be taken as fact and not as conventional compliment, then two "friends" are involved: the "private Friend," possibly but not necessarily Sadler, to whom the treatise was sent as a letter; and the friend of both Brooke and the "private Friend," who may be responsible for some of the contents of the book. The identity of such a second friend cannot from the evidence at hand be conjectured.[3]

[2] *The Nature of Truth,* pp. 173–4.
[3] Unless it is someone like Henry Darley, who was acquainted with both Brooke and Wallis (see Chapter II above, pp. 15–16 and note 15).

The opening page of Brooke's tract reveals that his philosophy was close to theology, a fact that was true of the writings of all Puritans, including Milton. Brooke explains that he has attempted to "finde out the true sense of the Spirit" in two chapters of the New Testament that provide him with a point of departure, Matthew 24 and Revelation 20, both of which contain matter pertinent to an investigation of the nature of truth.

Matthew 24 begins with the prophecy of Jesus that the temple will be destroyed. The disciples ask him when these things shall be, and Jesus tells them of wars and pestilence and other calamities in the future. Brooke probably was attracted especially by verse 11, "And many false prophets shall rise, and shall deceive many," and by verse 24, "For there shall arise false Christs, and false prophets, and shall shew great signs and wonders; insomuch that, if it were possible, they shall deceive the very elect." The chapter continues with the parable of the fig tree: that is, that just as when the fig tree puts forth its leaves one knows that summer is nigh, so one will know that when these calamities occur, the Day of Judgment will be even at the doors.

There is an affinity between this chapter and the book of Revelation, of course; indeed, Matthew 24 is probably nearer in tone and substance to the apocalyptic prophecies of Revelation than any other part of the New Testament. Revelation 20 describes the imprisonment of Satan during the thousand years of the kingdom. The third verse is pertinent: "And cast him into the bottomless pit, and shut him up, and set a seal upon him, that he should deceive the nations no more, till the thousand years should be fulfilled: and after that he must be loosed a little season." In verse 7 Satan is "loosed," and in verse 8 it is said that he "shall go out to deceive the nations which are in the four quarters of the earth, Gog and Magog, to gather them together to battle: the number of whom is as the sand of the sea."

Both chapters are concerned with deception, a subject obviously relevant to a study of truth. Brooke was no doubt disturbed over the amount of what seemed to him to be "deception" around him as the English civil war drew near. The Roman Catholics were to him, as to most Puritans, subjects of antichrist (the Pope), and the Laudian hierarchy must have seemed little better. Furthermore, as Professor Haller has shown, by 1640 many Puritans were fully expectant that the millennium was at hand, perhaps immediately heralded by the Long Parliament, and apocalyptic and millennial speculations were certain to fall on ready ears.[4] Brooke embarked on private studies, then, in a time of dire predictions that may have seemed to him about to be accomplished, to seek a philosophical basis and an avenue toward the truth that he felt was being obscured. He concluded that truth is finally the all-embracing and radiant reality of which all individuals and all factions are a part. All things are one with God, who is truth. If this transcendent truth were but known, factionalism and dissension of all kinds would of necessity vanish, as all rivers eventually flow into one ocean.

Truth, then, is a mystery, declares Brooke at the beginning of the discourse. Since Adam's fall we are in the darkness of ignorance and cannot be expected to reach truth, either religious or moral. Truth is a "glorious star" that cannot be found if we seek it too high, identifying it with God, nor if we seek it too low, confusing it with the creatures of God.

Truth reigns in us in the understanding, and appears to us both as form, or substance, on the one hand, and on the other as "those workings which breathe from thence," or the actions of the soul.[5] The very nature of the understanding is truth; both the understanding and truth are rays of the "Divine Nature," and are in fact light and life. Indeed, the understanding and truth are one.[6]

---

[4] Haller, *The Rise of Puritanism*, p. 269.

[5] Cf. Aristotle, *De anima*, II, i, 412a (ed. and tr. W. S. Hett, Loeb Classical Library, p. 67): "We describe one class of existing things as substance; and this we subdivide into three: (1) matter, which is in itself not any particular thing; (2) shape or form, in virtue of which it is called some particular thing; and (3) a compound of the two. Matter is . . . potentiality, while form is realization or actuality." Brooke also uses the terms *actus primus* and *actus secundus* as his argument advances. He further reduces the "workings" of all three of Aristotle's souls (vegetative, sensitive, and rational, as explained in *De anima*, II) to one category. Everything emanates from the first Being.

[6] Brooke's emphasis on "light" in this context is distinctly Neo-Platonic. Plotinus, for example, discusses "divine light," which enables the intelligence to see, as the light of the sun enables the eye: "When Intelligence perceives this divine light, it is impossible to discern whence this light comes" (*Enneads*, V, vii-viii). Aristotle describes the soul (*De anima*, II, i, 412a, and II, ii, 414a) as the first actuality or form of the body, or "the form of that which has the capacity of hav-

In the second chapter Brooke takes issue with the scholastic classification of the understanding as a faculty through which the soul receives truth. In the next few chapters he enumerates the difficulties that he finds attendant upon such a classification. These obstacles drive him to a skepticism that forces him to reject the prevailing faculty psychology and to deny the distinctions between different kinds of knowledge, to maintain and reiterate that the soul and the understanding are one with light and truth.[7] The entire reasonable creature, the *totum existens*, is the recipient of light and truth, and it can be said that the recipient and the thing received, the reasonable creature and truth, are in themselves but one. All things, then, are one with light and truth and one with God, and "All Being seemeth to breath and catch after unity."[8] The argument through these chapters is illustrated richly with examples from the Bible, Puritan theology and the tomes of Mede and Brightman on the Apocalypse, classical and Renaissance philosophy, scientific experiment, music, mathematics, and contemporary belletristic literature.

In the eighth chapter Brooke argues the acceptability of the "doctrine of habits," provided that one understand both "infused" and "acquisite" habits to be the same, that "all the actings [of the soul] are onely new discoveries."[9] This conclusion, which amounts to an acceptance of the existence of innate ideas, is followed by a statement of agreement with the Platonic doctrine

---

ing a soul." The idea had wide currency in the Renaissance; see, for example, Spenser's "Hymne in Honour of Beautie," 132–133:

> For of the soule the bodie forme doth take:
> For soule is forme, and doth the bodie make.

One might say that here Brooke has Platonized this Aristotelian principle: as the soul is the form of the man, so light (or, as it appears later, Being, or God, or Truth, or One) is the form of the soul.

[7] Howard Schultz (*Milton and Forbidden Knowledge* [New York, 1955], p. 159) is quite correct in saying that this skepticism of Brooke's negates all of Lord Herbert's "compartmentalized epistemology." But it is unlikely that Brooke intended *The Nature of Truth* as "an escape from Lord Herbert" specifically, as Schultz hypothesizes. Brooke scarcely mentions him, and in one marginal gloss (*The Nature of Truth*, p. 40) alludes to an idea that he has been "informed" is expressed in *De veritate*, but apologizes that "I am not so happy as to have that booke by me, nor doe I remember it since my last reading it, so that I dare not say it confidently."

[8] *The Nature of Truth*, p. 32.

[9] *The Nature of Truth*, p. 47.

of reminiscence, which leads him in turn to the conclusion that faith and reason are the same, differing only in degree. Both faith and reason are gifts of God. It is therefore impossible to fall away from grace. Brooke agrees entirely with Calvin and Samuel Rutherford, upon whom Milton was to confer a dubious immortality in the sonnet "On the New Forcers of Conscience," that "spontaneity" rather than "free will" is the proper description of the motivation for human actions. For it is impossible to have great knowledge and little faith; if one knows the good one must do the good, or, as it may be put, the will necessarily follows the understanding. This point of view owes much to the Socratic notion of virtue, but Brooke, proceeding logically from his belief in the unity of being, carries the argument a step further, namely, to the point that the will is seen to be the same as the understanding. "I might adde," he concludes, "what good we know, we are: our act of understanding being an act of union, which (as before) being Metaphysicall in the soule, must be entire." [10]

After demonstrating in the ninth chapter that knowledge and the "affections" [11] are likewise one and the same, Brooke proceeds from his analysis of the "form and nature" of the understanding to the next major subdivision of his argument, consideration of what he calls "the particular and various workings" of the understanding. In the tenth chapter he begins his demonstration that the "workings" are one and the same as well, that they are "all conjoyned in one Being of light and truth," in the way that the fountain and the stream make but one river.[12] His

[10] *The Nature of Truth*, pp. 58–59. The Socratic notion of virtue is common in Puritan thought and elsewhere. William Ames wrote that the will "cannot will or nill any thing unless reason have first judged it to be willed or nilled" (Perry Miller, *The New England Mind*, p. 248). Hooker declares that "reason is the director of man's will, by discovering in action what is good" (*The Laws of Ecclesiastical Polity*, I, vii, 4). The idea was universal enough in the Renaissance to find expression in La Primaudaye's compendium, in which the understanding is described as "captain" over the will (*The French Academie* [London, 1602], p. 23).

[11] Brooke's use of the term "affections" in this chapter does not appear to be in a scholastic sense, for it would be a mixture of terms to maintain that the "affections" are the "activity" (or actuality) of the soul. He seems to mean "affections" more in the sense of love, perhaps both Christian and Platonic, possibly in the Ramist sense of the "glue" by which are held together the disparate entities in the world, that is, as a unifying force (cf. Miller, p. 131, quoting Alexander Richardson). Cf. Brooke's use of Ficino's idea of love, discussed later.

[12] *The Nature of Truth*, p. 82. The "fountain and stream" image was a favorite

argument carries him to the conclusion that the scholastic distinction between substance and accident, as that between *actus primus* and *actus secundus*, has no meaning; and from the implications of this conclusion he proceeds to the position that neither time nor place has real existence, a notion which stated thus is philosophically advanced, but which has clear antecedents in the Platonic heritage of Brooke's thought. Time and place seem to him to be "nothing but an extrinsecall modification of a thing." [13]

Brooke recognizes further that if time and place do not exist beyond the mind, if all our actions are but one, then it is difficult to explain the existence of evil and good. In answer to this hypothetical objection he maintains, with Augustine and other Platonists, that evil has no existence, that it is merely a "privation" of the good. Good and evil coexist in the same entities, just as both light and darkness coexist in the twilight. The senses may seem to tell us that a certain act consists of many parts or has many aspects, and yet the act is really but one, just as a prism may show many colors in some object that really possesses only one. Indeed, the senses themselves are not to be trusted in such matters; the Copernican theory, for example, if it is true, confutes the evidence that the senses have provided from time immemorial.[14]

The soul, Brooke continues in the twelfth chapter, cannot act falsely because falsehood has no existence. When the soul takes a false position it is not acting at all, as a man who mistakes an object he sees in the twilight cannot be said to be seeing the object. In the same way, pain has no existence but is only a privation of spirit and strength. To live in perpetual pain is better, as

---

one with Brooke and many Puritans and Platonists. Cf. Plotinus (*Enneads,* III, viii, 10): "The first Principle may indeed be conceived of as a spring of water which is its own origin, and which pours its water into many streams without itself becoming exhausted by what it yields, or even without running low, because the streams that it forms, before flowing away each in its own direction, and while knowing which direction it is to follow, yet mingles its waters with the spring."

[13] *The Nature of Truth,* p. 92.

[14] *The Nature of Truth,* p. 106: "The three leading Senses have confuted Copernicus these many yeares; for the eye seeth the circulations of the Heavens; we feele our selves upon a stable and firme foundation; and our eares heare not from the volutations of the Earth such a black Cant as her heavy rowlings would rumble forth: and yet now if we will beleeve our new Masters, sense hath done as sense will doe, misguided our Reason." Bacon's distrust of the senses has already been noted (p. 85 above).

the Puritan preacher and writer William Twisse maintained, echoing Milton's Belial, than not to live at all.

The consequences of these conclusions are mainly twofold practical and theoretical, just as happiness consists of both doing and knowing. Of the practical consequences, two considerations are relevant: first, our actions depend upon knowledge; and secondly, if we knew for a certainty that all things are one, then "how cheerfully, with what modest courage should wee undertake any action, reincounter any occurrence, knowing that that distinction of misery and happinesse, which now so perplexeth us, hath no Being, except in the Brain?" [15] For then we should know that misery does not exist, that it is a mere privation, and we should know as well that everything that is is good, and that all Being is one emanation from above.

As for the theoretical consequences, it is clear that the division of knowledge into many sciences is a vain pursuit. Further, knowledge is divided into a science of things and a science of causes, and since little is known even of the first, it is fruitless to attempt to comprehend the second, which is beyond understanding. Bacon contented himself with experiment, leaving the search for final causes to others. If one sees, maintains Brooke, that all things are really only one, he will improve in what he knows and then stop, short of the vain pursuits, the "nice, unnecessary prying into those things which profit not" that Bacon also condemns. [16]

In the sixteenth chapter Brooke lists some of the "unhappy fruits of division" in the parts of learning, drawing examples from science, philosophy, and theology. In the seventeenth he concludes that if we could "lay aside foolish questions" and "seek into our hearts . . . and not into the causes," then "We might have an Heaven here." [17] A postscript serves as an apologia, with remarks on the beliefs of the millenarians to bring the discourse back to the scriptural point from which he departed.

Brooke never strays far from his inclusive vision of all creation as a single emanation of the divine. The springs of his intellectual nourishment are various, for in his ideas one reads traces of

[15] *The Nature of Truth*, p. 118.
[16] *Ibid.*, p. 142.
[17] *Ibid.*, p. 169.

Platonism, scholasticism, and Puritanism, blended with lofty patriotism, stern Calvinist faith, and an acquaintance with the literature, the new science, and the philosophy of his time. On occasion his argument, it must be acknowledged, is little more than verbal gymnastic; but at other times he shows a close and careful logic, and here and there anticipates sound philosophical developments of the years ahead. But through his variety and his sporadic unevenness there gleams his single vision, the unvarying belief in unity that he proclaimed as the key to happiness in a time of upheaval and discord.

IX

SOURCES AND AFFINITIES

In attempting to trace the sources of Brooke's ideas one must use extreme caution. It cannot actually be said that he had many definable "sources" as such, for although Brooke's range of reference and annotation is broad, he appears to have learned much of his philosophy at second hand or perhaps at even greater remove. There are, however, many resemblances and affinities between certain of Brooke's points of view and underlying ideas and certain notions evident in ancient and scholastic philosophy and Puritan theology. Though one cannot safely maintain that such affinities are strictly indications of source, it is nevertheless illuminating to examine them.

It seems wise, then, to make a distinction between those writers whose works represent true "sources" of Brooke's thought, those whose works show important similarities to ideas in Brooke's writings and to whom he may be indirectly indebted, and, finally, those to whom Brooke simply alludes but from whom it cannot be said that he drew ideas of significance. In the first category there are three bodies of thought: Platonism, specifically Plato himself and Ficino, upon both of whom Brooke drew directly; Aristotle and the great body of scholastic philosophy, whose unacknowledged influence is prominent in Brooke's reasoning; and the huge system of Puritan theology, particularly that which shows the influence of Peter Ramus. It is mainly with these three groups that this chapter will be concerned. In the second category one may include Plotinus and Augustine, though Brooke mentions neither by name,[1] and some consideration of such writers will be relevant. The third group, those writers to whom Brooke merely alludes, is immense: major classical figures; the Bible and biblical

---

[1] With one exception: Augustine is included in a list of millenarians (*The Nature of Truth*, p. 175).

commentary; minor classical, medieval, and Renaissance writers of impressive variety, from Anaxagoras to Zabarella; the giants of the new science; theologians of many hues, from Cardinal Bellarmine to the obscure Puritan Ephraim Huit; and contemporary literary and philosophical figures like Barclay, Suckling, and Lord Herbert. Full treatment of individuals in this category would be appropriate only in annotations to an edition, and they will be mentioned in this discussion only as needed.

To proceed immediately to Brooke's sources, the author of *The Nature of Truth* leaves his reader in little doubt as to his greatest master. Brooke was a Platonist. It is true that no single label does him justice, but "Platonist" comes as close to describing him accurately as it comes to describing the Cambridge group whose published works were shortly to follow his. The extent to which Brooke actually knew the dialogues of Plato cannot be adequately measured. If one accepts, however, Dean Inge's definition of the essence of the Platonic movement, "the recognition of an unseen world of unchanging reality behind the flux of phenomena, a spiritual universe compared with which the world of appearance grew pale and unsubstantial and became only a symbol or even an illusion," [2] it is clear that one can be a Platonist without knowing Plato directly at all. Entirely aside from his occasional allusions to the Platonic dialogues and to Neo-Platonic writings, Brooke, who was a firm believer in an unseen and unchanging world of reality and unity behind the world of diversity in which he lived, is most certainly by this standard a Platonist.

It is not only his fundamental other-worldliness, however, that demonstrates Brooke's Platonism. The influence of other Platonic doctrines pervades *The Nature of Truth*. It has already been briefly noted that the Socratic notion of virtue is reflected in Brooke's insistence that "the will doth necessarily follow the understanding," with the clear and partially stated implication that to know the good is to do the good. [3] The Socratic corollary to this belief, the paradox of the "involuntariness of evil," which

[2] W. R. Inge, *The Platonic Tradition in English Religious Thought* (New York, 1926), p. 8. Dean Inge devotes a page or so to Brooke, explaining the two or three principal ideas in *The Nature of Truth* (though he does not refer to the treatise by name) that show Platonic origin (pp. 46–47).

[3] *The Nature of Truth*, p. 58.

in turn implies that evil has only a negative existence, is reflected in Brooke's statement that when the soul acts falsely it is not acting at all: "He that in the twilight, mistaketh a man for a tree, acteth right in what he seeth; and when he raiseth a false conclusion upon the premises, he acteth not." [4] As another example of pervasive Platonic influence, Brooke accepts the doctrine of reminiscence,[5] and the Neo-Platonic notion, labeled by Lovejoy as the "metaphysical pathos," that all knowledge and indeed all reality are one.[6]

It may be that Brooke's Platonism is traceable in the main to Neo-Platonic and other Renaissance sources, but in several instances Brooke did refer specifically to Platonic dialogues. He was familiar with the *Symposium* and the *Timaeus*, through Ficino if not directly, and he seems to have been acquainted with the *Philebus*. It is true that some of the ideas Brooke owes to Plato are expounded in dialogues other than these three: the fullest expressions of the doctrine of reminiscence, for example, appear in the *Phaedo* and the *Meno*. Yet the doctrine of reminiscence must have been so well known in the Renaissance to those who were at all acquainted with Platonic thought that one could surely have alluded to it without having read it in Plato, perhaps as in the atomic age one can with some comprehension quote the formula $E = mc^2$ without having read Einstein. One cannot assume, then, that Brooke knew any more Plato at first hand than appears in his actual references to the three dialogues.

That Brooke was acquainted with the *Symposium* is demonstrable from his specific allusions to Ficino's commentary on it. Platonic love as a unifying force that can reconcile the hostile elements in the universe is a notion consonant with a belief in the unity of all being.[7] It will be appropriate, however,

---

[4] *Ibid.*, p. 110. The "involuntariness of evil" simply means that one cannot know the good and do the bad, and therefore, that one commits the bad only by wrongly supposing it to be the good. Cf. Taylor, *Plato, the Man and His Work* (New York, 1936), pp. 26–27.

[5] *The Nature of Truth*, p. 46.

[6] The notion so fully pervades the treatise that one need not cite specific references. For Lovejoy's comment see *The Great Chain of Being*, pp. 12–13.

[7] Brooke alludes to the speech made by Eryximachus in the *Symposium* (186–187), a discussion of love as a unifying and harmonizing force, in *The Nature of Truth*, pp. 42–43. (In citing Plato I have used unvaryingly the Jowett translation and the standard Stephanus pagination.)

to evaluate Brooke's particular application of the notion in the discussion of Ficino later on.

The *Timaeus*, especially its mystical pronouncements on harmonies and proportions, must have been attractive to Brooke, whether he knew it directly or only through Ficino, for the concept of the universe as basically a harmony of disparate elements is in sympathy with Brooke's view of the universe as unified in its very diversity.[8] Further, the portions of the *Timaeus* that describe the universe as composed of both the limited and the unlimited, and those that express the idea that the action of the soul is one of turning in upon itself, are closely related to Brooke's thought. The following passage from the *Timaeus* is representative:

> Now when the Creator had framed the soul according to his will, he formed within her the corporeal universe, and brought the two together, and united them centre to centre. The soul, interfused everywhere from the centre to the circumference of heaven, of which also she is the external envelopment, herself turning in herself, began a divine beginning of never-ceasing and rational life enduring throughout all time. The body of heaven is visible, but the soul is invisible, and partakes of reason and harmony, and being made by the best of intellectual and everlasting natures, is the best of things created. And because she is composed of the same and of the other and of the essence, these three, and is divided and united in due proportion, and in her revolutions returns upon herself, the soul, when touching anything which has essence, whether dispersed in parts or undivided, is stirred through all her powers, to declare the sameness or difference of that thing and some other.[9]

Brooke's system shows some influence of the *Philebus*, a dialogue that he cites several times in the marginal gloss. The belief that the one and the many inhere in each thing that exists is congenial to Brooke's metaphysics, and one finds in the *Philebus* a number of representative explanations of the idea. For example, Socrates at one point describes a way of arriving at truth:

> The ancients, who were our betters and nearer the gods than we are,

---

[8] This notion is similar, of course, to the idea expressed by Eryximachus in the *Symposium* cited above: "The One is united by disunion," etc.

[9] *Timaeus*, 36–37. Cf. *The Nature of Truth*, pp. 4, 9–10, 28, and elsewhere. On pp. 9–10 Brooke may be alluding in his gloss to this passage. The notion of an entity's turning back upon itself was particularly attractive to Brooke, for such an idea displayed a belief in some sort of inclusive unity.

handed down the tradition, that whatever things are said to be are composed of one and many, and have the finite and infinite implanted in them: seeing, then, that such is the order of the world, we too ought in every inquiry to begin by laying down one idea of that which is the subject of enquiry; this unity we shall find in everything. Having found it, we may next proceed to look for two, if there be two, or, if not, then for three or some other number, subdividing each of these units, until at last the unity with which we began is seen not only to be one and many and infinite, but also a definite number; the infinite must not be suffered to approach the many until the entire number of the species intermediate between unity and infinity has been discovered, — then, and not till then, we may rest from division, and without further troubling ourselves about the endless individuals may allow them to drop into infinity.[10]

Brooke may have this passage in mind when he says that "Plato most excellently, most acutely, most truly hath made all Being of Terminus and Infinitum." [11]

One or two other sections of the *Philebus* have bearing on Brooke's thought. One concerns pleasure and pain. Socrates says that pain is caused by a dissolution of the harmony that inheres in a being, and "the restoration of harmony and return to nature is the source of pleasure." For example, hunger and thirst are pain, to be remedied by replenishment; excessive cold and heat may be seen to be remedied similarly. This notion can be compared to Brooke's view that pain, like evil, is merely a privation.[12] Another relevant passage, toward the end of the dialogue, is that in which Socrates asks whether pleasure or mind is more akin to truth. Protarchus replies, "pleasures, like children, have not the least particle of reason in them; whereas mind is either the same as truth, or the most like truth, and the truest." [13] Brooke and Plato probably are not construing truth to mean the same thing, but there is at least an interesting verbal parallel between this remark and Brooke's central insistence that the understanding and truth are one.

It need not be assumed that Brooke was acquainted only with those Platonic dialogues to which he refers specifically. It might

[10] *Philebus*, 16.
[11] *The Nature of Truth*, p. 28. Brooke may also have had in mind *Philebus* 23–24.
[12] *Philebus*, 31–32; and *The Nature of Truth*, p. 112.
[13] *Philebus*, 65.

appear likely, for example, that he had read the lengthy disquisition on the one and the many in the *Parmenides*. To be sure, the dialogue is a carefully executed attack on the Eleatic theory of "the one," as represented by Parmenides and Zeno, and it could be said that Brooke's monism has something in common with their doctrine. Actually, however, Brooke does not deny the many, and his own doctrine is probably nearer to the theory Socrates professes, that everything is a mixture of like and unlike, just as the one and the many inhere in every being, as Socrates puts it in the *Philebus*. Such a belief would do no damage to a belief in an underlying and all-pervasive unity.[14] Yet it is perfectly possible that Brooke had not read the *Parmenides*; his friend Sadler had, for he mentions it in the preface, but one cannot assume that they had read the same things. Besides, both could have found out from an allusion in Aristotle what Parmenides believed, and it was probably well known that the *Parmenides* was a refutation of the Eleatic school.[15] In fact, an attempt to determine which dialogues Brooke knew at first hand would be a profitless and rather pedantic task. It is clear enough that Brooke had Platonic affinities, wherever he might have absorbed them.

Among the Renaissance Platonists to whom Brooke was indebted none rivals Marsilio Ficino, the fifteenth-century Florentine. Not only is Ficino mentioned several times in Brooke's marginal gloss, but his unacknowledged influence is apparent throughout *The Nature of Truth*. Indeed, it is not too much to maintain that Ficino's writings are the true "source" of many of the Platonic ideas in the treatise, even including those that may be directly traced to the three dialogues to which Brooke specifically alludes.

Brooke found in Ficino expressions of an idea of unity similar to that in which he himself so rapturously believed. It is true, as Professor Kristeller points out, that Ficino is not thoroughly a monist.[16] Yet one can assert without levity that he often writes as if he were one and that he shows a preoccupation with the notion of unity too fervent to be merely academic. Examples are numerous, but for a striking verbal demonstration one might

[14] See especially *Parmenides*, 126–130.

[15] Aristotle, *Physics*, I, 2–3; 184b–187a.

[16] Paul O. Kristeller, *The Philosophy of Marsilio Ficino*, tr. Virginia Conant (New York, 1943), p. 46.

turn to a passage near the beginning of the eleventh chapter of
the commentary on the *Timaeus*, a chapter partly entitled
"Singuli ordines ad singula capita reducuntur": "Cuncta enim
mundi corpora ad corpus unum: Naturae omnes ad unam quoque
naturam: Animae ad animam: Mentes ad mentem: ad bonum
denique bona et quia bona, ideo cuncta." [17] One must, however,
examine under certain recurrent headings Ficino's concept of
unity to see what he really meant by it.

Ficino's belief in unity is explained by Professor Kristeller
in terms of two principles: continuity, or the notion that all of
being is connected within itself through a sequence of intermediate numbers; and affinity, or the notion that all thinking is
the result of an affinity between the mind and its objects.[18] These
two principles establish, first, the physical proximity of all the
entities that make up the world, and secondly, a reciprocal relationship and interaction among them. The central figure in this
closely interrelated structure is God, who is, to summarize rapidly,
the totality of goodness; all things proceed from God and return
to Him, for He is the origin of goodness.[19] There is, then, a continuous attraction between God and the world and, in turn, God
once more; and the force that literally "makes the world go
around" (an unfortunate banality, perhaps, but an accurate description) is love. An important passage in the *Commentary on
the Symposium* may be taken as representative:

Certainly the great Creator first creates everything, then He attracts,
and third He finishes. Everything also, when it is born, flows from that
eternal source; then it flows back to the same source when it seeks its own
origin; and finally it is finished when it has returned to its own source. . .
This single circle, from God to the world and from the world to God, is
identified by three names. Inasmuch as it begins in God and attracts to
Him, it is Beauty; inasmuch as, going across into the world, it captivates
the world, we call it Love; and inasmuch as it returns to its source and with
Him joins its labors, then we call it Pleasure. In this way Love begins in
Beauty and ends in Pleasure. It is this that Hierotheus and Dionysius the
Areopagite mean in the famous hymn in which they sing, 'Love is a circle
of good, revolving from good to good perpetually.' [20]

[17] Ficino, *Omnia divini Platonis opera tralatione* (Lyons, 1548), p. 459.
[18] Kristeller, pp. 99, 109, *et passim*.
[19] Kristeller, pp. 143–145 ff.
[20] Second speech, from chapters 1 and 2; see Ficino, p. 259. I have quoted the

The nature of the world, then, is a transcendent unity held together by love.

All the parts of the world, because they are the works of one artist, the parts of one creation, like each other in life and essence, are bound to each other by a certain mutual affection so that it may justly be said that love is a perpetual knot and binder of the world, the immovable support of its parts and the firm foundation of the whole creation.[21]

In this system nothing is simpler than unity, nothing is better than the good, and they are one with God.[22] The centrality of God is the preeminently important fact.

Who will deny that God is rightly called the center of everything, since He is located, single, simple, and motionless within them all; but that everything that is produced from Him is multiple, complex, and movable, and that as these things flow from Him, they flow back to Him in the image of the lines and circumference? Thus Mind, Soul, Nature, and Matter, proceeding from God, strive to return to Him, and they revolve toward Him from every possible direction. Just as the central point is found everywhere in the lines and in the whole circle, and through this central point, the separate lines touch the middle point of the circle, so God, the center of everything, who is the simplest unity and the purest actuality, is infused into everything.[23]

I have quoted these passages at length because Brooke's debt to the principal idea expressed in them is clearly discernible. In the sixth chapter of *The Nature of Truth* Brooke maintains that "all Beeing is derived from the same fountaine," and that "All Being is the same in nature, (*scil.*) a beame of that excellent light." [24] At the end of the fifth chapter he declares that "Unity is

---

translation by Sears Jayne, *Marsilio Ficino's Commentary on Plato's Symposium* (Columbia, Mo., 1944), pp. 133–134. Brooke quotes the hymn of Dionysius in *The Nature of Truth*, p. 145.

[21] Third speech, chapter 3, Ficino, p. 263; quoted from Jayne's translation, p. 152. The title of chapter 4 is concisely illustrative: "Nullum mundi membrum odit aliud membrum."

[22] *Commentary on the Timaeus*, chapter 8, Ficino, p. 458: "Nihil autem vel unitate simplicius, vel melius bonitate. Neque etiam unitas melior bonitate, neque bonitas unitate simplicior. Unum ergo sunt ambo summusque Deus."

[23] *Commentary on the Symposium*, second speech, chapter 3, Ficino, p. 260; quoted from Jayne's translation, p. 136.

[24] *The Nature of Truth*, pp. 26–27. The use of the word "debt" is justifiable in that Brooke acknowledges in his marginal gloss both the commentaries (on the *Symposium* and the *Timaeus*) to which I have alluded.

Gods Essence. Unity is all what we are." [25] He is shortly to state that "The power of God is the unity of all Being in one point." [26] From this position, after certain digressive but pertinent illustrations of the unity of all being, he proceeds to a consideration of love in the ninth chapter. "Love is lovely in Gods eye, he is stiled the God of Love, the God Love." [27] By the end of the chapter he has demonstrated that knowledge and love (variously called the affections) are the same, differing only in degree, and that both are but "the Truth, that spirituall ray of heavenly light which God is pleased to present to our view under several shapes, yet is but one and the same Being, *scil.* light and truth." [28] It will be readily granted that each of these passages from Brooke, simply as isolated quotations, could have come to his mind from sources other than Ficino. Yet the comprehensive system that Brooke is endeavoring to construct bears a resemblance too close to the system of Ficino to be ignored.

As Brooke's insistence that "all Being is . . . a beame of that excellent light" depends upon a belief in something like Ficino's principle of continuity, one can see in Brooke's incipient idealism a relationship to Ficino's principle of affinity. Kristeller explains that Ficino develops his attitude from the position of Parmenides and Plato that true being is accessible only to thought, and he quotes a significant passage from the *Commentary on the Philebus*: "Truth is the correspondence of the thing and the mind . . . and the truth of the mind is its correspondence to the objects, the truth of the things is their correspondence to the mind." [29] One recalls the title of Brooke's first chapter: "The Understanding and the Truth-understood, are one." One thinks also of the conclusions Brooke reaches after accepting this principle, the most boldly stated of which is that "Time and Place seeme to me nothing but an extrinsecall modification of a thing," for "the Soule is but one Act distinguished to our notion by severall apparitions." [30] In-

[25] *The Nature of Truth*, p. 24.

[26] *Ibid.*, p. 36.

[27] *Ibid.*, pp. 67–68.

[28] *Ibid.*, pp. 80–81.

[29] Kristeller, p. 51. Cf. chapter 39 of the *Commentary on the Timaeus*: "Mundus est ex intellectu et necessitate compositus, id est ex ipso formarum ordine atque materia" (Ficino, p. 472).

[30] *The Nature of Truth*, p. 92.

deed, regarding time, "*aeternum* and *tempus* are all one in eternity: and this succession is but to our apprehension." [31]

Similarities between smaller figures in the carpet may be seen. Brooke is fond of images that involve the reflecting or turning back of an entity upon itself. For example:

> For the Beauty of Truths character is, that she is a shadow, a resemblance of the first, the best forme; that she is light, the species, the sparkling of primitive light; that she is life, the sublimation of light, that she may reflect upon her selfe.[32]

Kristeller has shown how to Ficino thought is a kind of "reflection":

> It is even called 'infinite reflection' in so far as it thinks that it thinks and so repeats over and over again the act of awareness and of return to oneself. It follows, then, that life and thought have a fixed relation to one another as *actus rectus* and *actus reflexus*.[33]

Or again in the third chapter Brooke goes to some length to prove that the fourth vial in Revelation 16 is emptied upon itself and is therefore both receiver and received. One might expect such an image to occur in the exposition of a monistic system, but it is at least arresting that something like it occurs in Ficino with great regularity.[34]

Brooke's identification of the soul with truth and with light is sometimes expressed in terms strikingly similar to those used by Ficino. One thinks of a passage in the *Commentary on the Symposium*:

> But what do I bid you love in the soul? — the beauty of the soul. The beauty of bodies is a visible light, the beauty of the soul is an invisible light; *the light of the soul is truth.* . . . Plato declares that the beauty of the soul consists in truth and wisdom; and that this is given men by God. One and the same Truth given to us all by God, acquires the names of various virtues according to its various powers. According as it shows divine things, it is

[31] *The Nature of Truth*, p. 99.

[32] *Ibid.*, p. 4. Brooke glosses this passage with a sentence, "Vita est in se reflectio," that he appears to attribute to Seneca's *Epistles*. There is nothing in Seneca quite like that idea, and the mystifying gloss may be merely another of Brooke's frequent errors in his rather haphazard annotation. He may have had in mind a passage from Ficino: "Vita motus, quia iam exit in actum. Mens reflexio, quia sine hac vita in externum opus efflueret" (Ficino, *Opera omnia*, Basle, 1576, p. 199), a reference for which I am indebted to Professor Kristeller.

[33] Kristeller, pp. 44–45.

[34] *The Nature of Truth*, p. 14; and cf. the passage from Ficino, n. 23 above.

called Wisdom, which Plato asked of God above all else. According as it shows natural things, it is called Knowledge; as human things, Prudence; as it makes men equal, Justice; as it makes them unconquered, Courage; and as tranquil, Temperance. . . That single light of the single truth is the beauty of the Angelic Mind, which you must worship above the beauty of the soul. . . It excels the beauty of the soul because it is fundamentally eternal and is not disturbed by the passage of time, but since the light of the Angelic Mind shines in the series of innumerable ideas, and it is fitting that there be a unity above all the multitude of everything, a unity which is the origin of all number; this light necessarily flows from one single principle of everything, which we call the One Itself.[35]

Light, soul, truth, unity — these terms, occurring again and again in the early chapters of Brooke's treatise, are synonymous, and the meanings attached to them by both Brooke and Ficino are, if not actually parallel, at least analogous. With the account of the various names under which "truth" is known, in the preceding passage from Ficino, one may compare the following from Brooke:

I shall not agree to confound the names of particular Beings, though I doe conjoyne their natures. For, all Being may be compared to light; in such a body it is styled the Sunne; in another it is called the Moone; in the third it beareth the name of a Starre, and under various shapes, the names of various Stars, as Syrius, Canopus, etc. but all is light, and it is but light. The body of waters is by us called Seas; when they beate upon such a coast, it beareth one name; when it coasteth upon another soyle, it receiveth a severall denomination. All Being is this light, this truth; but contained within those Circles, it appeareth to us under this name; and againe, it hath another style when it beateth upon a various object.[36]

Brooke thought of the universe as an emanation from God, perhaps, in the words of another Platonist, as "a great ring of pure and endless light," turning and reflecting upon itself through all eternity. Whether Ficino directly provided him with this lovely vision or not, it is likely that Brooke absorbed at least some of the radiance from the writings of the "alter Plato." [37]

[35] *Commentary on the Symposium*, sixth speech, chapter 18, Ficino, pp. 277–278; quoted from Jayne's translation, pp. 213–215 (italics mine).

[36] *The Nature of Truth*, pp. 27–28.

[37] I do not consider it necessary to "prove" Ficino's direct influence on Brooke more fully than I have done. It is interesting, however, that Brooke felt as Ficino did on the subject of the "nonbeing" of evil, and on the close relationship of the will and the intellect (understanding). Cf. Kristeller, pp. 351–352, and 256–258. The basis of both ideas, of course, is to be found in the writings of Plato, and such similarities of belief are to be found among Platonists of all hues.

It is tempting to hypothesize that Brooke drew upon the works of other Platonists than Ficino in formulating his system. Of evidence that he had read Plotinus or Augustine at first hand there is little or none; and yet certain affinities between their writings and Brooke's thought may be noted. Perhaps the point is simply that these affinities exist among all the Platonists, for they, in turn, drew upon a single source. A few such resemblances, nevertheless, merit being pointed out, in that they sharpen the focus on Brooke's ideas and bring him into clearer perspective with his intellectual heritage.[38]

One would like to think, for example, that Brooke had read in the Fifth Ennead of Plotinus that "Spirit, the whole of reality, and truth, are one nature." [39] The Platonic notion of the identity of thought with the objects of thought, an idea of great importance to Brooke, appears in Plotinus with striking clarity:

> Since contemplation rises by degrees, from nature to the Soul, from the Soul to intelligence; and as within it thought becomes more and more . . . interior, more and more united to the thinker; and as in the perfect Soul the things known are identical with the knower; and because they aspire to Intelligence, the subject must then evidently within Intelligence be identical with the object . . . because of the identity between thinking and being.[40]

A compelling view of the universe as a divine unity is expressed by Nicholas of Cusa, and one feels that Brooke would have seized eagerly on his demonstrations of the unity of diverse aspects of being, such as:

> Circulus est figura perfecta unitatis et simplicitatis. Et iam ostensum est superius, triangulum esse circulum: et ita trinitas, est unitas. Ista autem

[38] J. Freudenthal, the German scholar whose detailed criticism of *The Nature of Truth* has already been cited ("Beiträge zur Geschichte der englischen Philosophie," *Archiv für Geschichte der Philosophie* 6:190 ff.), confidently lists a great many authorities as "sources" whom Brooke does not mention at all. Among these are Plotinus and Nicholas of Cusa. Freudenthal evidently makes no allowance for Brooke's having drawn on the great body of Platonic and scholastic thought indirectly. It becomes increasingly clear to the investigator, however, that Brooke need not have had more than a handful of direct "sources."

[39] *Enneads*, V, v, 3. I have in this instance used Dean Inge's translation of the phrase (Inge, *The Philosophy of Plotinus* [London, 1929], II, 41); for other quotations from Plotinus, unless otherwise noted, I have used the translation by K. S. Guthrie, *Plotinus* (London, 1918).

[40] *Enneads*, III, viii, 8.

unitas est infinita, sicut circulus infinitus. . . Omnis enim diversitas, in ipso est identitas.[41]

Such resemblances, though they do not "prove" that Brooke had read Plotinus or Cusa, serve to link Brooke with the Platonic tradition.

Brooke does not allude directly to Augustine, yet one would expect that he had read him. As Professor Miller has shown, Augustine is the "arch-exemplar" of the religious frame of mind of which Puritanism is one of the strongest subsequent manifestations.[42] One need not read far into the *Confessions* to find a concept of light and truth that rings changes familiar to the reader of Brooke's treatise:

> Into myself I went, and with the eyes of my soul (such as it was) I discovered over the same eye of my soul, over my mind, the unchangeable light of the Lord: not this vulgar light, which all flesh may look upon. . . This light was none of that, but another, yea clean another from all these. Nor was it in that manner above my mind, as oil is upon water, nor yet as the heaven is above the earth: but superior to my soul because it made me; and I was inferior to it because I was made by it. *He that knows what truth is, knows what that light is; and he that knows it, knows eternity.*[43]

One is reminded, too, of the early pages of the *Corpus Hermeticum,* in which truth is revealed to the seeker through a "holy Word" that comes forth from "Light," [44] and of the "divine light" that enables the intellect to see which pervades the *Enneads* of Plotinus.[45]

Two of the notions of Platonic origin that Brooke develops in the elaboration of his own system are, as already noted, the nonreality of evil and the subjectivity of time and space. Augus-

[41] *De docta ignorantia,* I, xxi (Cusa, *Opera* [Basle, 1565], p. 16). Cusa appears to have identified truth and the intellect as well; cf. *De filiatione Dei:* "Non erit . . . veritas aliud aliquod, ab intellectu, neque vita qua vivit, alia erit ab ipso vivente intellectu, secundum omnem vim et naturam intellectualis vigoris, quae omnia secundum se ambit, et omnia se facit, quando omnia in ipso ipse" (*Opera,* p. 123).

[42] Miller, *The New England Mind,* p. 4.

[43] Augustine, *Confessions,* VII, x, tr. William Watts, Loeb Classical Library (London, 1931), I, 371–372 (italics mine).

[44] *Hermetica,* ed. Scott, I, 117–118. Brooke did allude to the Hermetic writings. He may have known them in Ficino's widely read translation, of which there were twenty editions by 1641, including an English translation in 1611.

[45] Cf. *Enneads,* V, v. 7–8.

tine's belief in the nonreality of evil is well known, and at times he explains it in terms of a "privation of good," as Brooke describes sin as "onely a Privation, a Non-Entity." [46] In a passage in the *Confessions* Augustine points up the absurdity of certain questions put to him by adherents of the Manichean heresy:

> For I knew not that . . . I was, as it were, in some subtle way persuaded to give my consent to those foolish deceivers when they put their questions to me: Whence comes evil? and whether God were made up in a bodily shape, and had hair and nails? and whether those were to be esteemed righteous men, who had many wives at once, and did kill men, and offered sacrifices of living creatures? At which things ignorant I was much troubled; and while I went quite from the truth, I seemed to myself to be making towards it: because I yet knew not how that *evil was nothing else but a privation of good*, next indeed to that which has no being.[47]

Plotinus likewise concludes that "evil must be located in nonbeing," but that, as Dionysius the Areopagite had also determined, all degrees of privation must be necessary to fulfill the plenitude of the universe.[48] As for the subjectivity of observable phenomena, Plotinus suggests that "Intelligence, by its mere real existence, thinks beings, and makes them exist," and in his explanation of time in the Third Ennead, asks, "Is time also within us?" [49] Augustine suggests that we measure time in our minds: "The future therefore is not a long time, for it is not: but the long future time is merely a long expectation of the future." [50] And Nicholas of Cusa, according to Cassirer, considered time to be in as close relation to the mind as seeing is to the eye.[51]

[46] *The Nature of Truth*, p. 101.

[47] *Confessions*, III, vii (italics mine).

[48] *Enneads*, I, viii, 3; II, iii, 18; and III, ii, 7. Cf. Dionysius the Areopagite, *De divinis nominibus*, chapter 4, sections 19–32, noting especially the definition of evil: "Le mal est privation, défaillance, faiblesse, disharmonie, erreur, irreflexion, absence de beauté, de vie, d'intelligence, de raison" etc. (from the translation by Maurice de Gandillac, *Oeuvres complètes du Pseudo Denys L'Areopagite* [Paris, 1943], pp. 111–125). Brooke may or may not have known this work, but Sadler alludes to it in the preface (sig. A6v). See also Lovejoy, *The Great Chain of Being*, pp. 64–66.

[49] *Enneads*, V, ix, 5, and III, vii, 10.

[50] *Confessions*, XI, xxviii.

[51] Ernst Cassirer, *Individuum und Kosmos in der Philosophie der Renaissance* (Leipzig, 1927), pp. 44–45: "Wie das Auge zum Sehen, so verhält sich demnach die Zeit zur Seele: die Zeit ist das Organ, dessen sich die Seele bedient, um ihre Grundfunktion: die Funktion der Ordnung und Sichtung des Mannigfalten, vielfältig Verstreuten erfüllen zu können."

Brooke's ties, then, with Platonic thought are manifold and strong, and he can make ample claim to be included in the roster of seventeenth-century Christian Platonists in England. In recognizing, however, the great extent to which the core of Brooke's thought was adumbrated by both ancient and Renaissance Platonism, one must not be misled into thinking that he learned only from these masters. One has only to glance through the pages of *The Nature of Truth* to become aware that Brooke owed far more to Aristotle and scholastic thought than his marginal gloss ever acknowledges.

Scholasticism still ran strong in the intellectual currents of the seventeenth century, and the inheritors of the Renaissance revolt could not but be diverted by it even as they pulled against it. Indeed, one could agree with Professor Randall that scholasticism was still developing and that it was to reach its fullest growth "in the very different structure of Spinoza." [52] Its still continuing force can be seen clearly in the works of some of the century's great figures, perhaps most prominently in Donne, about whose poetry, especially the *Anniversaries*, it has been said that in it one breathes the air of the Middle Ages.[53] It is to be expected, then, that one should find traces even stronger in a writer whose purpose was principally rather than secondarily philosophical, a writer who was in a humbler way as representative of the bold many-sidedness of the century as was Donne.

The role played by Aristotelianism and scholastic thought in the writings of Brooke is, however, a different sort of role from that played by Platonism. It might be said that the Platonic philosophers had inspired Brooke with the light that never was on sea or land, and had revealed to him the first glimpses of the radiant unity that was to pervade his thought. The Aristotelian and scholastic philosophers, on the other hand, had furnished him with modes of thought, organizational categories, and a basic terminology which served as a framework for the expression of his ineffable vision. The conclusions Brooke reached can usually be recognized as Platonic, but the premises and the form of the argument can as often be recognized as scholastic.

[52] J. H. Randall, Jr., *The Making of the Modern Mind* (Boston, 1940), p. 93.

[53] Cf. *The Poems of John Donne*, ed. H. J. C. Grierson, II, 33–34, and elsewhere. See also M. P. Ramsay, *Les Doctrines médiévales chez Donne* (Paris, 1917), p. 83.

In the opening chapter of *The Nature of Truth* Brooke embarks upon a proof that the understanding and the "truth-understood" are one, a hypothesis clearly related to the Platonic notion that thought and the objects of thought are identical. Brooke immediately describes the understanding as appearing under two aspects, the form or substance, and the effects of a reasonable soul, a patently scholastic distinction. In the course of his argument Brooke disputes the classification of the understanding as a faculty, shows familiarity with the three souls of Aristotle's *De anima*, and calls up as axiomatic truth the law that whatever is received is received in the manner of the recipient.[54] He condemns argument whose certain outcome is infinite regression, and cites as authority the "razor" of William of Ockham, the principle of economy which would deny a large number of elements in an explanation when fewer would suffice.[55] Is the soul the container and the body the contained, or is it the other way around? Brooke brings up this ancient problem in order to prove the emptiness of the question, yet his answer, that neither is the container nor the contained but both make up the "compositum," is the solution of Thomas Aquinas.[56] He condemns the obscure distinctions made by the scholastics between the active intellect and the passive, yet follows the scholastic definition of God as "unus, purus, simplex actus," or pure actuality.[57]

Form, essence, cause, activity — these terms are common in *The Nature of Truth*. At one point Brooke feels it necessary to define "activity," and does so in scholastic terms, such as "potentia agendi," "ipsa actio," and "actus primus et actus secundus," only then to remark parenthetically that there is no difference between

[54] *The Nature of Truth*, pp. 1–10.

[55] *Ibid.*, p. 9: "Entia non sunt multiplicanda, nisi necessario." See McKeon, *Selections from Medieval Philosophers*, II, 357.

[56] *The Nature of Truth*, p. 16.

[57] *Ibid.*, pp. 19–23. It is interesting that the scholastic phrase "unus, purus, simplex actus" occurs in the text of Brooke's treatise only a few lines above a quotation from the great Puritan preacher, William Ames. On the page from which Brooke took his quotation (Ames, *The Marrow of Sacred Divinity*, which was the English translation of the *Medulla sacrae theologiae*, published in translation in 1638, chapter 4, pp. 9–10), Ames uses the same scholastic phrase. Such a coincidence affords no conclusive evidence, of course, but does mildly substantiate the feeling one has that Brooke became acquainted with much ancient, medieval, and Renaissance learning through his reading of such secondary works as contemporary theological tracts.

"actus primus" and "actus secundus" except a difference in time, which, he soon afterward argues, has no existence in itself.[58] The old distinction between substance and accident is brought out and examined along with the distinction between the two kinds of actuality, and both "aged impostures" are "set upon the Rack." [59] Brooke's acquaintance with the scholastic categories of "causes" leads him to exclaim, "How doth our great Master perplexe him-selfe in the inquiry of causes?" Such barren inquiries produce only the "unhappy fruits of division." [60]

From such examples one finds that Brooke reflects scholasti-cism principally in two ways. Most often he quotes or alludes to Aristotle or the scholastic philosophers only to refute them, since many of their principles point up his own by contrast. But sec-ondly, again and again Brooke uses scholastic statements as his authorities and scholastic distinctions in his argument. There are nearly as many instances of his concurrence with a scholastic point of view, though often tacit, as there are of his rejection of scholastic principles.

Brooke's relationship to scholasticism, then, is an ambivalent one. He considers his ideas as expressive of the revolt against scholasticism, and indeed, in their principal import, they are; and yet in many ways he has escaped from scholastic bounds hardly at all. In this respect Brooke is at one with many of his Puritan compatriots, for, in the words of Professor Miller, "though Puritan literature abounds with condemnations of scholasticism, almost no limits can be set to its actual influence." [61] In two other ways Brooke bears out Miller's evaluation of the part played by scho-lasticism in the intellectual heritage of Puritan literature. In the first place, Brooke rarely acknowledges his indebtedness to the scholastics. Occasionally he mentions Aristotle in his gloss, but never once does he cite by name Aquinas or any other medieval scholastic philosopher. And secondly, there is evidence that some, if not a great deal, of Brooke's acquaintance with medieval thought came to him from his reading in Puritan theology and

[58] *The Nature of Truth,* p. 83.
[59] *Ibid.,* pp. 86–88.
[60] *Ibid.,* pp. 140, 146, *et passim.*
[61] Miller, *The New England Mind,* p. 104.

other contemporary literature rather than from his reading of the medieval writers themselves. Brooke was acquainted, one remembers, with the monumental *Encylopaedia scientiarum omnium*, compiled by J. H. Alsted, in which he might have found any point in medieval theology or logic explained; and his reading in the equally monumental literature of contemporary theological controversy appears to have been more than cursory.[62] But regardless of how Brooke came by his scholastic knowledge, his indebtedness to the great body of scholastic thought must be taken into account in any attempt to define his own intellectual heritage.

It may well be, however, that the most significant influence on Brooke has not yet been discussed. Platonic thought was indubitably the "source" of many of his most fundamental ideas. Medieval scholasticism furnished him with many of his tools. But one must not — indeed, one is not permitted to do so — lose sight of the fact that Brooke was a Puritan. There are ways in which *The Nature of Truth* differs from Puritan controversial writing; the broad range of his inquiry, for example, stands as an exception to Professor Haller's generalization that "as a matter of conviction and of convention, the Puritans professed to disapprove the citation of human authors and to depend solely upon scripture." [63] But Brooke was thoroughly a Puritan and a fervent laborer in the Puritan vineyard. His record in Parliament and his brief career in the Parliamentary army speak for the depth of his belief in Puritan principles. The *Discourse on Episcopacy* was to merit the praise of the noblest Puritan of them all. The influential Puritan Thomas Goodwin thought so much of Brooke that he dedicated to him his treatise entitled *A Child of Light*

[62] Miller makes the point that the laity in New England in the seventeenth century could hardly suspect that much of what they heard delivered from the pulpits came from scholastic sources, and that "the ministers themselves were more aware that they had derived something from Anselm, Aquinas, or Duns Scotus, but even they never acknowledge their full indebtedness" (p. 100). And the second point: "In estimating the scholastic cast of the Puritan mind we must remember, not only that Puritans were unaware how much they naturally and inevitably took from medieval lore, but that they seldom went directly to medieval writers. Instead they generally used restatements by writers of their own day and their own persuasion" (p. 102). Cf. comment in n. 57 above, and see Miller in general, pp. 100–103 *et passim*. For Brooke's familiarity with Alsted, note his allusion to Alsted's millenarian speculations, *The Nature of Truth*, p. 177.

[63] Haller, *The Rise of Puritanism*, p. 23.

Walking in Darknesse.[64] It is more than reasonable to expect, then, to find evidence of a Puritan heritage and outlook in a treatise by one who retained the Puritan Platonist Peter Sterry as his chaplain, gave his protection to the "indefatigable compiler" of the lives of the saints and martyrs, Samuel Clarke,[65] and whose very coachman, though unlearned, was a theologian.[66]

Before one has read through Brooke's own preface to *The Nature of Truth* one is aware that he was acutely conscious of original sin, a doctrine certainly not exclusively Puritan but one which the Puritans embraced with more than ordinary zeal: "Alas, are we not all since Adams lapse buried under the shadow of death, and lost in the region of darknesse? Who is there that knoweth truth?"[67] But there are other respects more doctrinaire in which Brooke reveals the Puritan foundation of his thought. For one thing, his position on predestination is strongly Calvinistic. In a way, adherence to a belief in predestination is something of an anomaly for one who held reason in high regard. As Professor Bush says of Milton's insistence on the freedom of the will, "No humanist who had learned from the ancients the dignity of human reason could accept predestination and the depravity of man."[68] But Milton at the age at which Brooke composed his two tracts was still a Calvinist, and perhaps if Brooke had lived longer his own variety of Christian humanism would have led him to modify his orthodox position even as Milton outgrew his. Brooke was, however, both rationalist and Calvinist in 1640. Reason is for him not only endowed with dignity but is actually one with God, and Brooke conceives of it in terms learned from the ancients:

> That degree of light, which we enjoy in the inward man, is the specificall difference, which distinguisheth between us and brutes, deservedly called Reason, that ample Sphere of Truth, which is the All in us, and besides which we are wholly nothing.[69]

[64] Goodwin's tract was originally published as a sermon in 1636, perhaps preached as early as 1628; it appears, with the dedication to Brooke, in *Certaine Select Cases Resolved* (London, 1647), sig. A2v.

[65] Haller, pp. 102, 105.

[66] John Spencer, author of *A Short Treatise Concerning the lawfullnesse of every mans exercising his gift as God shall call him thereunto.* See Haller, p. 268.

[67] *The Nature of Truth*, sig. A11–A11v.

[68] Bush, *The Renaissance and English Humanism* (Toronto, 1939), p. 114.

[69] *The Nature of Truth*, pp. 22–23.

Yet one of the objectives of the quest for truth is to Brooke the
assurance "that you shall not dash your feete against the stone
of free will." [70]

Brooke believes that when grace is vouchsafed to the soul
by God, the soul cannot reject it, and he calls to his aid on this
point the testimony of the learned Dr. William Twisse, chaplain
to Elizabeth of Bohemia, future prolocutor of the Westminster
Assembly, and a strict doctrinal predestinarian who admitted no
compromise with pure Calvinism.[71] In the same way Brooke dis-
countenances "that unhappy opinion of falling away from
Grace." [72] In both instances he is objecting to doctrine similar to,
perhaps actually, that of the Dutch Remonstrants, led by Episcopius and Uyttenbogaert, who in 1610, the year following the
death of Arminius, declared their disapproval of "the orthodox
teaching on predestination, the statement that Christ had died
for the elect alone, the belief in irresistible grace, and the notion
that the saints could not fall from grace." [73] Brooke calls Calvin
himself to witness that the notion of God is incompatible with
the notion of free will, and he quotes the "new Presbyter" Samuel
Rutherford on the eternity and the absolute certitude of divine
decrees.[74]

On the matter of faith, which is of necessity closely related to
the doctrine of regeneration and God's grace, Brooke shows himself indebted to several Puritan theologians, including John Ball,
whose *Treatise of Faith* was widely used among New England
Puritans as a handbook, and his old acquaintance by correspondence, John Cotton.[75] Brooke's opinion on faith does not, however,
appear to be closely reasoned. He is principally concerned with
proving faith and reason to be but degrees of the same truth that

[70] *The Nature of Truth*, p. 163.

[71] *The Nature of Truth*, pp. 11–12; and William Twisse, *The Doctrine of the
Synod of Dort and Arles reduced to the Practice* (Oxford[?], 1650/51), pp. 24–26.
Brooke must have read this tract either in manuscript or in an edition of un-
specified date earlier than 1640, listed as STC 24403.

[72] *The Nature of Truth*, p. 50.

[73] W. K. Jordan, *The Development of Religious Toleration in England*, II, 333.
Brooke identifies the controversialists with whom he differs as Remonstrants and
Counter-Remonstrants, and one recalls that he was a student at Leyden soon after
the Synod of Dort.

[74] *The Nature of Truth*, pp. 51–53.

[75] *Ibid.*, pp. 48, 152–153. For an account of Ball see Miller, p. 25.

is one with God. It apparently troubles him little that in accepting
Cotton's belief that faith is "a laying hold of that promise which
God hath made," he is tacitly giving assent to the doctrine of the
Covenant of Grace that elicited gasps of horror from Twisse,
whom Brooke has cited in support of his own position on pre-
destination.[76]

Brooke shows awareness of a number of theological matters
over which Puritan controversy raged. He was, for example, well
read in the voluminous eschatological literature of the century.
This is to be expected, in view of the fact that Revelation 20 is
one of his original points of departure in his investigation of truth.
He expresses high admiration for "that bright man" Thomas
Brightman, whose "very Errors . . . have their beauty," [77] and
shows familiarity with the *Clavis apocalyptica* of Joseph Mede,
"the only man," according to Theobald Pontifex, "who ever really
understood the Book of Revelation." [78] Brooke touches briefly on
the question of whether the Sabbath is "inherently holy," adopt-
ing the position that the proper time and place for worship are
not preordained, but that worship at any time or in any place is
fitting in God's sight.[79] In a word or two he alludes to the thorny
matter of "Whether there be a prescript forme of Church-government," but leaves this difficulty, in the solution of which he is at
one with Milton, to be explored in the *Discourse on Episcopacy*.[80]

Probably the most organic aspect of the Puritan heritage discernible in *The Nature of Truth* is the influence of the logic of
Peter Ramus. Professor Miller has shown how deeply the Ramist
logic affected Puritan thought, particularly in New England, and

---

[76] *The Nature of Truth*, pp. 47, 152–153. To Twisse, as to Calvin, no "covenant"
between God and man is possible, for God elects or condemns simply according
to his pleasure. See Miller, pp. 404–405.

[77] *The Nature of Truth*, sig. A10v, and pp. 178–179. Brightman's *Apocalypsis
Apocalypseos* (1609) was translated as *A Revelation of the Revelation*, 1615.

[78] *The Nature of Truth*, pp. 14–15, where Brooke disagrees with Mede on a
small point (and aparently agrees with Brightman, whom he does not on this
occasion cite); but I see no reason to explore the interminable ramifications of
eschatological controversy beyond pointing out Brooke's awareness of the issues.
For Theobald Pontifex's opinion see Butler, *The Way of All Flesh*, Modern Library
ed., p. 68. It has been suggested that Mede is the "old Damoetas" of Milton's
"Lycidas." See Marjorie Nicolson, "Milton's 'Old Damoetas,' " *MLN* 41:293–300
(1926).

[79] *The Nature of Truth*, pp. 166–167.

[80] *Ibid.*, p. 155. And see Part III below.

has maintained that Ramus exerted on New England Puritanism an influence as great as that of Calvin and Augustine. The *Medulla sacrae theologiae* of William Ames, the "standard textbook survey of theology used by New England students," which Brooke knew and cited, applied the methodology of Ramus to theology.[81] It is reasonable, then, though of course not inevitable, that one should find in Brooke's thought some of the currents that were prominent in the theology of the New England Puritans.

The particular aspect of Ramist logic that appears to have influenced Brooke is the set of attitudes that Miller analyzes under the name of "technologia." [82] This doctrine, as reconstructed by Miller from the writings of Ames, Alexander Richardson, and others, will bear summarizing before Brooke's relationship to it can be made clear. It is in short a belief that the universe is the embodiment of a single plan in the mind of God; this universe is reflected through concrete objects and seems diverse and temporal to the human reason; but the principles of these diversities, which are the arts, can be gathered and arranged in order by men through their natural powers.[83] Once gathered, these principles lead men to understand the wisdom of God. "And this teacheth man thus much," wrote Alexander Richardson, "That he is to seek out, and find this wisdom of God in the world, and not to be idle; for the world, and the creatures therein are like a book wherein Gods wisdom is written, and there must we seek it out." Man learns these rules from "singulars, by analysis," and becomes aware that "Truth is first in God, then secondly, all things are so far forth true, as they answer to the *idaea* in God." [84] One sees immediately certain far-reaching implications, such as belief in a pattern of ideas in the mind of God to which the creatures correspond, and a conception of the unity and divine authorship of knowledge and, hence, of all things. Miller quotes, finally, a passage written by Samuel Mather in which the doctrine of "technologia" is summarized and universalized:

---

[81] Miller, pp. 48, 116–119. Brooke quotes the *Medulla*, disagreeing with Ames on a matter concerning the attributes of God, in *The Nature of Truth*, p. 23. And see n. 57 above.

[82] Miller, pp. 160–180 *et passim*.

[83] Paraphrasing from Miller, p. 116.

[84] Richardson, as quoted by Miller, pp. 162–166.

All the Arts are nothing else but the beams and rays of the Wisdom of the *first Being* in the Creatures, shining, and reflecting thence, upon the glass of man's understanding; and as from Him they come, so to him they tend: the circle of Arts is *a Deo ad Deum.* Hence there is an affinity and kindred of Arts (*omnes Artes vinculo & cognatione quadam inter se continentur*: Cicer. pro Arch. Poet.) which is according to the reference and subordination of their particular ends, to the utmost and last end: One makes use of another, one serves to another, till they all reach and return to *Him*, as Rivers to the Sea, whence they flow.[85]

The relationship between this complex of ideas and Brooke's thought will be best shown by comparing a quotation or two from *The Nature of Truth* with Samuel Mather's summary:

How would the soule improve, if all Aristotles *Materia prima*, Plato's *Mens Platonica*, Hermes Trismegistus his νοῦς and λόγος, were converted into some spirituall light? the soule might soare and raise it selfe up to Universall Being, bathe it selfe in those stately, deep, and glorious streames of Unity, see God in Iesus Christ, the first, chiefe, and sole cause of all Being: It would not then containe it selfe within particular rivulets, in whose shallow waters it can encounter nothing but sand or pebbles, seeing it may fully delight it selfe in the first rise of all delight, Iesus Christ.

Thus, when you see the face of Beauty, you will perfectly be assured how many the severall pieces which make it up, must be, what their nature, and their severall proportions. So shall you with certainty descend to knowledge of existences, essences, when you shall rest in one universall cause: and Metaphysicks, Mathematicks, and Logick will happily prove one, while they teach the variations of Unity through severall numbers. All particular Sciences will be subordinate, and particular applications of these. So all shall be, according to Ficinus, *Circulus boni per bonum in bonum rediens*; and the face of divine Beauty shall bee unveiled through all.[86]

Another passage has a likewise familiar ring: "If you follow this rule, and see all things in the glass of Unity, you will not lose all Arts and Sciences in the Wood of Divisions and Subdivisions *in infinitum.*" [87] One may note, too, Brooke's introductory remarks in the section in which, having established to his satisfaction the "nature" of the understanding, he essays to explain its "workings":

Now concerning the particular and various workings thereof, in conclusions, simple apprehensions, negations and affirmations, etc. which seeme to be the ofspring of the first and originall Being; even these, I hope to prove all one and the same, as with themselves, so with the former, all

[85] Miller, p. 180.
[86] *The Nature of Truth*, pp. 143–145.
[87] *Ibid.*, p. 164.

conjoyned in one Being of light and truth. *That* is a truth in the fountaine, *this* in the streames; and no man will deny the fountaine and streame to make one river.[88]

It is clear, then, that there is a similarity between the doctrine of "technologia" and Brooke's own theory of unity.

In examining *The Nature of Truth* more closely one experiences further shocks of recognition. At the very beginning Brooke defines truth in terms of the familiar "stream" image:

Truth is indeed of the seed Royall, of Progeny Divine . . . The Understanding is her throne, there she reigneth, and as she is there seated, as she shineth in that part of the soule; she appeareth to me under two notions, which are also her measure through the whole sphere of Being; as will be discovered more hereafter, when these lesser streames shall have emptied themselves by progresse into a larger river.[89]

Beyond the similarity in imagery one notices too that Truth only "appears" under two notions; that is, the diversity is apparent only to the human reason: in the eyes of God Truth is one.

This first Truth is the Understanding in its Essence; for what is the Understanding other than a Ray of the Divine Nature, warming and enlivening the Creature, conforming it to the likenesse of the Creator? And is not Truth the same?

As one reads further one is reminded of Brooke's fancy for notions that involve the reflection of an entity upon itself:

For the Beauty of Truths character is, that she is a shadow, a resemblance of the first, the best forme; that she is light, the species, the sparkling of primitive light; that she is life, the sublimation of light, that she may reflect upon her selfe.[90]

Remembering these last two passages one turns back to the opening sentence from the Mather quotation: "All the Arts are nothing else but the beams and rays of the Wisdom of the *first Being* in the Creatures, shining, and reflecting thence, upon the glass of man's understanding . . ." These striking similarities are beyond being merely coincidental.

Only by studying the objects that are visible to us do we

[88] *The Nature of Truth*, pp. 81–82.
[89] *Ibid.*, pp. 1–2.
[90] *Ibid.*, pp. 3–4.

glimpse the "preexistent pattern of ideas" in the mind of God, from whom all creation flows in its apparent diversity. As one of the "technologists" quoted by Miller puts it,

It is certain that the Arts are all of them imprinted in the *Book of the Creature*; and from thence it is that Men's Reasoning Power Collects them, by Observation and Experience, the Foundation of them is laid in the Nature of things, and is gathered from thence by curious inquiry . . .[91]

Brooke, though in a somewhat different context, seems to echo this attitude when he enters in his gloss that "Experience [is the] collection of particular lights," opposite a question in the text couched in language that reminds us startlingly of Bacon: "For what . . . is experiment, but the daughter of light, gathered by frequent observation?"[92]

Brooke's affinity with the Puritan doctrine of "technologia" points illuminatingly in two directions. In the first place, the resemblance of this attitude to Platonic thought is too obvious to require elucidation. Ames could protest that "the theory of a pre-existent platform of ideas was not a species of Platonism"[93] — the resemblance is none the less arresting. Besides, it cannot be accidental that Ames reached a conclusion of another sort, also reached by Brooke, that has Platonic overtones: namely, that the will must of necessity follow the understanding.[94] In these two respects, if in no other, both Ames and Brooke were Platonists, a fact that suggests a great deal more than it tells concerning the extent to which Platonism figures in the make-up of the Puritan mind.

The other direction in which this affinity points is, perhaps strangely, toward Bacon. One recognizes, with due caution, that to interpret *The Nature of Truth* as a plea for the advancement of learning would distort its import violently, just as one must realize that Ramus and his followers were, as Miller warns one to remember, humanists and not scientists.[95] Yet as the doctrine

---

[91] Miller, p. 169.
[92] *The Nature of Truth*, p. 55.
[93] Miller, p. 177.
[94] Miller, p. 248. Brooke's position on this matter has been outlined, p. 98 above.
[95] Miller, p. 143.

of "technologia," while recognizing the divine unity that infuses all of being, turns man's attention to the concrete objects within the range of his powers of observation so that he can gather from them sufficient to enable him to comprehend even to a small degree the wisdom of God, so Brooke, while conceiving of the unity that pervades existence as so transcendent and inclusive as to defy the ordinary comprehension of man, is not disposed to "reject an industrious search after wisedome," though, with Bacon himself, at the same time condemning "nice, unnecessary prying into those things which profit not." [96] For Brooke, as indebted as he is to tradition of many sorts, gives sympathetic attention to the new science, granting the feasibility of searching for "effects," though with "that learned wit, Sir Francis Bacon . . . leaving the search of causes to those, who are content, with Icarus, to burne their wings at a fire too hot for them." [97]

The fact that Brooke's Puritan heritage is broadly inclusive of the most ancient and the most modern elements in his thought is significant, for it suggests a fact of great importance to the evaluation of his treatise; and that is that Brooke, like his greatest contemporary, was both a Puritan and a broad-minded humanist. Nor was he, any more than Milton, an ivory-tower philosopher, but a controversialist in the pamphlet war and an active soldier in the real war. Yet his manner in controversy, befitting a humanist, was dignified, courteous, and tolerant, so much so as to lead Milton to say of him, "I cannot call to mind where I have read or heard words more mild and peaceful." [98] One is strongly impressed, then, with Brooke's calm reasonableness and with the scope of his inquiry. In *The Nature of Truth* his points of departure were strictly theological, yet his subject led him into many secular paths. As Professor Bush has noted, his "range of reference is almost as broad as his theme." [99]

The Nature of Truth does not reveal dependence by Brooke on any two or three actual "sources." Rather, it reveals a well-blended synthesis of three major intellectual strains: Platonic, scholastic, and Puritan. All three are important in the formation

---

[96] *The Nature of Truth*, p. 142.
[97] *Ibid.*, p. 125.
[98] Milton, "Areopagitica," *Works*, IV, 346.
[99] Bush, *English Literature in the Earlier Seventeenth Century*, p. 341.

of Brooke's system, and whether he drew upon the Platonists and scholastics directly or absorbed their points of view from second-hand acquaintance through Puritan literature is of little moment. With these three strong influences one must take account of Brooke's familiarity with the Bible. The extent to which all the influences are synthesized in his writing should by now be evident; but it can be dramatized by a quotation from *The Nature of Truth* in which the synthesis is fully achieved, a recapitulation that sees Plato and Ficino, the scholastics and the prophets, and even the Calvinists themselves, bow hurriedly to each other and rush on:

And if you long, with the Israelites, to have a King, as your neighbours have; and you desire to speak in their language: When the soule entertaineth light, say it doth understand. When it doth exercise any morall vertue, say it willeth. When you see some things precede others, call the one a cause, the other an effect: but travell not far in the search of the source of this cause. Doe not make the will and the understanding two faculties, *Fratrum concordia rara*; Iacob will supplant Esau in the Womb. Make therefore the severall Actings of the soule, as Rayes of this one soule; make these rayes, and the soule sending forth these rayes, a perpetuall emanation Divine: and so by these degrees of truth, mount up into the armes of Eternity, and he will take care of you, that you shall not dash your feete against the stone of free will: that you shall not overthrow all faith, by starting so many nice questions in the point of faith. If you follow this rule, and see all things in the glasse of Unity, you will not lose all Arts and Sciences in the Wood of Divisions and Subdivisions *in infinitum*.[100]

[100] *The Nature of Truth*, pp. 162–164.

X

CONTEMPORARY PERSPECTIVES

John Wallis, the mathematician, was not by any means a
Platonist. In his reply to *The Nature of Truth*, a tract published
in 1643 entitled *Truth Tried: or, Animadversions On a Treatise
published by the Right Honorable Robert Lord Brooke, entituled,
The Nature of Truth, Its Union and Unity with the Soule*, Wallis
betrays decided annoyance with Brooke's inspired vision of unity.
In view of the fact, however, that Wallis's answer is the only
contemporary full-scale critique of Brooke's treatise, one must
take some account of his objections before attempting to evaluate
the position of Brooke among other literary figures of seventeenth-
century England.

Though Wallis expresses great respect for Brooke's accomplishments and genuinely laments his sudden death,[1] he is pointedly critical of his philosophical views. One of the aspects of
Brooke's treatise that most disturbs him is the looseness of some
of its terminology. He confesses himself to be in great doubt as
to what Brooke means by "truth" in his contention that "truth"
and the "soul" are one. Perhaps, he concedes, if one takes Brooke's
"truth" to mean "the power of being known," or "knowability"
(Wallis uses the scholastic term *cognoscibilitas*), then one may
come close to Brooke's meaning, in that "Truth in the Things and
Knowledge in the Understanding have relation to each other as
Objectum and *Potentia*." Truth in this sense is an "affection of
Being." Yet the "Truth of Being" and the "Truth of Knowledge"
are really one and the same with "that Being, which truly Is,
and is truly Known to be" — which is just as true and just as

---

[1] *Truth Tried*, sig. A1, in a letter written after Brooke's death and inserted in
the book after it had gone to press: "A sad losse it was, had it been in the Best
times, to loose so many Accomplishments in one Noble Breast; but Now most Unhappy, when there is so much work and so few hands; in which, I am confident,
None was guided by a more single Eye, with lesse Obliquity to collateral aimes."
Wallis's elegy, also appended to this tract, has been noted (pp. 75–76 above).

knowable when no understanding takes notice of it as when it is understood; "and therefore this truth cannot be One with the Understanding, because it may be then and there where the Understanding is not." [2]

One can see at the root of the difficulty a refusal on the part of Wallis to accept in any form the Platonic-idealistic notion of the identity of thought and the object of thought, a notion of central significance in Brooke's incipiently idealistic system. If truth is one with the thing known, asks Wallis, is the soul one with the stone? Are all the souls understanding the stone then one with the stone, and with each other? Such an identity of souls and of objects is not only absurd, he pursues, but it is a notion with which Brooke himself is inconsistent enough to disagree; for God, then, being known by the soul, must be one with the soul, and "all things else are one with God, because they are all known by Him" — and hence Brooke falls into an error against which he himself warns, namely, "by mounting too high in the exalting of Truth, to confound the Creator with the Creature by making her God." [3]

The trouble lies in Brooke's insistence that "the truth" and "the truth-understood" are one. If, maintains Wallis, Brooke means only that "truth" is the "power of knowing," his theory might be more admissible. If only Brooke did not continually vary the "acceptation of truth" from the "truth-understanding" to the "truth-understood," or in other words, from "innate truth" to "advenient truth" (as in "those sweet beames of light, which beat upon us continually"), there would be relatively little difficulty in following him. [4] But how can the "truth-understood" have any conjunction with the understanding until it is actually understood? "And even Then, we cannot make it to be One with the Understanding, except we make those things to be One, which have neither coexistence of Place, nor coexistence of Time; For those things may be understood, which were many thousand Yeares past, and many thousand Miles distant." [5] The obstacle, one realizes, is still the same; for if Wallis could accept the Platonic

[2] *Truth Tried*, pp. 4–5.
[3] *Ibid.*, p. 7; and see *The Nature of Truth*, sig. A12.
[4] *Truth Tried*, p. 22; and see *The Nature of Truth*, p. 7.
[5] *Truth Tried*, p. 28.

basis of Brooke's reasoning, he could also accept Brooke's subsequent demonstration that time and place themselves do not exist outside the realm of thought. Philosophical idealism was as impossible for Wallis to comprehend as the nonexistence of Bishop Berkeley's stone was to be for Dr. Johnson.

Finally, when Brooke concludes in the sixth chapter that "All things are this one light or truth," the hardheaded mathematician is left gasping.

> I confesse, I was at a stand a great while, and could not imagine any shew of Consequence between these propositions: If Truth or Reason be the same with the Soule or Understanding; then is it also the same with All things else.[6]

The insuperable gap between the Platonic idealist and the practical Aristotelian is probably nowhere more effectively dramatized than in Wallis's plaintive, and on his terms justifiable, outburst: suppose all things do indeed have the same "Specificall Essence," he declares:

> Yet doth it not follow that they must be all One and the Same. For are there not many Individualls under the same Species, whereof One is not the Other? Doth not the Soule of Peter and the Soule of Judas agree in all the same Specificall and Essentiall Praedicates, whilst notwithstanding it may be truly said, that the Soule of Peter is not the Soule of Judas, and again, that the Soule of Judas is not the soule of Peter? What Essentiall difference is there between water in the Baltick Sea, and that in the Mediterranean, since they both are but Integrall Parts of the same Homogeneall Ocean: Yet how true it is withall, That the Baltick is not the Mediterranean sea; and That the Water which is now in the Baltick, is distinct from that which at the same time is in the Mediterranean Sea? Two drops of Water taken out of the same spoonfull, be they in their Essentialls never so Consonant, in their Accidents never so Like; Yet we may truly say This is not the Other, nor the Other This. How then can it follow, That Truth is One with the Understanding, and that All things are this One Truth, Because all Being is but a Ray of Divinity?[7]

If this absurd proposition is true, then whence comes, he would like to know, the "great Variety in the Creation"? "For my own judgement," he impatiently concludes,

> I am as confident, that Unity is Nothing; as his Lordship is, That it is

[6] *Truth Tried,* p. 28.
[7] *Ibid.,* pp. 30–31.

All things. 'Tis a meer rationall, nominall Notion, that hath no more Reality in it, then Darknesse, then *non esse*. Yea, to be One, is a pure Negative Proposition; and what Reality you can allow to a Negation, so much you may allow to Unity.[8]

With mounting indignation Wallis reviews the many points on which he and Brooke disagree: free will, the question of whether the will must follow the understanding, the existence of time and place, the positive existence of evil.[9] The abyss between them emerges more clearly and becomes wider. Wallis cannot subscribe, with Brooke, to the effort of the Platonists

to make Knowledge nothing but a Remembrance. (As if there were naturally in our Understanding, the Pictures or Pourtraictures of all Truths, but so obscured and covered as it were with dust, that these glorious Colours doe not appear, till such time as they be rubbed and washed over anew.) I approve rather of Aristotle's *Rasa Tabula*, (then Plato's *Reminiscentia*) making the Understanding, of it selfe, to have no such Idea or Picture at all, but capable of all.[10]

As a final trial to the mathematician's patience, Brooke ecstatically describes the joy of knowing that all is one:

if wee knew this truth, that all things are one; how cheerfully, with what modest courage should wee undertake any action, re-incounter any occurrence, knowing that that distinction of misery and happinesse, which now so perplexeth us, hath no Being, except in the Brain.[11]

To this Wallis acidly concludes:

That all things are one; That the difference between Happinesse and Misery is only in the Brain . . . I have allready denied. I will only adde, That by this discourse you prove the Devills as happy as the blessed Angels: And if it be a Good Consequent of this Position, That it will make us not afraid of Misery and Danger: I am sure it is as Bad a Consequent, That it will make us not afraid of Sinning . . . My judgement cannot assent to make the Torments of the damned, onely Imaginary; To make Hell a Fansie.[12]

If a modern reader, imbued as he must be with the scientific and pragmatic attitudes characteristic of the twentieth century, were

[8] *Ibid.*, pp. 36, 43.
[9] *Ibid.*, pp. 54, 56 (misnumbered 44), 69, 72.
[10] *Ibid.*, p. 49.
[11] *The Nature of Truth*, p. 118.
[12] *Truth Tried*, pp. 90–91.

to judge the significance of Brooke's treatise for seventeenth-century thought from the only full contemporary critique of it, his impulse would be to consign it to the misty mid-regions of Weir and go on about more serious business. One need not, however, depend upon Wallis for the last word. He is merely the star witness for the prosecution. More eminent authorities than he may be called to testify for the defense.

Bacon, for one, whose concern is with a visible world rather than an invisible one, is scarcely a Platonist. When he declares that men "have made too untimely a departure and too remote a recess from particulars,"[13] he is implicitly criticizing Platonic emphasis on ideas and forms. Furthermore, if Robert Hooke praised Bacon,[14] Wallis would have been unlikely to scorn him. Yet one finds in the *Advancement of Learning* and the *Novum Organum* evidence that Bacon and Brooke were at least not poles apart. Their mutual mistrust of the senses has already been noted. "By far the greatest hindrance and aberration of the human understanding," Bacon argues in the explication of the Idol of the Tribe, "proceeds from the dulness, incompetency, and deceptions of the senses."[15] On another occasion Bacon explains that

the third vice or disease of learning, which concerneth deceit or untruth, it is of all the rest the foulest; as that which doth destroy the essential form of knowledge, which is nothing but a representation of truth: for the truth of being and the truth of knowing are one, differing no more than the direct beam and the beam reflected.[16]

This opinion is not far removed from the Platonic notion that knowing the good necessitates doing the good; and Bacon elsewhere implies that the will depends upon the understanding, such as when he declares that "the commandment of knowledge is yet higher than the commandment over the will; for it is a commandment over the reason, belief, and understanding of man, which is the highest part of the mind, and giveth law to the will itself."[17] The idea is further delineated in the essay, "Of Goodness and

---

[13] Bacon, *Works*, ed. Spedding, Ellis, and Heath (Boston, 1860–63), VI, 221.
[14] Bush, *English Literature in the Earlier Seventeenth Century*, p. 265.
[15] Bacon, *Works*, VIII, 82.
[16] Bacon, VI, 125.
[17] Bacon, VI, 166.

THE
NATURE
OF
TRUTH

Its Union and Unity
with the SOULE,

Which is
One in its Essence, Faculties,
Acts; One with TRUTH.

Discussed by the Right Honorable
ROBERT Lord BROOK,
in a Letter to a private Friend.

By whom it is now published for
the Publick Good.

Printed by *R. Bishop*, for *Samuel
Cartwright*, at the Bible in
Duck-lane, 1641.

Goodness of Nature," in which Bacon alludes to the "habit of goodness, directed by right reason," and maintains that "Goodness answers to the theological virtue Charity, and admits no excess, but error." [18] Professor Craig sees in this essay a doctrine of evil akin to that expressed by Hooker, that "if reason err, we fall into evil," [19] a doctrine that clearly has affinities with the Augustinian-Platonic notion of evil as a privation.

There are, then, certain areas in which Bacon, the practical proponent of scientific inquiry, voices Platonic doctrine audibly enough so that he may be linked at a few junctures with such Platonists as Brooke. This Platonic tendency in Bacon's thought has been substantiated by the researches of Professor Anderson, who finds that Bacon's philosophy, while it is principally materialistic, is often Platonic in its methodology. [20]

On the question of final causes the practical man and the Platonist are sufficiently at one for Brooke to have quoted in his support "that learned wit, Sir Francis Bacon," who, "in his naturall Philosophy, bringeth onely experiments, leaving the search of causes to those, who are content, with Icarus, to burne their wings at a fire too hot for them." [21] One recalls that Bacon quoted Philo in his opinion that

the sense of man carrieth a resemblance with the sun, which (as we see) openeth and revealeth all the terrestrial globe; but then again it obscureth and concealeth the stars and celestial globe: so doth the sense discover natural things, but it darkeneth and shutteth up the divine.

Bacon goes on from this admission to conclude: "And hence it is true that it hath proceeded, that divers great learned men have been heretical, whilst they have sought to fly up to the secrets of the Deity by the waxen wings of the senses." [22] One remembers, too, Bacon's warning: "We ought not to attempt to draw down or submit the mysteries of God to our reason; but contrariwise to raise and advance our reason to the divine truth." [23] Bacon appears to see a theoretical relationship between reason and faith,

---

[18] Bacon, XII, 118.
[19] Hardin Craig, *The Enchanted Glass*, p. 26.
[20] F. H. Anderson, *The Philosophy of Francis Bacon* (Chicago, 1948), p. 124.
[21] *The Nature of Truth*, p. 125.
[22] Bacon, VI, 96.
[23] Bacon, VI, 213.

though he is far from equating them, a fact that tended in the long run, as Professor Bush has pointed out, to diminish the power of religion among the followers of Baconian science.[24] Brooke (and Bacon himself) would have been aghast at this turn of events, and one cannot call Brooke a Baconian any more accurately than one can call Bacon a Platonist. Yet both would, one believes, have conceded a mutual respect. Neither was disposed to solicit his thoughts with matters hid, but both saw in the matters hid a relevance to matters discernible.

Brooke is much closer to Sir Thomas Browne, who felt with "the Philosophy of Hermes" that "this visible World is but a Picture of the invisible, wherein as in a Pourtraict, things are not truely, but in equivocal shapes, and as they counterfeit some more real substance in that invisible Fabrick." [25] Browne's religious beliefs depend upon Scripture, the tenets of the Church of England, and the dictates of his reason; but he loves to pursue his reason "to an *O altitudo!*" and to teach his "haggard and unreclaimed reason to stoop unto the lure of Faith." [26] Unlike Brooke, Browne was an Anglican, but like Brooke he was a Platonist and rationalist whose rationalism was tempered with an almost mystical faith.

In other matters there is further community of feeling between them. Scientific investigation, up to a point, is sanctioned by Browne, who sees, as does Bacon, two Scriptures from whence to collect "Divinity" — the book of God and the book of Nature.[27] The book of Nature is not only well worth study in itself, but even further:

the wisdom of God receives small honour from those vulgar Heads that rudely stare about, and with a gross rusticity admire his works; those highly magnifie him, whose judicious inquiry into His Acts, and deliberate research into His Creatures, return the duty of a devout and learned admiration.[28]

[24] Bush, *English Literature in the Earlier Seventeenth Century*, p. 268.

[25] Browne, *Religio Medici*, I, xii. Brooke does not allude to the *Religio Medici*, but it is possible that he read it. Though it was not published until 1642, it was written in 1635 and was circulated widely in manuscript.

[26] *Religio Medici*, I, v: "Where the Scripture is silent, the Church is my Text; where that speaks, 'tis but my comment: where there is a joynt silence of both, I borrow not the rules of my Religion from Rome or Geneva, but the dictates of my own reason." And see also I, ix–x.

[27] *Religio Medici*, I, xvi; see also Bacon, VI, 144.

[28] *Religio Medici*, I, xiii.

Both appear to agree on the subjectivity of time. To Browne there is in eternity "no distinction of tenses," and Brooke's attitude is certainly similar: "In the Deity wee have creation, preservation, redemption, decree, and execution of that decree. All these to our apprehension are distinguisht by time: and yet no man will say, that in God they are two." [29] Browne's reasoning from his position on this matter does, however, reduce one of Brooke's theological tenets, one that measures the difference between an Anglican and a Calvinist, to meaninglessness:

> In Eternity there is no distinction of Tenses; and therefore that terrible term Predestination, which hath troubled so many weak heads to conceive, and the wisest to explain, is in respect to God no prescious determination of our Estates to come, but a definitive blast of his Will already fulfilled, and at the instant that he first decreed it; for to his Eternity which is indivisible and all together, the last Trump is already sounded, the reprobates in the flame, and the blessed in Abraham's bosome.[30]

Brooke and Browne do indeed diverge on crucial matters. The vigorous young Puritan could not accept the polity of Anglicanism, as the *Discourse on Episcopacy* would reveal, and the contemplative physician of Norwich could not allow himself to be troubled by the doctrine of predestination. Brooke was an active reformer who not only could not ignore political currents but allowed himself to be fully swept into them, Browne a retiring antiquarian who was more interested in basilisks and griffins than in Cromwell, who was busily and delightedly speculating upon some newly unearthed burial urns as the Commonwealth was crumbling. But they are not so very far apart in their intellectual positions. And though John Wallis would have shaken his head, no doubt, over the good doctor's yearnings for an "*O altitudo!*" just as he stood agape at Brooke's manifestations of Platonic idealism, he would not have scorned the intellectual company of either the widely read Puritan nobleman or the ingenious and learned virtuoso scientist, whose curious minds would have been at home among Wallis's colleagues in the early meetings that grew into the Royal Society.

The most eminent witness to the high regard in which Brooke's

---

[29] *The Nature of Truth*, p. 96.
[30] *Religio Medici*, I, xi.

thought could be held by his contemporaries is of course Milton.
It is true that the great poet was drawn to Brooke by the "mild
and peaceful" words of the *Discourse on Episcopacy* rather than
by the radiant vision of *The Nature of Truth*. It is also true that
Milton was soon to dash his foot against the Arminian stone of
free will, and one would distort the picture of both men in
rationalizing an inclusive community of agreement between them.
Yet apart from their mutual position on the reform of church
government, which is their most striking area of common outlook, to be discussed in detail later on, in their Platonic rationalism one also may discern a philosophical affinity.

Reason was, to Milton, the "light within his own clear breast"
whose possessor might "sit i' th' centre, and enjoy bright day." [31]
It was reason that made virtue possible. The Lady resisted the
wiles of the enchanter Comus partly because her reason was
impregnable, as Eve was to fail to resist the blandishments of
the glozing tempter because her reason was beguiled. Reason "is
but choosing," [32] and if Milton could allow Adam, his reason
unbeguiled, to will an evil choice — a length to which the Platonist Brooke could probably not have accompanied him — he
could still maintain that Adam, in so doing, recognized the
difference between truth and falsehood, good and evil. If man
has fallen on evil days, it is not because "that intellectual ray
which God hath planted in us" has failed to reveal the truth;
for, as the fine passage in *Of Reformation* continues:

> The very essence of Truth is plainnesse, and brightnes; the darknes
> and crookednesse is our own. The wisedome of God created understanding,
> fit and proportionable to Truth the object, and end of it, as the eye to the
> thing visible. If our understanding have a film of ignorance over it, or be
> blear with gazing on other false glisterings, what is that to Truth? [33]

One thinks back to the eulogy of the "certain divine breath"
implanted in man "as it were a part of Himself, immortal, imper-
ishable, immune from death and destruction" in the Seventh
Prolusion, and to the Lady's "unpolluted temple of the mind,"
and forward to the "true wayfaring Christian" whose virtue,

---

[31] "Comus," line 381, *Works*, I, 99.
[32] "Areopagitica," *Works*, IV, 319.
[33] "Of Reformation," *Works*, III, 33.

neither fugitive nor cloistered, depends upon choice determined by reason.[34]

These passages illuminate Milton's attitude toward reason from several points of view, and their collective import is that Milton's position is, if not by any means identical with, at least not antagonistic to Brooke's representation of the understanding as a "ray of the Divine Nature, warming and enlivening the Creature, conforming it to the likenesse of the Creator," [35] and at the same time one with truth itself, whose very essence, according to Milton, is plainness and brightness. Milton, who wrote that the understanding is "fit and proportionable to Truth the object, and end of it, as the eye to the thing visible," is not likely to have been as shocked as Wallis was at Brooke's identification of the "Truth" with the "Truth-understood." Professor Barker maintains that Milton actually shared Brooke's opinion that the understanding and truth are one, but did not fully see the connection between the understanding so conceived and those things considered "indifferent" in church government until Brooke's *Discourse on Episcopacy* pointed it out. In fact, he goes so far as to argue that Brooke is as much as anyone the source of the rationalism of the *Areopagitica*.[36] Without making so strong a claim, however, one may recognize that a bond between the rationalism of Milton and that of Brooke does exist.

Both Milton and Brooke recognize the limitations of reason as clearly as they recognize its divine heritage. Eve knows that "Our Reason is our Law," [37] yet she fails to heed Raphael's warning:

> Solicit not thy thoughts with matters hid,
> Leave them to God above, him serve and fear.[38]

Reason is God's image in man, yet it is intended to lead man only so far; when he aspires too high he commits the sin of pride. Brooke likewise admits that "Our spirits are mighty Nimrods,

[34] "Seventh Prolusion," *Works*, XII, 255; "Comus," line 461, *Works*, I, 102; "Areopagitica," *Works*, IV, 310–311.

[35] *The Nature of Truth*, pp. 3–4.

[36] Barker, *Milton and the Puritan Dilemma*, pp. 58, 82–83. This matter will receive full treatment in Part III.

[37] *Paradise Lost*, IX, 654.

[38] *Paradise Lost*, VIII, 167–168.

hunting after knowledge, venturing all, to eate of the tree of knowledge of good and evill." [39] Further, Milton allows that reason can be overborne, and he has Raphael caution Adam "lest Passion sway thy Judgment"; [40] and when Adam "scrupl'd not to eat," it was

> Against his better knowledge, not deceiv'd,
> But fondly overcome with Female charm. [41]

Eve's reason is actually deceived, but to Adam, swayed by his "Passion," other values temporarily seem of greater consequence than those dictated by reason and obedience. Brooke would have said that in thus acting falsely the reason was not acting at all, as the sense of sight cannot be properly said to be acting when in the twilight one mistakes a man for a tree; yet the result, an action against the dictates of reason, would be the same. The senses (and the passions) are always capable of "misguiding" the reason. [42] But these aberrations do not, either for Milton or for Brooke, impugn the sovereignty of reason. Reason is still the mansion of truth.

Any further comparison of Brooke with Milton, however, on grounds apart from their sympathy on the reform of church government, must be necessarily somewhat forced. One could demonstrate a number of resemblances, some of them of great interest, such as Milton's belief in a monistic unity of matter and spirit as expressed in one of the most overt philosophical statements in *Paradise Lost*, Raphael's explanation to Adam of the structure of creation:

> O Adam, one Almighty is, from whom
> All things proceed, and up to him return,
> If not deprav'd from good, created all
> Such to perfection, one first matter all,
> Indu'd with various forms, various degrees
> Of substance, and in things that live, of life;
> But more refin'd, more spiritous, and pure,
> As nearer to him plac't or nearer tending
> Each in thir several active Spheres assign'd,

[39] *The Nature of Truth*, p. 126.
[40] *Paradise Lost*, VIII, 635–636.
[41] *Paradise Lost*, IX, 997–999.
[42] *The Nature of Truth*, pp. 106–110.

Till body up to spirit work, in bounds
Proportion'd to each kind. So from the root
Springs lighter the green stalk, from thence the leaves
More aery, last the bright consummate flow'r
Spirits odorous breathes: flow'rs and thir fruit
Man's nourishment, by gradual scale sublim'd
To vital Spirits aspire, to animal,
To intellectual, give both life and sense,
Fancy and understanding, whence the Soul
Reason receives, and reason is her being,
Discursive, or Intuitive; discourse
Is oftest yours, the latter most is ours,
Differing but in degree, of kind the same.[43]

But in order to find contemporary literary figures toward whom Brooke reveals more than an occasional resemblance, with whom he has a really profound philosophical affinity, one turns to the Cambridge Platonists.

If Brooke knew at Cambridge any of the writers who came to make up this school, no record of their association has come to light, unless one includes among the Cambridge Platonists Brooke's personal chaplain, Peter Sterry. It is not only in their common Platonism that Brooke is related to this group. One may note other resemblances, though perhaps even these are ultimately dependent upon their common Platonic outlook. A comparison of some of Brooke's ideas with the ideas of several of the Cambridge Platonists is useful in that it both illuminates Brooke's strength and reveals his weakness. In considering his relationship to these philosophers one is allowing Brooke to be met on his own ground; for the ultimate aim of the Cambridge Platonists, unlike that of Bacon, Browne, Milton, or Wallis, was, if it can be reduced to so simple a statement, the reconciliation of religion and philosophy, or more directly, of faith and reason.

Since he has been mentioned, one might begin with Peter Sterry, who may possibly have influenced Brooke in the formu-

---

[43] *Paradise Lost*, V, 468–490. This monistic belief is quite clearly explained elsewhere in prose, in the *De Doctrina Christiana*, I, vii: "It is objected . . . that body cannot emanate from spirit. I reply, much less then can body emanate from nothing. For spirit being the more excellent substance, virtually and essentially contains within itself the inferior one; as the spiritual and rational faculty contains the corporeal, that is, the sentient and vegetative faculty" (*Works*, XV, 25).

lation of ideas that emerged in *The Nature of Truth*.[44] The principal point of intellectual contact between the noble lord and his chaplain is their common acceptance of the unity of being, a resemblance that is not surprising when one considers that both were Platonists and Puritans. To Sterry,

God is Being it self in its simplicity and absoluteness, the first, the supreme, the universal Being. . . Being it self in its absoluteness, undivided, unrestrained, unconfined, unalloyed by any differences of mixtures. . . Being it self in its Truth, in its substance; the only true Being, the universal Being.[45]

Sterry's vision of the unity of God and all Being includes and accounts for the diversity of creation:

Unity without distinction or variety, is a barrenness, a melancholy, a solitude, a blackness of Darkness. . . God is not a Solitary Unity, without Society or Solace; but a Unity richly Replenished, and Eternally entertain'd, with a Variety, as true and boundless as the Unity itself.[46]

In one respect Sterry's monism differs from the belief in unity exhibited by most of the Cambridge Platonists and resembles that expressed by Brooke: neither Sterry nor Brooke is willing to accept free will. According to Brooke, God dispenses grace freely; the soul cannot reject grace, nor can the soul, having received grace, subsequently reject it.[47] This attitude not only stems from his Calvinist theology but also appears to him as a necessary consequence of his monism, in that the recipient and the thing received must be the same. Sterry puts the belief on a more clearly philosophical basis by maintaining that in a creation utterly unified in one inclusive Being, liberty and determinism meet. Liberty is freedom to follow that "endeavour

---

[44] V. de Sola Pinto, *Peter Sterry, Platonist and Puritan* (Cambridge, 1934), pp. 12–13. Pinto's conjecture is based upon a remark of Antony Wood's, that Brooke was helped in the composition of both his treatises by "some Puritanical minister" (Wood, II, cols. 432–434). Wood asserted that Brooke had become "unhappily attainted with fanatic and antimonarchial principles, by the influence of one of his near relations and some schismatical preachers, (tho' in his own nature a very civil and well-humour'd person)." The near relation may have been his father-in-law, the Earl of Bedford, or perhaps his brother-in-law, Sir Arthur Haselrig; and one of the "schismatical preachers" may have been Sterry.

[45] Pinto, pp. 89–90.
[46] Pinto, p. 90.
[47] *The Nature of Truth*, pp. 12, 50.

wherewith a thing endeavours to persist in its being." The Will, driven by an inward necessity, a "reason from within," is thus "divinely free." In this way freedom and necessity are really one.[48]

It is principally in the objective of reconciling reason and faith that Brooke and the Cambridge Platonists are at one. By implication, a conflict between reason and faith involves further conflicts between science and religion, matter and spirit. To bridge these gaps was the aim of the Cambridge Platonists, whose purpose, it has been said, was "comprehension, and not exclusion." [49] A significant result of their resolution of such conflicts was their espousal of the cause of toleration, and in this respect, even though most of the Cambridge Platonists were bitterly opposed to the doctrine of predestination as an insult to the dignity of man,[50] one may link them even more closely with Brooke. In the writings of all of them, as in the writings of Brooke, there is manifest a fervent desire to harmonize the discordant elements of the universe, and with this end in view all of them tend toward a conception of being as one divine unity.

To the elder statesman of the group, Benjamin Whichcote, whose favorite and often-repeated text was "The Spirit of man is the Candle of the Lord," [51] not only can reason not oppose faith, but neither faith nor reason can exist without the other. In a sermon entitled "The Work of Reason" Whichcote reiterates this attitude eloquently:

> In the state of Religion, Spirituals and Naturals joyn and mingle in their Subjects; so that if a Man be once in a true State of Religion, he cannot distinguish between Religion and the Reason of his Mind; so that his Religion is the Reason of his Mind, and the Reason of his Mind is his Religion. They are not two things now; they do not go two several ways, but concur and agree; they both run into one Principle, they make one Spirit, make one Stream.[52]

[48] Pinto, pp. 105–106: a Calvinist version of "Christian liberty."

[49] John Tulloch, *Rational Theology and Christian Philosophy in England in the Seventeenth Century* (Edinburgh, 1872), II, 3. The conflict with science did not emerge, however, in the early writings of the group.

[50] Jordan, *Religious Toleration*, IV, 98.

[51] See the selection from Whichcote's "Aphorisms" in E. T. Campagnac, *The Cambridge Platonists* (Oxford, 1901), p. 70. The text (Proverbs 20:27) was used at one time or another by other members of the group as well.

[52] Campagnac, p. 57.

One notes in this passage the image, common among Platonists and Puritans, of the fountains that make up one stream and the streams that flow to make up one river, and one may recognize the affinity between Brooke and Whichcote even more clearly from passages concerning the relationship between truth and the soul. Although Whichcote considers that truth is revealed by two kinds of emanation from God (Brooke would insist that even these are but one), the "truth of first inscription" and the "truth of after-revelation," he regards truth as practically identical with the soul: "Truth is so near to the Soul; [so much] the very Image and Form of it; that it may be said of Truth; that as the Soul is by *Derivation* from God, so Truth by *Communication*." [53] Truth depends upon both reason and faith, between which there can be no antagonism. "To go against Reason, is to go against God." [54] Whichcote's faith was a rational faith, a fact that made him abhor Catholicism because it demanded an implicit faith.[55] And yet his faith was no less spiritual because it was rational. As Brooke had put it earlier, faith and reason differ only in degree, not in nature.[56]

The attempt to ground truth upon reason was not, to be sure, an unusual phenomenon in the seventeenth century. There is no evidence that Brooke was directly familiar with the works of Descartes, but he is perhaps the most influential of the philosophers who tried to determine a rational basis for truth. His efforts eventuated in developments that he could not have foreseen and which he would have viewed with misgiving. For Descartes' system, though it admitted the existence of a spiritual realm in *res cogitans,* was to prove in due course a real threat to religion. Descartes evolved the entity *res cogitans* principally to explain such matters as sense perception and the existence of secondary qualities that could not be explained satisfactorily by a universe of *res extensa* alone.[57] His explanation of the connection between

[53] Campagnac, pp. 3–4 (bracketed words represent an emendation by the editor). Whichcote, it should be noted, actually qualifies this statement and may see the two emanations he describes as ultimately one: "For I cannot distinguish Truth in itself; but in way of descent to us."

[54] Campagnac, p. 67.

[55] Tulloch, II, 109.

[56] *The Nature of Truth,* p. 47.

[57] Useful evaluations of Descartes' general position may be found in Basil

the two realms, however, was far from satisfactory, and the result was that among later thinkers *res cogitans*, as the less obvious, intangible concept, began to lose all but its nominal importance. One development of this tendency was the materialism of Hobbes, who courageously explained the troublesome secondary qualities in terms of matter alone. The consequence for religion was disastrous, for the mode of thought represented by Hobbes seemed both to remove the spiritual *res cogitans* and to obviate the necessity for it. It was against this tendency, though not necessarily against Hobbes himself, that the Cambridge Platonists bent their efforts. Hence it is that truth, to the Cambridge Platonists, while it is grounded upon reason no less than it is for Descartes, is also grounded upon faith.

One may glance at a few of the characteristic notions of other Cambridge Platonists to see how they adopt basically the position of Whichcote. The general similarity to Brooke's system is evident. Ralph Cudworth, like his old friend Whichcote, continually stresses the harmony of philosophy and religion, of reason and faith.[58] His theory of being as a sort of "plastic nature," a kind of world-soul, emphasizes his acceptance of the unity of matter and spirit [59] — a metaphysical position that leads him, one might note in passing, to an attitude on the nonreality of falsehood and evil that is strongly reminiscent of Brooke:

> Pure falsehood is pure nonentity, and could not subsist alone by itself; therefore it always twines up together about some truth . . . like an ivy that grows upon some wall. . . There is always some truth which gives being to every error.[60]

Henry More insisted upon the literal reality of a sphere of spiritual being, attributing to it such measurable qualities as "penetrability" and "indiscerptibility" and, in short, extension.[61] John Smith, who resembles Brooke more strongly than either

Willey, *The Seventeenth Century Background*, chapter 5; and E. A. Burtt, *The Metaphysical Foundations of Modern Physical Science*, chapter 4.

[58] Tulloch, II, 233–234. Cudworth did argue specifically against Descartes and Hobbes. See F. J. Powicke, *The Cambridge Platonists* (Cambridge, Mass., 1926), pp. 119–120.

[59] Tulloch, II, 269 ff.

[60] Tulloch, II, 199.

[61] Tulloch, II, 377–384.

More or Cudworth does, is not unwilling to assign the quality of extension to spirit;[62] and his concept of "Divinity," which is to be understood "by a Spiritual sensation," is closely allied to his idea of reason:

Divinity indeed is a true Efflux from the Eternal light, which, like the Sun-beams, does not only enlighten, but heat and enliven; and therefore our Saviour hath in his Beatitudes connext Purity of heart with the Beatifical Vision. And as the Eye cannot behold the Sun . . . unless it be Sunlike, and hath the form and resemblance of the Sun drawn in it; so neither can the Soul of man behold God . . . unless it be Godlike, hath God formed in it, and be made partaker of the Divine Nature.[63]

One may compare with this passage a statement on reason:

Reason in man being *Lumen de Lumine*, a Light flowing from the Fountain and Father of Lights, and being, as Tully phraseth it, *participata similitudo Rationis aeternae* . . . it was to enable Man to work out of himself all those Notions of God which are the true Ground-work of Love and Obedience to God, and conformity to him: and in molding the inward man into the greatest conformity to the Nature of God was the Perfection and Efficacy of the Religion of Nature.[64]

With these expressions Brooke would have been more than sympathetic. Indeed, Smith echoes Brooke in more ways than one. Recalling especially the first of the two selections from Smith quoted above, one turns to the early chapters of Brooke's treatise:

What is the Understanding other than a Ray of the Divine Nature, warming and enlivening the Creature, conforming it to the likenesse of the Creator?

God doth not communicate light . . . but to light. . . And if the understanding have not light, it cannot take it, unlesse by being turned into the nature of it.

In this our shadowy resemblance of the Deity, I shall not challenge perfection; for though the Scripture say, We shall hereafter be perfect as he is perfect, and doth here style us, partakers of divine nature; yet all this is to be understood according to our little modell. Unity is that wherein wee carry some touches, some lineaments of his Majesty.[65]

Although Smith probably resembles Brooke more closely than

[62] Smith, *A Discourse Demonstrating the Immortality of the Soul*, chapter 2, in Campagnac, p. 109.

[63] Smith, *A Discourse Concerning the True Way or Method of Attaining to Divine Knowledge*, Section I, in Campagnac, p. 80.

[64] Smith, *The Excellence and Nobleness of True Religion*, chapter 1, in Campagnac, p. 181.

[65] *The Nature of Truth*, pp. 3–4, 10, 24.

any other of the Cambridge Platonists, it must not be forgotten that the points of doctrine on which their resemblance most depends were common to the Cambridge Platonists as a group. Henry More, the most metaphysical among them, often differs sharply from the others; and yet More believed that "to exclude the use of reason in the search to divine truth was . . . simply to destroy the light by which divine truth can alone be recognized." [66] The principal point to be made is simply that both Brooke and the Cambridge Platonists recognized an identity rather than a disparity between reason and faith, matter and spirit, philosophy (or science) and religion, and each sought to construct a system of thought that would incorporate these entities into one divine unity.

There was one Cambridge Platonist who had the strange distinction of being an Aristotelian: namely, Nathanael Culverwel. The points of agreement and disagreement between Brooke and Culverwel are significant. They agree with each other and with the other Cambridge Platonists in maintaining that reason and faith have no conflict. They agree with each other and disagree with all their fellow Platonists except Sterry in that they deny the freedom of the will. They disagree, however, on the Platonic doctrine of reminiscence.

Culverwel reveals early in his *Discourse of the Light of Nature* his indebtedness to Whichcote; his text is the favorite text of Whichcote, "the Spirit of man is the Candle of the Lord," and Culverwel develops it as the basis for his definition of reason. In the "porch" to his *Discourse* he states immediately the point of departure for his argument:

It is . . . a thing very material, and desirable, to give unto Reason the things, that are Reason's, and unto Faith the things, that are Faith's, to give Faith her full scope, and latitude, and to give Reason also her just bounds, and limits; this is the first-borne, but the other has the blessing. And yet there is no such a vast hiatus neither . . . between them, as some would imagine: there is no such implacable antipathy, no such irreconcileable jarring between them, as some do fancy to themselves; they may very well salute one another . . . Reason, and Faith may kiss each other. There is a twin-light springing from both, and they both spring from the same Fountain of light, and they both sweetly conspire in the same end, the

[66] Tulloch, II, 355.

glory of that being, from which they shine, and the welfare, and happiness of that being, upon which they shine.[67]

The similarity between this point of view and that of Brooke and the other Platonists need not be labored.

Culverwel does, however, take account of the weakness of man's reason since the fall, and he defends this human predicament in prose more distinguished than Brooke's. Even in its fallen state reason is yet the candle of the Lord. Suppose this "daughter of the morning" is indeed fallen, he asks, from her primitive glory:

> What, though it cannot enter into the *Sanctum Sanctorum*, and pierce within the Veil; may it not, notwithstanding, ly in the Porch, at the gate of the Temple called Beautiful, and be a Door-keeper in the House of its God? Its wings are clipt indeed, it cannot flie so high, as it might have done; it cannot flie so swiftly, so strongly, as once it could; will they not therefore allow it to move, to stir, to flutter up and down, as well as it can? [68]

Reason has retained its dignity and it still may be considered one with faith as an emanation from God; but since its corruption in the fall it can be led into error. This qualification suggests Culverwel's strongly Puritan attitude, and in doing so it prepares one for the unequivocal expressions of Calvinistic determinism that one reads in Culverwel's sermons.

Like Brooke, Culverwel sees no inconsistency between the Platonic vision of unity and the doctrine of God's free grace, though neither of them states the doctrine of predestination as an inevitable consequence of a belief in unity as Sterry did. Culverwel leaves one in no doubt concerning his Calvinism. In a sermon entitled "The Schism" he observes that a preacher can wield a forceful style and fail to succeed while a weaker preacher may succeed spectacularly, for "the Spirit breatheth when it pleases, and blowes where it lists." [69] The text of a sermon

[67] Campagnac, p. 213. The greater part of Culverwel's *Discourse* is reprinted in the Campagnac anthology, and all quotations from the *Discourse* (though not from the sermons) will be taken from that volume, as generally more accessible than the original.

[68] Campagnac, p. 217. Brooke also, it will be remembered, admits the limitations of the understanding "since Adam's lapse" (*The Nature of Truth*, sigs. A11–A11v).

[69] "The Schism," p. 17. Eight of Culverwel's sermons are printed with the early editions of the *Discourse of the Light of Nature*. Page references for the

entitled "The White Stone" is "Make your Calling or Election sure." [70] In "The Act of Oblivion" Culverwel argues that God's grace is entirely a free grace, for otherwise why would Jacob have been chosen before Esau? Election, furthermore, takes place before birth and does not depend upon "any prevision of worth and excellence in thee more then in another." The argument most convincing to his hearers may have been this: "Give a reason, if thou canst, why thou wert not plac't in some obscure corner of America, and left only to the weak and glimmering light of nature?" [71] One would think to have found in Culverwel, then, the seventeenth-century thinker whose affinities with the thought of Brooke are closest of all, for both are Platonists who strive to harmonize reason and faith, and both are Calvinists. Yet there is one important difference, and an examination of it reveals matter of much interest.

In explaining the "law of nature" that the "light of nature" illuminates for man, Culverwel postulates that "There are stamp'd and printed upon the Being of Man some clear and indelible Principles, some first Alphabetical Notions; by putting together of which it can spell out the Law of Nature." [72] There is a universality in these "common notions" evidenced by the "consent of nations"; that is, all nations and peoples develop similar fundamental moral principles:

> Look upon the diversities of Nations, and there you will see a rough and barbarous Scythian, a wild American, an unpolish'd Indian, a superstitious Aegyptian, a subtle Aethiopian, a cunning Arabian, a luxurious Persian, a treacherous Carthaginian, a lying Cretian, an elegant Athenian, a wanton Corinthian, a desperate Italian, a fighting German, and many other heaps of Nations, whose titles I shall now spare: and tell me, whether it must not be some admirable and efficacious Truth, that shall so overpower them all, as to pass current amongst them, and be owned and acknowledged by them. [73]

Up to this point Culverwel appears to be voicing respectable Platonic doctrine. But at the next corner he takes the road less

---

sermons to which I have alluded are those of the 1652 edition of the *Discourse*.

[70] "The White Stone," p. 97.
[71] "The Act of Oblivion," pp. 37–38, 41.
[72] Campagnac, p. 255.
[73] Campagnac, p. 277.

traveled, at least by his Cambridge compatriots. These common notions may indeed be aspects, individual wicks perhaps, of the candle of the Lord; but before they can be efficacious something must light them. Since no one is willing to admit, implies Culverwel, that these "connate species" were discernible from the cradle, then "you plainly have recourse to the sensitive powers, and must needs subscribe to this, that all knowledg[e] comes flourishing in at these Lattices." If the senses are necessary to light the candle, then one reaches the inescapable conclusion that "no other innate light, but onely the power and principle of Knowing and reasoning is the Candle of the Lord." [74] And here Culverwel is at one with Brooke no longer, but is instead expressing his agreement with Brooke's Aristotelian critic, John Wallis. Culverwel alludes, in fact, to both Brooke and Wallis specifically. After a brief and perceptive criticism of the position of Lord Herbert on the subject of the "common notions," he proceeds:

> Yet that other Noble Author of our own [Brooke], that has the same Title of Truth, not without a competent mixture of Errour too, doth choose to resolve all into a Platonical Remembrance: which yet that acute Answerer of him [Wallis] doth shew to be a meer vanity; for, as for matters of fact, to be sure, they have no implanted Ideas: and, if Historical Knowledge may be acquired without them, why then should discursive knowledge have such a dependence upon them? And, I wish, that the Platonists would but once determine, whether a Blind Man be a competent Judge of Colours by virtue of his connate Species; and whether, by supply of these Ideas, a Deaf Man may have the true notion of Musick, and Harmony? If not, then they must ingenuously confess, that the Soul, for the present, wants so much of Light, as it wants of the window of Sense.[75]

Even though he was himself one of them, Culverwel speaks in this passage almost contemptuously of "the Platonists" in respect to this one vital area of disagreement with them, and appears strongly drawn to Lord Herbert, with his "common notions" and "natural instincts" which require the stimulation of sensory contact with external objects to become operative.[76] Yet, Culverwel concedes with due magnanimity, "the Platonists in this were

[74] Campagnac, pp. 287–289.
[75] Campagnac, pp. 291–292 (bracketed insertions mine).
[76] See E. N. S. Thompson, "Richard Hooker among the Controversialists," *PQ* 20:457 (1941).

commendable, that they look'd upon the Spirit of a Man as the Candle of the Lord; though they were deceiv'd in the time when 'twas lighted." [77]

In Culverwel, as far as his relationship to Brooke is concerned, one might say that the wheel has come full circle. Wallis appears to represent a position utterly opposed to that of Brooke, whom he reduces almost to the status of a bewildered mystic. Yet under scrutiny Brooke's thought stands up with dignity beside that of Bacon, Browne, Milton, and the Cambridge Platonists, among whom especially he seems to come into his own. One would expect to find the most complete agreement in comparing his thought to that of Culverwel, for both of them reflected an intellectual heritage at once Platonic and Calvinistic. But Culverwel the Platonist is also an Aristotelian, if somewhat disguised, and while in some matters he and Brooke are in enthusiastic unanimity, on the question of innate ideas and the Platonic doctrine of reminiscence they sharply part company.

One may see in this divergence more than one implication. For one, it reinforces the thesis that Platonism and Aristotelianism were not by any means distinctly disparate philosophical strains in the Renaissance and seventeenth century. Wallis and Brooke could disagree violently, but Culverwel could agree with them both. For another, it suggests that Wallis had good cause for part of his argument. Culverwel is a clearheaded and generally consistent thinker, and this disagreement with Brooke, with whom on the face of it he ought to have agreed, points up the fact that Brooke, it must be admitted, is not always clearheaded or consistent. On the subject of innate ideas, for example, Brooke does not express himself with clarity, as one or two quotations will reveal. Early in the treatise Brooke begins to touch on the subject: "If the truth come from God, then why is it not immediately, intrinsecally, infused into the soule it selfe?" But without following up this question or its implications he sidesteps the issue, reverting quickly to his principal thesis: "But however the understanding bee enrich with this treasure of Truth, if it be imparted to it, then is it, it selfe that Truth, that light which

[77] Campagnac, p. 292.

I contend for." [78] A passage somewhat later suggests that he does not accept the doctrine of innate ideas: "Where is the power of our five senses, which are in their nature so honourable, that *nihil cadit in intellectum, quod non prius cadet in sensum?*" [79] Brooke is listing various kinds of evidence to witness the unity of all things, and here he suggests that the "power" of the senses resides in one "common sense," which may in turn have its station in the sense of touch. [80] But he fails to note the dangerous implications of the scholastic dictum that he has quoted in making his point; it appears to be used as little more than a rhetorical question. Finally, in the eighth chapter, Brooke states that he does not refuse "the doctrine of Habits, either Infused or Acquisite":

> For when the soule by vertue of its Being, is cleare in such a truth, it is said to be an infused habit. When by frequent action, such a truth is connaturall to the soule, it may be stiled an habit acquisite: though indeed all is but light more or lesse glorious, discovering it selfe frequently or rarely, and by divine appointment, at such a conjunction of time, and not any other, not that the soule is informed by its owne action; for what hath the streame which it derives not from the source? What can those workings adde to that, from which they receive themselves? And therefore I wholly subscribe to the Platonists, who make all *scientia* nothing but *reminiscentia*; for when it appeareth not, it is not; the soule being but an activity, it must be no more than it acteth: and though we seeme by frequent actings to helpe the soule, and so to create in it acquisite habits, yet these are but a Phaenomenon. This is but the way which God discloseth to our eye, whereas all the actings are onely new discoveries. [81]

This is orthodox Platonism, but Brooke uses the conclusion at which he has arrived — that is, that the habits are one with the soul and the understanding, whether they are "infused" or "ac-quisite," — to back up his next point, that faith and reason do not

[78] *The Nature of Truth*, pp. 9-10.

[79] *Ibid.*, p. 40. This well-known idea arises from Aristotle, *De anima*, III, iv, 430a, where the mind is described as a blank sheet on which the senses write. Aquinas begins from this premise; see *Summa theologiae*, I, i, 1, and the discussion of epistemology in I, lxxxv. For a Renaissance occurrence of the phrase see Burton, *Anatomy of Melancholy*, Part I, Sec. i, Mem. 2, Subsect. x, in which he quotes (in English, surprisingly), "There is nothing in the understanding which was not first in the sense."

[80] On this point Brooke alludes briefly to Lord Herbert in his gloss (see p. 92 above, n. 7).

[81] *The Nature of Truth*, pp. 45–47.

differ except in degree. This conclusion may be justifiable enough, but there is an element of vagueness in Brooke's progression of thought that stands in marked contrast to the clear logic of Culverwel's treatment. One must admit, much as one may admire the loftiness and radiance of Brooke's vision of unity, that his reasoning was sometimes vaguely roundabout. Brooke is perhaps too much the mystic to be always accurately logical. "Mystic" may be too strong a word, but if it is used in the sense in which Pinto applied it to Sterry it is suitable: "If we use the word 'mysticism' in a wider sense and apply it to the experiences of such men as Dante, Spinoza, Goethe, and Wordsworth, who begin with rationality, and then transcend its limits, Sterry is certainly a mystic." [82] Brooke was to some extent this sort of mystic, and if in transcending the limits of rationality he failed to clarify his attitude toward a doctrine as significant for Platonists as the existence of innate ideas, he may perhaps be justified by the sublimity of his total vision.

Brooke's great contemporaries furnish the points of reference from which one can proceed to an evaluation of *The Nature of Truth*. In his passionate striving toward unity he resembles most of all the Cambridge Platonists; in his glorification of reason he can be compared to Milton as well; in his open-mindedness toward science he reveals a mildly Baconian tendency that also characterized the "Latitude-Men" of Cambridge.[83] Brooke was as well read as Culverwel, as devoted to his ends as Milton. On the debit side of the ledger, Brooke's thought is not always lucid nor is his logic unassailable. As a prose stylist he cannot be said to have the vigor of Milton, the clarity of Bacon, the beauty of Browne, Smith, or Culverwel. He occasionally loses himself in a sentence and his exposition is often obscured by an overuse of metaphor, a characteristic that bewildered John Wallis.[84]

[82] Pinto, p. 114.

[83] For the collective attitude of the later Cambridge Platonists on science see the letter from "S. P. of Cambridge," dated June 12, 1662, to his friends at Oxford, entitled "A Brief Account of the New Sect of Latitude-Men," reprinted in *The Phenix* (London, 1707–08), II, 499–518.

[84] Wallis, *Truth Tried*, p. 1: "One thing that may make it [Brooke's treatise] seem somewhat dark, is, that his Lordship speaking of a matter somewhat unusuall, is forced to use such Metaphors, for want of native words, which may somwhat

His limitations do not, however, vitiate the force of his treatise any more than some of his aristocratic habits of mind nullify his essentially liberal outlook. Brooke translated into action his philosophical integration of nature and spirit as successfully as Milton and more successfully than most, for with his belief in the unity of all being he developed an attitude of toleration that lifted him above the bitter factionalism that pervaded the atmosphere of England in the 1640's.[85] His concept of the divinity and unity of truth was worthy of its Platonic and Puritan heritage, and in exploring its implications to such extremes as to maintain the subjectivity of time and space, he joins the long procession of thinkers who led the way toward Berkeleyan idealism. If he does not tower among the highest in that century of greatness, his stature is more commanding than one might expect in one of his years. His confident rationalism, borne out by his life, sharpens his all-embracing vision of unity that stands in contrast to the disruptive forces in philosophy that were already beginning to make themselves evident.

---

obscure it: And his Lordship was the lesse carefull to avoid it, because they being with himselfe of frequent use, and sufficiently understood by him to whom hee wrote, there was the lesse feare of being not understood, or mis-understood: And so the lesse need to prevent it, by seeking for such words as might better sute with an ordinary Reader."

[85] See Jordan, *Religious Toleration*, II, 444–446.

Part Three

"A Discourse Opening the Nature of Episcopacy"

The occasion of Lord Brooke's second treatise, *A Discourse Opening the Nature of that Episcopacie, which is Exercised in England,* differed notably from that of his first. Whereas in *The Nature of Truth* Brooke wrote as a calm and dispassionate seeker of eternal verities, in the *Discourse* he entered actively into a fray that occupied the attention of the reading public on a far wider scale, and one that had attracted the talents of men as different as William Prynne and John Milton, as Dr. Bastwick and Bishop Hall. As a glance at the Thomason catalogue will show, antiepiscopal tracts were in the early 1640's flooding the presses.

A time of violent controversy engenders a number of unfortunate characteristics in polemical literature. Among these one finds, to mention a few, intemperateness of language, intolerance of the principles of the opposition, the device of refutation by quoting out of context, a tendency to repeat endlessly and often pointlessly the main arguments. That these characteristics were evident during this agitated period scarcely needs demonstration. Milton himself was at one time or another guilty of all of them, particularly in the *Animadversions,* and he was a less serious offender than many. It is one of the marks of distinction of Brooke's *Discourse* that he chose to conduct it for the most part on a higher plane than his principal cohorts and antagonists achieved. His language is generally dignified and measured,

"the grave, elaborate style of a seventeenth-century grandee";[1]
his respect for the opposition is, while qualified, at least apparent;
his documentation is careful; and he contributes to the current
argument two lines of thought that had not been usually so
well stated. It was characteristics such as these that aroused the
admiration of Milton and led him, in the *Areopagitica*, to describe
Brooke's argument as "so full of meekness and breathing charity,
that next to his last testament, who bequeathed love and peace
to his Disciples, I cannot call to mind where I have read or
heard words more mild and peaceful." [2] And yet at the same
time Brooke's plane did not always remain lofty. The only remark
that Fuller in his *Church History* chooses to make about the
Discourse concerns a complaint of Brooke's that bishops are not
of sufficiently good breeding for their lordly estate. "Yea, about
this time," says Fuller,

> came forth the lord Brooke his book against bishops, accusing them in
> respect of their parentage to be *de faece populi*, "of the dregs of the people,"
> and in respect of their studies no way fit for government, or to be barons
> in parliament.[3]

As in all controversy, those who were in sympathy with Brooke's
point of view were more disposed to recognize the larger issues
in his argument, while those who were not could dismiss it
contemptuously as that "book against bishops."

In order fairly to estimate the importance of Brooke's treatise,
then, one must not only examine the content of it with care, but
must attempt to see it in relation to the polemical literature that
immediately preceded it and can be said to have impelled Brooke
to enter the lists. Only then can the modern reader recognize
the extent of Brooke's particular contribution and evaluate the
significance of his second tract in relation to its contemporaries.

In this discussion, therefore, I propose first to summarize in

---

[1] Haller, *The Rise of Puritanism*, p. 333.

[2] Milton, "Areopagitica," *Works*, IV, 346.

[3] Fuller, *Church History of Britain*, ed. J. S. Brewer (Oxford, 1845), VI, 212.
The offensive phrase as used by Brooke is *"ex faece plebis"* (*Discourse*, p. 3).
Fuller was hardly an admirer of Brooke. In his dedication of the 8th Book of the
Church History to Brooke's son, Francis, then third Lord Brooke, Fuller remarks
that Robert Greville, "notorious for his hostility to the church and the throne,"
met "the death which he deserved at the siege of Lichfield."

some detail the argument of the *Discourse*. Second, I shall outline enough of the background of the controversy, from the
Cartwright-Hooker dispute in the preceding century through
the events of the 1630's that dramatized the disagreement
between the bishops and the Puritans, to enable the reader to
discern the shape and size of the storm-clouds. Third, I intend
to describe the principal tracts in the early 1640's that bear on
the issue of episcopacy, with particular emphasis on the Hall-
Smectymnuus debate. Only with this perspective can Brooke's
special contribution be properly discerned. For it should by this
means be made clear that, in the first place, Brooke defined the
problem of "indifferency" and its implications more clearly than
any of the pamphleteers had done, and in the second, his attitude
on the thorny subject of toleration of the sects was considerably
more advanced than the attitude of most of the controversialists
on the Puritan side. Finally, one may then see precisely what
Brooke's relationship to Milton was on this issue and at this
stage in Milton's development. Brooke and Milton were almost
exact contemporaries, and Brooke's importance at the time of
his death may be somewhat more nearly appreciated when one
sees why his treatise does not, as Professor Haller puts it, "yield
in importance to Milton's tracts of the same year." [4]

[4] Haller, *Tracts on Liberty,* I, 20.

XI

THE ARGUMENT

Brooke explains in the Epistle Dedicatory that the *Discourse* was a product of the "Retirements of Your Humble Servant in the Last Recesse," [1] namely, the Parliamentary recess from September 9 to October 20, 1641. At this stage in the controversy over episcopacy, Milton's *Of Reformation* and *Of Prelatical Episcopacy* had been published and the Smectymnuan controversy had been pursued as far as Milton's *Animadversions*, which appeared more or less simultaneously with the Smectymnuan *Vindication* and with Bishop Hall's *Short Answer to the Tedious Vindication*. Archbishop Ussher had joined issue as well.[2] Brooke addressed his work to the Parliament. Unlike *The Nature of Truth*, originally a "letter to a private friend," the *Discourse* was manifestly written for publication.

The *Discourse* consists of two sections. In the first, the author describes what he conceives episcopacy to be, and argues that it is incongruous to "State-policy." In the second he follows the line of attack most common among Puritan pamphleteers, the

[1] *Discourse*, sig. A3. All references cite the second edition, which differed from the first in the correction of a number of errata; the addition of English translations of Latin quotations, probably supplied by the stationer, as a newly appended note from "the Stationer to the Reader" explains (sig. Q4); the addition of section and chapter headings throughout the text, following those in the table of contents (which is identical in the two editions); the transposition of two sentences to improve the emphasis in one short paragraph (p. 22); and the addition in the final chapter (pp. 115–116) of two short but significant passages, which appear to be Brooke's own. The first edition appeared in 1641, probably November; the second in 1642. Both were printed by "R. C. for Samuel Cartwright" (probably Richard Cartwright). I have followed the text of the second edition as reproduced in facsimile in Haller, *Tracts on Liberty* (Columbia University Press, 1933–34), II, 37–163, collated with a copy of the first edition in the Harvard University Library and with one in my own possession.

[2] See the chronological table of these publications in Parker, *Milton's Contemporary Reputation* (Columbus, 1940), pp. 263–265. The content of these tracts will be discussed later.

argument that episcopacy cannot be said properly to be based upon either antiquity or Scripture.

Brooke devotes the first four chapters specifically to the subject of bishops. It is the office rather than merely the name of a bishop that he holds up for criticism, for, as he says in an opening sentence once again reminiscent of Bacon, "I ayme not at words, but Things." It is the *kind* of bishop we now have, he maintains, that is dangerous to the state. A bishop is no longer the kind that he is confident Christ intended, the "true faithfull Overseer, that, over one single Congregation, hath a joynt care with the Elders, Deacons, and rest of the Assembly." [3]

For one thing, he argues in the chapter that aroused the ire of Fuller, the low birth of most of the bishops is a disadvantage, for it encourages pride and affectation in those who thus rise so suddenly to high degree. [4] Furthermore, a bishop does not counteract this disadvantage by "good breeding" and industry; he has undergone no preparation for assuming civil power, which the present interpretation of his office bestows upon him, for his studies have not been of that character. Some may argue, to be sure, as Brooke himself had argued in *The Nature of Truth*, that all truths are "of neere consanguinity," and that thorough acquaintance with one kind of truth, such as in theology, would prepare a man so learned for action in the realm of another, such as in philosophy or politics.

"I confesse," says Brooke, "did they improve their Studies to the ripening of Reason, and inlarging of their understanding, This might in some sense be true." But their studies as now pursued, such as "criticall, Cabalisticall, Scepticall, Scholasticall Learning," do not provide nourishment for "the Reasonable part of man," and one must recognize that even if they did, "State Policy is the Daughter of Converse, Observation, Industry, Experience, Practice." [5]

Brooke postpones most of what he has to say about the well-known vexed question as to the election of bishops until the

[3] *Discourse*, p. 2.

[4] This argument does Brooke no credit among modern democratic readers; but it is hardly surprising to find one of the authors of the conditions for removal to New England making a point such as this one.

[5] *Discourse*, pp. 9–10.

second half of the treatise, but he examines quite thoroughly
the matter of the conduct of the bishop's office in its twofold
aspect of civil and religious duties. As his principal exhibit he
portrays the way in which a bishop, representing the Church
at large, has power to make "indifferent" things, such as the
"Subjects Liberty, or propriety in goods," necessary, not only
in the Church but in general. The power to enforce obedience
in matters that are indifferent, even if they should be in themselves sinful, he inveighs against as "unreasonable," "unbrotherly," and "favouring of self." Unreasonable, because only man's
own conscience, directed by right reason, can validly judge
what is indifferent, and it ill behooves the Church to usurp that
prerogative. Unbrotherly, because in this way the bishops "make
themselves the Church, excluding all others" from salvation,
exercising greater power, complains Brooke, than the angels were
given in the Book of Revelation. "Favouring of self," because
such a power leads to pride, for with "the chaines of Indifferency"
they bind the liberty of the people and threaten the sovereignty
of the King himself. And in their practice according to these
principles, the bishops have called some indifferent things, such
as cassocks and gowns, sitting and standing for the congregation,
and the like, necessary; and some actually unlawful things they
have enforced "under the maske of Indifferent," such as the
reading of the Book of Sports and the imposition of certain
oaths that violate both the positive and the natural law. In this
way the bishops encroach upon the Crown, for by insisting upon
episcopacy as *jure divino* and by practicing it under this assumption, "they seeme to affirme Themselves to stand upon a surer
Rocke than Kings." [6]

This analysis of the place and power of the bishop leads the
author in the fifth and sixth chapters into the brilliant and closely
reasoned explanation of the nature of "indifferency." In view of
the fact that there is in the pamphlet literature of the time no
comparable discussion of this complex subject, one may see in
these two chapters an important and unique contribution to
the episcopal controversy. For that reason a full evaluation of
them will be reserved until later. It is sufficient for the moment

[6] *Discourse,* pp. 12–17.

to summarize them. Brooke argues from the sovereign power of right reason, which he describes, as one remembering his philosophical affinity with the Cambridge Platonists might expect him to do, as "The Candle of God, which he hath lighted in man, lest man groaping in the darke should stumble, and fall." [7] The conclusion toward which Brooke moves is that there is no such thing as an indifferent act. "Nothing is Indifferent *in Re, in Se;* but to our Understanding some things seeme so, for want of Good light." [8] Consequently the Church has no right to force compliance in matters not clearly prescribed in Scripture; for the Church must also follow the dictates of reason, and her reason is as fallible as the ordinary man's: hence if a man doubts the validity of the judgment of the Church on the ground of his own reason, the Church sins by forcing his obedience on such a matter. The error of the bishops thus becomes manifest. Even if the bishops could be said to constitute the Church (which Brooke will not admit in any case), they have no power to determine indifference arbitrarily, or to enforce those matters that they decree to be indifferent and thus necessary, "on paine of Imprisonment, losse of Eares, yea life it selfe." [9]

In the remaining four chapters of the first section Brooke returns to the bishops, particularly regarding their relation to the state. Their dependence upon the court for their position and their revenues limits their freedom of action, and the fact that their honors are not hereditary tempts them to seek private enrichment of themselves and their families. But they actually endanger the Crown itself through their weapon of excommunication and by erecting episcopal courts and exercising sentences under their own seals rather than the King's.[10] Indeed, the annals of ecclesiastical history reveal many instances of insolence and even treason on the part of bishops toward kings, both before and after the Reformation. Brooke disputes the claim made by episcopal apologists that a monarchical system of church govern-

---

[7] *Discourse,* p. 25.

[8] *Discourse,* p. 27.

[9] *Discourse,* p. 31.

[10] Cf. Neal, *History of the Puritans,* I, 324–325, in which he describes the framing of articles of visitation during the 1630's in the names of the bishops themselves, without the King's seal and authority.

ment is the only kind consonant with a monarchical civil government, and points out examples of happy cooperation between
Continental princes and the churches of the reformed discipline.
Just as no civil power should dictate to a church in doctrine,
civil determination of church discipline is equally indefensible.
Only the Church should have the right to determine its policy
on church membership, excommunication, and selection of its
officers. So long as the Church "intermedleth not" with matters
of state, then the magistrate should have nothing to say in regu-
lation of the Church. Brooke concludes the first section by
maintaining that episcopacy, far from being consonant with
monarchy, is destructive to it; and in enlarging upon a text
from Second Thessalonians he claims, as many Puritans were
claiming, that the Pope is antichrist because of his encroachment
on the offices of Christ himself, and that the bishops are following directly in his tradition.[11] For their aim is to ascend to the
power of the princes themselves; under the "maske of Indifference" they have enslaved the consciences of men; and in wield-
ing both sword and keys have been busier in cutting off ears
than he was "whom they bragge to have beene their first Predecessor." [12]

In the second section Brooke reviews the authorities of Scripture and, as Milton called it, "that indigested heap, and frie of
Authors, which they call Antiquity." [13] As might be expected he
finds in them no valid basis for the episcopacy that is "exercised
in England." First he examines a defense of episcopacy by "a most
Reverend man, famous for learning," by whom he means Archbishop Ussher,[14] and discredits most of his testimony drawn from

---

[11] *Discourse*, p. 49. The text is II Thessalonians 2:3–4, especially: "Who
opposeth and exalteth himselfe above all that is called God, or is worshipped."

[12] *Discourse*, p. 61.

[13] Milton, "Of Prelatical Episcopacy," *Works*, III, 82.

[14] *Discourse*, p. 66. Professor Haller assumes that Brooke means Bishop Hall
(see *Tracts on Liberty*, I, 20 and 152). Brooke does allude to Hall later (*Discourse*, p. 72), but in this section he reviews almost statement for statement the
arguments of Ussher in *The Originall of Bishops and Metropolitans*, one of the
tracts included in *Certain Briefe Treatises written by Diverse Learned Men*, published about the time of the beginning of the Parliamentary recess in September,
1641 (Parker, p. 264). Milton was also answering Ussher in *Of Prelatical Episcopacy*. G. W. Whiting's argument that Brooke was influenced by, if not actually
copying, Milton's tract in this section is supported by his citation of a number of
closely parallel passages (*Milton's Literary Milieu*, pp. 301–310). But the parallels

Timothy, Ignatius, Tertullian, and others. From this discussion
Brooke ranges over the arguments of other disputants, first pointing out that most of them are concerned only with the relatively
unimportant question of the antiquity of the bishop's name, or at
best of his ecclesiastical power, but that they do not show a precedent in antiquity for the English bishops' civil power that the
Puritans especially deplore.[15] In ecclesiastical matters, the institutions that he finds most disturbing are the election of bishops by
a small number of church officers instead of by the church at
large, the improper delegation of authority by the bishops to lesser
clergy, and the custom of "sole ordination." On the second of
these issues Brooke indulges in one of his rare thrusts of irony. He
argues that a diocese is an unwieldly as well as an arbitrary division, and that the evil of delegation has arisen from the fact that
a diocese

of it selfe is oft so large, that no one man living could sufficiently Visit
and Over-see it, except he could get the Pope to Transubstantiate him also,
and so get a Ubiquitarian Body. To supply which he is oft forced to puffe
up his wide sleeves, and looke very big: And yet much, yea most of all his
Office, must be done by Delegates; who are oft, yea usually the lowest
dregs of basest men.[16]

He cites a number of authorities to demonstrate that ordination
was not solely the right of bishops in antiquity, that if presbyters
have the power to administer the major sacraments they should
also be given the right of the lesser sacrament of ordination, and
agrees with Bucer that the commission of the power of ordination to the whole Church rather than to particular persons is
"most agreeable to Right Reason, Scripture, and All Good (un-
tainted) Antiquity." [17]

A chapter is devoted to argument from scriptural references
that the name and office of bishops as presently understood have
no clear scriptural basis, followed by a discussion of the sort of
church government that Scripture does seem to approve. He con-

can be explained on the ground that Brooke and Milton were answering the same
tract from the same point of view. Arthur Barker (*Milton and the Puritan Dilemma*,
pp. 350–351) finds Brooke much more heavily indebted to the Smectymnuan
Answer.

[15] *Discourse*, p. 69.
[16] *Discourse*, p. 71.
[17] *Discourse*, p. 74.

cludes that in three important matters — namely, election, decision in such problems as cases of conscience, and excommunication — "the whole Church disposeth every thing, not the Bishops, not the Presbyters alone," and that the form of church government most consonant to Scripture is clearly "Democraticall" rather than "Monarchicall" or "Aristocraticall." [18]

In the final two chapters Brooke considers the possible consequences of a change of church government, and it is this subject that leads him to an extended consideration of sects and schisms, a notable contribution to the literature of toleration in its time,[19] and one of the two sections of the *Discourse* that lifts it in distinction above the sphere inhabited by the great majority of the controversialists on both sides. After concluding that from the point of view of "State-policy, Antiquity and Scripture," civil government and the episcopacy that is practiced in England are incompatible, and expressing the hope that "we shall never hereafter be choaked with that Proverbe, No Bishop, no King," [20] he raises a hypothetical objection. Suppose one does allow for certain inconveniences in the present system, would not the removal of it open the way for much worse, such as the more widespread outbreak of schism and heresy? Is not tyranny preferable to anarchy? Brooke's reply to the objection he poses is in three parts.

First, he maintains that whatever is done about church government, heresies and schisms are going to arise anyway. He reviews the history of the Jews and the heathen Greeks, the early Christians and the Papacy, and points, to demonstrate his contention, to the divisions among the Protestants in his own day both on the Continent and in England. For it is man's propensity in his pride to claim, as Manicheus did, that he alone is possessed of the spirit, and the mere continuation of episcopacy will not

[18] *Discourse*, p. 83, and chapter heading, p. 79.

[19] As Professor Jordan recognizes: see Jordan, *Religious Toleration*, II, 444–446. Professor Merritt Y. Hughes, it should be noted, sees Brooke's *Discourse* as considerably more intolerant than Milton's *Areopagitica* (Hughes, *John Milton: Prose Selections* [New York, 1947], introd., pp. lxxii–lxxiii), for reasons which will appear.

[20] *Discourse*, p. 84. The "Proverbe" is of course the famous rejoinder of James I to Dr. Reynolds at the Hampton Court Conference, 1604. For a full account of the interchange see Fuller, *Church History*, V, 267–303, especially 296.

prevent him from doing so. Besides, a forced unity, such as the
Spanish Inquisition imposed, is even more abhorrent than divisions.[21]

Secondly, Brooke argues that episcopacy can actually be seen
as a kind of efficient cause for the sects and schisms that have
arisen during its tenure as the recognized system of church government. Some of the bishops are Arminians and Socinians, some
take orders from Rome, and divisions have thereby arisen even
among themselves. By suppressing preaching, praying, and ex-
pounding, and by wounding the consciences of good men with
things "so far from being indifferent that many of them were
point blank unlawfull," [22] they have forced many of their brethren
into separation. Brooke lists a number of the causes of division
during the preceding three reigns, but makes it clear that he
does not blame the sovereigns themselves. He finds ground for
hope in the events of the past few years, and concludes this particular argument with a statement of optimism worthy of comparison in tone if not in style with some of the similar passages
in Milton:

> For, now I hope the Clouds begin to breake away. Light springeth up,
> while Dark Iniquity is forced not only to shut her mouth, but hide her
> selfe and disappeare. Now the Sun againe mounteth up in our Horizon,
> and quickeneth the drooping spirits; so that many that were Bed-rid some
> moneths since, now begin to take up their Beds and walke, leaping up and
> blessing God.
>
> Fire and Water may be restrained, but Light cannot; it will in at every
> cranny, and the more it is opposed, it shines the brighter: so that now to
> stint it, is to resist an enlightened, enflamed Multitude . . .[23]

In the final chapter of the treatise Brooke considers a third
answer to the hypothetical objection. He wonders whether the
dangers that will attend a change of church government are
really of consequence. Having demonstrated to his satisfaction
that prelacy is attended by the evils of Arminianism, Socinianism,
superstition, idolatry, and popery, he turns his attention to what
he considers the three principal dangers attendant upon a re-

[21] *Discourse,* pp. 86–91.
[22] *Discourse,* p. 92.
[23] *Discourse,* pp. 94–95. The expectation among Puritans that the millennium
was at hand in 1640 has already been noted (see p. 91 above).

A
DISCOVRSE
OPENING
THE NATVRE
OF THAT
EPISCOPACIE,
WHICH IS EXERCISED
IN ENGLAND.

Wherein,

With all Humility, are reprefented
fome Confiderations tending to the much-
defired Peace, and long expected Reformation, of This our Mother Church.

By the Right Honourable ROBERT
LORD BROOKE.

LONDON,
Printed by *R. C.* for *Samuel Cartwright*, and are
to be fold at the figne of the Hand and Bible
in *Ducke-Lane.* 1641.

formed church polity, namely, Anabaptism, Brownism or Separatism, and unlicensed preaching. Brooke professes himself to be aware of those aspects of each which are unjustifiable and deserving of repression, but he does not find that any of the three is an unmitigated evil. A detailed discussion of this chapter will follow later on, when it is appropriate to consider Brooke's contribution to toleration. For the moment it will suffice to indicate his conclusion, the "mild and peaceful" words that Milton praised, the overtones of which clearly recall the plea for unity embodied in *The Nature of Truth.*

Those who are branded dangers to the Church and the state, the Anabaptists and Brownists and unlicensed preachers,

may maintaine some errors, may not carry on the truth in the glory of it; who is so perfect? but oft-times in the midst of thickest ore we finde the purest gold: discover their errors and reject them; but doe not refuse what is good, because they hold it forth but darkly: no truth can shine in its perfect lustre at the first; light is darknesse when it first appeareth.[24]

Truth manifests itself in various ways. Cannot Christians differ in judgment as to what truth is without also disagreeing in affection? Cannot we honor the image of Christ in whatever form it appears? "To this end," he concludes,

God assisting me, my desire, prayer, endeavour shall still be, as much as in me lies, to follow peace and holinesse; and though there may haply be some little dissent betweene my darke judgement, weake conscience, and other Good men, that are much more cleare and strong; yet my prayer still shall be, to *keepe the Unity of the Spirit in the Bond of Peace.* And as many as walke after this Rule, Peace I hope shall still be on them, and the whole Israel of God.[25]

[24] *Discourse,* p. 115. This is one of the passages added in the second edition.
[25] *Discourse,* p. 118. The text, Ephesians 3:4, italicized by Brooke, was often quoted in Puritan literature; it appears, for example, in the *Areopagitica* (Milton, *Works,* IV, 350).

XII

REASON AND SCRIPTURE IN CHURCH POLITY

The debate into which Brooke entered with his *Discourse* was scarcely new. As time went on, new issues of course continued to emerge within the broad bounds of the dispute, and some of these were rather strictly localized. But Puritans had been inveighing against the Church government under which they felt themselves chafed even during the preceding century, and Brooke, Milton, and the Smectymnuans appeared only as the spiritual malaise gathered itself to a head. An account of the steps by which this dispute grew to the proportions it had attained by 1640 is largely the history of Puritanism itself, and there is no need to reiterate at length matters that have already been many times fully and capably elucidated. The character of the argument had changed, however, in certain respects since the sixteenth-century antiepiscopalians had had their say; and in view of the fact that Brooke and Milton aptly point up at least one, and perhaps more, of the shifts that had occurred, it will be helpful to review briefly the early stages of the controversy.

The more familiar one becomes with the history of Puritanism, the more clearly one realizes the active character of this religious outlook. Not for Puritans was the merely contemplative life. Rather, one sees at every turn in their often violent annals the tendency of the religious man to live his religion vigorously in the arena of the world. Some of the more extreme among them made themselves vulnerable to caricature, as Ben Jonson so gleefully knew, and some of them, like the prolific Prynne, sank to mere furious iconoclasm. But it was characteristic of all of them to witness to the world their faith, whether in the tremendous output of huge tomes of theology or in the more attractive records of their spiritual experience (as George Fox and John Bunyan were to do with such distinction later on), whether in reforming and colonizing activities or in strong political or economic drive toward the Puritan ideal of fulfillment of the calling. As Professor Tawney so convincingly demonstrated, Calvinism was "a creed which sought, not merely to purify the individual, but to reconstruct Church and State, and to renew society by penetrating every department of life, public as well as private, with the influence of religion." [1] The calling not only involved repentance and belief but imposed as well a life of action.[2]

Coincidental with the rise of militant Puritanism in the sixteenth century there was growing steadily stronger a tendency in English intellectual life toward skepticism, described by the historian Buckle as the "rise of the spirit of doubt." [3] There had been, admittedly, a good deal of "doubt" since the fourteenth century and before, but as the seventeenth century approached, skepticism ran more strongly than ever in the currents of politics, science, and religion. One of the established institutions that was to come under more searching critical scrutiny, now that the Reformation both on the Continent and in England had opened the floodgates, was church government. It is not surprising that the Puritans, who bolstered their special variety of skepticism with the powerful authority of the Scriptures, should have directed their energies, fulfilling their fervently felt need for action in the service of the Lord, toward this vulnerable bulwark of the civil and religious authority in power.

The corruptions among the lower clergy and the lordliness of the higher ecclesiastics had of course been a subject for concern and a vehicle for satire since the time of Chaucer and Wycliffe. But general discontent had grown greatly since that time, and it is symptomatic of the confidence with which Puritans in the sixteenth century unabashedly attacked established institutions that Edward Dering could in 1570 have had the temerity to preach his famous sermon before Elizabeth herself, even though it not unexpectedly resulted in his being forbidden to preach again. He dwelt in lurid detail on the abuses in benefices and country parishes, pointing out that some of the incumbents were

---

[1] Tawney, *Religion and the Rise of Capitalism*, p. 102.
[2] Haller, *The Rise of Puritanism*, pp. 123–124.
[3] Buckle, *History of Civilization in England* (London, 1885), I, 336.

"ruffians," "hawkers and hunters," "dicers and carders," who could be described as "blind guides, and can not see . . . dumb dogs and will not bark." After further imprecations and a bitter castigation of the Queen, to her face, for doing nothing about these abuses, he concluded that the only remedy would be removal of the bishops and the institution of "a truly learned preaching ministry." [4]

It was not only corruption and ignorance among the lower clergy nor lordliness among the bishops, however, that aroused Puritan protest. The acts enforcing uniformity in worship and the supremacy of the Crown during the first two years of Elizabeth's reign rankled dangerously, as did any manifestation that smacked to them of Rome. Neal summarizes the major areas of disagreement between the Puritans and the court during these years, and it would be appropriate to review them in substance.

First, the court invested the monarch with all matters of doctrine and worship as well as discipline in church affairs; the Puritans felt it unreasonable that one person should thus have jurisdiction over the religion of an entire nation. Secondly, the court conceded that Rome was a true church, though in some respects corrupt both in doctrine and discipline, partly if not mainly because only by such a concession could the apostolic succession be assured; but to the Puritans Rome was no true church and the Pope was antichrist, and they "durst not risk the validity of their ordinations upon an uninterrupted line of succession from the apostles through their hands." In the third place, the court, while agreeing that Scripture determined the rule of faith, argued that church government should be left to the discretion of the civil magistrate; but the Puritans maintained that Scripture governed discipline as well as doctrine, and that nothing should be imposed as necessary except what was explicitly found in Scripture — and that if a matter should arise for which scriptural authority could not be found, the power in determining it should rest not with the civil magistrate but with the officers of the Church. Fourth, the court insisted that the government of the Church during the first few centuries of its existence was actually

---

[4] Haller gives a full account of this historic sermon, *The Rise of Puritanism*, pp. 12–13.

better suited to modern times than the government during apostolic years when the Church was an infant; but the Puritans
asseverated that the apostolic forms were meant to be models
for the later Church, and that no deviation would be acceptable
which did not precisely correspond with scriptural direction. And
finally, the court asserted that "things indifferent in their own
nature, which are neither commanded nor forbidden in the Holy
Scriptures, such as rites, ceremonies, habits, etc., might be settled,
determined, and made necessary by the command of the civil
magistrate"; but to the Puritans, no human law should decree
as necessary anything that Christ had left unspecified, "and
farther . . . such rites and ceremonies as had been abused to
idolatry, and manifestly tended to lead men back to popery and
superstition, were no longer indifferent, but to be rejected as
unlawful." [5]

As principal spokesman for the sixteenth-century Puritan point
of view, in whose works most of the areas of disagreement summarized by Neal are delineated, one recognizes inevitably the
great Thomas Cartwright. In 1569 Cartwright was elected to the
Lady Margaret Divinity Professorship at Cambridge.[6] His first
official act was to deliver a series of lectures on the first two chapters of the Acts of the Apostles; in these lectures he clearly advo-
cated the radical alteration of the governmental structure of
the Church of England in the direction of Presbyterianism. While
the import of his lectures was the occasion of a good deal of
shocked surprise among his Cambridge colleagues, it should not
be too astonishing to one who with the advantage of several centuries of hindsight understands the compulsion of Puritans toward
action in fulfillment of the calling. If to Cartwright the only honest
solution to the vital question of curing the ills of the church was
total reform it would have been inconsistent for him not to take
advantage of his new position to advance it. He could neither
acquiesce tacitly in the present state of the Church, nor betray

[5] Neal, *History of the Puritans*, I, 78–79.
[6] A. F. S. Pearson, *Thomas Cartwright and Elizabethan Puritanism* (Cambridge, 1925), p. 25 and ff. Cartwright was elected to fill the vacancy created
by William Chaderton's elevation to the Regius Professorship in Divinity, recently resigned by Dr. Whitgift, eventually to become Elizabeth's primate. I am
heavily indebted to the Rev. Dr. Pearson's definitive account for an understanding
of Cartwright's position.

his calling by resigning his post. Cartwright accordingly persisted in his unorthodox teaching, actually proposing that the Church of England be reorganized along Presbyterian lines, which to him typified the structure of the apostolic church as revealed in Scripture.[7] He was willing to acknowledge as an accurate summary of his views six articles that were transmitted to the court by Whitgift, then Master of Trinity, as follows:

I. The names and functions of archbishops and archdeacons ought to be suppressed.

II. The names of lawful ministers in the Church, such as bishops and deacons, when abstracted from the office described in Holy Scripture, are likewise to be rejected, and the whole brought back to apostolical institution. And thus the bishops' functions ought to be limited to praying and preaching, and the deacons' to taking care of the poor.

III. The government of the Church ought not to be entrusted with bishops' chancellors, or archdeacons' officials, but lodged in the hands of the ministers and elders of the same Church.

IV. That the ministry ought not to go loose and at large; but that everyone ought to be tied to a particular congregation.

V. That nobody ought to solicit for the functions of a minister, nor stand candidate, as it were, for that employment.

VI. That ministers ought not to be ordained by the sole authority of the bishop, much less are they to receive orders in a study, or such private place; but this office ought to be conferred by a public choice of the congregation.[8]

The repercussions were not slow in being felt. Before a year was up Cartwright had been deprived of his chair, whereupon he removed himself for a time to Geneva; and in 1572, perhaps because he was suspected (wrongly, according to Pearson) of having written at least part of the Puritan *Admonition to the Parliament*, he lost his fellowship at Trinity College.[9] The cele-

---

[7] Pearson, pp. 27–29, 89.

[8] As quoted from various original sources by Powel M. Dawley, *John Whitgift and the English Reformation* (New York, 1954), pp. 82–83.

[9] Pearson, pp. 42–43, 63. Whitgift removed him on technical grounds, and it may be true that the *Admonition* had nothing directly to do with his removal. But Cartwright was looked upon by the ecclesiastical authorities as a principal divisive force in the Church, and the appearance of the *Admonition* was certainly related in Whitgift's mind to Cartwright's efforts toward reform. Dawley says that the authorities had little doubt that Cartwright was at least the "chief instigator," though their surmise could not be proved (Dawley, pp. 89–90).

brated controversy in print between Whitgift and Cartwright followed shortly.[10]

Some of the issues over which the antagonists differed are illuminating. Probably the most fundamental is their clash over the authority of Scripture regarding church discipline. Whereas Cartwright maintained that God had made provision for Presbyterian church government in Scripture just as clearly as He had laid down rules for the minutiae of ceremonial ritual in the Old Testament, Whitgift finds "no one certain and perfect kind of government prescribed or commanded in the scriptures to the church of Christ; which no doubt should have been done, if it had been a matter necessary unto the salvation of the church." [11] Cartwright, who later in his *Confutation of the Rhemists* in 1618 was to brand the Pope as antichrist, saw in the Book of Common Prayer only the finger of Rome rather than the dictate of uncorrupted Scripture, and saw in diocesan episcopacy only a reflection of the papal hierarchy.[12] Equally "popish" were the unpreaching ministry, the "obnoxious apparel" that clergy were forced to wear, and the whole system of polity involving election, excommunication, and the decision in matters regarding corruptions in doctrine and discipline. He particularly deplored the "meddling" of ecclesiastical officers in civil affairs.[13]

Cartwright, furthermore, was anything but tolerant in his outlook. One of his main indictments against episcopacy was that it encouraged such evils as Anabaptism and the heresies of other sects; the English ministry, arraigned by Cartwright as generally inefficient and even drunken and immoral, were not so fortunate as to have the elders of Geneva to keep watch over them and admonish the offenders, and were hence ineffective in preventing

---

[10] Whitgift wrote a confutation entitled *An Answere to a certen Libel entituled An Admonition to the Parliament* (1572); a *Second Admonition* appeared later in 1572, marked by a bitter antipathy toward the bishops, but also probably not by Cartwright (Pearson, pp. 73–74); Cartwright's *A Replye to an Answere* appeared in 1573; Whitgift's *The Defense of the Aunswere* in 1574, a generally impressive work in eight hundred folio pages summarizing the whole debate, which seriously damaged the Puritan cause and contributed to their relative eclipse in that year (Pearson, pp. 88, 129; and Dawley, pp. 98–99), and Cartwright's *Second Reply*, published in two parts, 1575 and 1577, round out the debate.

[11] Whitgift, *Works* (Cambridge, 1851), I, 184; and Pearson, p. 90.

[12] Pearson, pp. 93–96.

[13] Pearson, pp. 97–100.

the spread of heresy among their charges.[14] But it was not only of such overt forms of heresy as Anabaptism that Cartwright was intolerant. He was so rigid a literalist in his insistence upon the Bible as authority that he was willing to brook no deviation from it by anyone. For example, he went so far as to defend even the judicial laws of the Old Testament that demanded the death penalty for blasphemy, murder, adultery, and heresy.[15] It is impossible for one who condones, or indeed even goes so far as to advocate, persecution for heresy to show tolerance in religious matters in any respect. It must also be remembered that Cartwright had resided for a time in Geneva, where uniformity of belief permeated not only religious life but the entire social structure, a state of affairs that contrasted sharply with the degree of toleration that obtained in England. There, owing to the careful course pursued by Elizabeth, a policy of comprehension, to which Whitgift was committed, was maintained in the Church as a kind of insurance toward political security.[16] For Cartwright there could be no toleration on the basis of expediency nor, evidently, on any other ground, and the "nascent germs of rationalism" that were making their appearance during his century left him unimpressed.[17] All men he looked upon as equally sinful and equally deserving of damnation; but this outlook, far from leading his thoughts toward democracy, strengthened his conception of the duty of the ministers to instruct the people as to what they should think and to permit no dissent. Besides, under a system of national Puritanism, the permissible degree of toleration would be determined by the Church rather than the state, which Cartwright was careful to dissociate from the Church as far as ecclesiastical government was concerned; and one could scarcely expect much in the way of toleration from a church controlled by Puritans of Cartwright's persuasion.[18] To modern readers, especially those who have grown to maturity within a democratic tradition, much of Cartwright seems so authoritarian and intransigeant as to be repellent. But it must at least be acknowledged

[14] Pearson, p. 100.
[15] Pearson, p. 90.
[16] Haller, *The Rise of Puritanism*, p. 84; and Dawley, p. 186.
[17] Jordan, *Religious Toleration*, I, 150.
[18] Haller, p. 12; Jordan, I, 140.

that his intolerance sprang, as it usually does, from devoutness and conviction, not from mere bigotry. He thought of himself as an expositor of Scripture, nor would he shrink from any of the implications that his literal reading confronted him with.

History has not been especially kind to Whitgift — Neal, for example, comments with sarcasm on the way Whitgift "routed his adversary" by depriving him of his professorship and expelling him from the University [19] — and it may surprise a modern reader to find in his contribution to the debate with Cartwright a notable degree of reasonableness and toleration. He was the official apologist for the regime, and his defense of the Erastian character of the Church of England is constructed on practical grounds. Though he accepts, of course, the authority of the Bible as supreme in church affairs, he sees no reason for the uncompromising literalism that impelled Cartwright to defend the severity of the judicial law of the Old Testament.[20] As a practical man, he is unwilling to accept Cartwright's view of church polity as rigidly fixed and unalterable, but recognizes the possibility of advantageous change. Indeed, his "vindication of rationalism," as the foremost authority on toleration in England acknowledges, "is almost as far-reaching as that of the more famous Hooker." [21]

One does not entirely need, then, the testimony of Hooker to support Jordan's argument that at this time "Anglicanism, even when under attack, could portray itself in a far more moderate guise than Puritan extremism." [22] But a glance at Hooker in this regard will prove useful. It is not, of course, true to maintain that Hooker was wholly tolerant in ecclesiastical matters. He made it quite clear that allowing members of the Church to think as they pleased could lead only to schism, and that "chaos must ensue upon the triumph of the principle of private judgment." [23] This strain of illiberalism in the great liberal Anglican will be examined in a more relevant context shortly. But one can surely discern a less faint glimmering of toleration in Hooker

[19] Neal, *History of the Puritans*, I, 124.
[20] Whitgift, *Works*, I, 265.
[21] Jordan, I, 139. I am indebted to Jordan's remarks as well as to Dawley's thorough study for an understanding of Whitgift's position.
[22] Jordan, I, 149.
[23] Jordan, I, 224–225. Cf. Hooker, *Ecclesiastical Polity*, VIII, iv, *et passim*.

than in any pronouncement of Cartwright's, a fact that is manifestly due to Hooker's championship of *reason*. Yet in view of
the fact that Hooker is hardly a rationalist of the sort that later
seventeenth-century philosophers became, his qualified trust in
reason requires scrutiny.

Hooker was, rationalist or not, still something of a scripturalist.
He could scarcely have been comfortable in the company of his
fellow churchman Bishop Jewel in this regard; Hooker would not
have been content to test the validity of traditions solely on the
basis of scriptural authority, as Jewel could and did.[24] Yet to
Hooker the Scriptures had in them everything that man might
require for his salvation, if not indeed his total well-being. To him
the Scriptures

> are with such absolute perfection framed, that in them there neither wanteth
> any thing the lack whereof might deprive us of life, nor any thing in such
> wise aboundeth, that as being superfluous, unfruitful, and altogether need-
> less, we should think it no loss or danger at all if we did want it.[25]

What Hooker clearly meant by this evaluation was not, as Cartwright believed, that anything not specifically described in Scripture was therefore sinful, but that the Scriptures reveal to mankind everything necessary *beyond* what the light of reason can
tell him. Specific matters of doctrine (such as the Trinity or infant
baptism) as are not explicitly stated in Scripture can be held
true if they can be deduced from Scripture by reason; for Scripture can be said to *comprehend* these matters even when it does
not actually *contain* them.[26] It is not that the Scriptures contain
every trivial thing, or that God directs us even in the "taking
up of a rush or straw," for "it sufficeth if [our] actions be framed
according to a law of Reason." [27] But the point is that when reason
no longer is sufficient to direct us, then we must turn to the word
of God. Just as reason, in the classical hierarchy derived from
Aristotle that all the Renaissance recognized, is a higher faculty
than sense, revelation is to Hooker a higher authority than
reason.[28]

[24] Buckle, I, 340–343.
[25] Hooker, I, xiii, 3.
[26] Hooker, I, xiv, 1-2.
[27] II, i, 2. Hooker specifically answers Cartwright's claim, that "the word of
God containeth whatsoever things can fall into any part of man's life," in II, i, 4.
[28] I, xv, 2, 4.

The Scriptures are therefore seen by Hooker as backing up reason ("the evidence of God's own testimony added to the natural assent of reason" [29]); and even though the reason must be supplemented by a "diviner light," the reason is no less essential.[30] How else may we know, for that matter, that the Scriptures are the Word of God but by the operation of the sovereign reason? [31] Reason may lead us to recognize the Scriptures as truth, and may also reveal what laws ought to be made over and above those that can be found in Scripture. And on the difficult matter of the validity of tradition, such as apostolic rites and ceremonies, the criterion of their truth was not to Hooker strict scriptural authority as it was to Jewel, but whether the traditions could be proved *by reason* to be of God.[32] If traditions are not supported by reason, they are to be rejected.

It is reason, then, that frames law. The "drift and purpose" of this entire work, Hooker explains in the concluding section of the first book, is "to shew in what manner, as every good and perfect gift, so this very gift of good and perfect laws is derived from the Father of lights; to teach men a reason why just and reasonable laws are of so great force, of so great use in the world." [33] But it is precisely Hooker's reverential respect for law derived from reason that keeps him from allowing a fuller measure of the toleration that his rational outlook partially directed him toward; for he was unwilling to admit that an individual, on the strength of his own *private* reason, had a valid basis for gainsaying a law framed according to the reason of earlier authorities. Men in society must respect all the different kinds of law in that society. By "following the law of private reason, where the law of public should take place, they breed disturbance." [34]

One of the most striking applications of Hooker's conviction on this point is in regard to "indifferent things." Those aspects of discipline and doctrine including ritual, vestments, order of worship, prescribed prayer, and the like, over which the Puritans

[29] I, xii, 1.
[30] I, xiv, 4.
[31] III, viii, 12–13, 17–18, and elsewhere.
[32] I, xiv, 5. Apostolic rites and customs are valid because it can be historically (i.e., rationally) demonstrated that they were really apostolic in origin.
[33] I, xvi, 1.
[34] I, xvi, 6.

choked, were not matters on which Scripture dictated particular practices; the Puritans, therefore, maintained that they were illegal, and the Anglicans argued that they were, rather, "indifferent." Hooker's position, that indifferent matters should be enforced, may be summarized in the following way. Just as we must depend upon some authority outside the Scriptures in determining the truth of Scripture, it is possible that there may be kinds of belief grounded on such authority rather than on the specific assurance of Scripture. This authority is reason. We must believe that certain obvious necessities, such as food and raiment, either secular or ecclesiastical, which God neither expressly forbids nor commands, are matters of indifference to Him. Now, how shall we determine the proper course in such instances? The rigid scripturalist would argue that the only true light is the word of God, and that anything done and not commanded expressly by God is sin: on such a premise there can be no such thing as an indifferent matter.[35] Cartwright says that,

> Whereas the heathen did send men for the difference of good and evil to the light of Reason, in such things the Apostle sendeth us to the school of Christ in his word, which *only* is able through faith to give us assurance and resolution in our doings.[36]

Hooker calls attention to the real stumbling block in his next sentence: "Which word *only*, is utterly without possibility of ever being proved." If Hooker cannot accept the word "only," then it is clear that to him the truth can also be determined by reason. God cannot but be delighted when we use that mark of God's favor toward man, as Milton's God was pleased by Adam's demonstration of his power of reason:

> Thus far to try thee, Adam, I was pleas'd,
> And find thee knowing not of Beasts alone,
> Which thou hast rightly nam'd, but of thyself,
> Expressing well the spirit within thee free,
> My Image, not imparted to the Brute . . .[37]

Furthermore, since the law depends upon reason, "to allege reason

[35] II, iv, 3. It will be noted that Brooke reached the same conclusion, but from a quite different point of departure from that of the scripturalists, and for a very different purpose.

[36] II, iv, 5, quoting Cartwright (italics mine).

[37] *Paradise Lost*, VIII, 437–441.

serveth as well as to cite Scripture"; [38] and we cannot "so far reject the authority of men as to reckon it nothing." [39] Admitting, then, that the reason is an instrument inferior to the Scriptures and less infallibly a guide to truth, Hooker anticipates the Cambridge Platonists, Milton, and Brooke, by putting his trust in it, "even as in darkness candlelight may serve to guide men's steps, which to use in the day were madness." [40] One can follow Augustine, who would not credit any point in Christianity "unless he confirmed his sentence by the Scriptures, *or by some reason not contrary to them.*" [41]

Yet one must keep in mind that Hooker was not disposed to put his trust in the private reason of the individual. Just as he felt that no one had the right to disobey or ignore a law simply on the basis of his conviction, however strong, Hooker argued that matters not specifically dictated by Scripture and hence in the category of "indifferent things" should be referred, in the interest of good order, to the historical — that is to say, the rational — authority of the church. His reluctance to give free license to the individual reason made it impossible for him to admit freedom of choice in indifferent matters, and it thus kept him from achieving the full measure of toleration that a modern student, with the advantage of hindsight, might have expected from a liberal rationalist.

Here Hooker and Cartwright are, ironically, in some agreement, though for different reasons. To Hooker, conformity in indifferent things should be enforced in the interest of decency and order; to Cartwright, conformity in indifferent things would be absolutely unlawful, as such matters had not been demonstrated by Scripture unequivocally as necessary. It would appear that the two positions are poles apart. But the thread of agreement that connects the antagonists is this: neither would permit an appeal to the individual reason for guidance in such instances, nor did either appear to be concerned over the broader issue of liberty of conscience that clearly lies behind the controversy.[42]

[38] II, v, 7.
[39] II, vii, 8.
[40] II, iv, 7.
[41] II, iv, 7 (Hooker's italics).
[42] Pearson points out, quite aptly, that Cartwright did indeed stand for liberty

It remained for the pamphleteers and controversialists of half a century later to illuminate this broader issue fully, and the brilliance of that shaft of light was to relegate to dim obscurity the earlier points on which the debate turned. The fact that theologians so far apart as Hooker and Cartwright should exhibit even a faint similarity in this matter, namely, a lack of concern over liberty of conscience, will prove significant in a strange shift of emphasis that took place among the Anglican spokesmen and the Puritan pamphleteers between the late sixteenth century and the middle of the seventeenth.

For it is evident that in general the Puritans of the Cartwright era, as exemplified principally by Cartwright himself, were intolerant of the views of others, while the Anglicans, exemplified by Hooker and Whitgift, were relatively tolerant. It is also evident that Cartwright insisted upon sole dependence on Biblical authority as the proper prescription for church polity as well as doctrine, allowing no question to be settled by an appeal to the reason; and that Hooker and Whitgift, representing Anglicanism, did permit dependence upon reason with less emphasis on Biblical authority.[43]

One may well ask, therefore, how it happens that by the 1640's one finds Anglicans like Hall and Ussher forsaking the surer ground of reason in favor of argument from Scripture, and Puritans like Milton and Brooke appealing to reason. "Strange it may seem," asserted a scholar in recent years, "that the fundamental position of the *Ecclesiastical Polity* should become within fifty years the staple argument of one of the Cambridge Platonists with at least some Puritan leanings and connections."[44] Further,

of conscience, "not because he believed in its intrinsic value, but because he bravely endeavoured to secure it for himself" (Pearson, p. 406). Yet it is clear that Cartwright did not see the controversy over indifferent things in the light of liberty of conscience. What he really wanted was the ascendancy of his own system rather than liberty of conscience for every man. Woodhouse too has acknowledged that "a concern for liberty does not appear to be a constant feature of the Puritan mind, and that it runs counter to another and the most universally recognized of traits, the passionate zeal for positive reform, with the will, if necessary, to dragoon men into righteousness — or the semblance of righteousness" (A. S. P. Woodhouse, *Puritanism and Liberty* [London, 1938], introd., p. 51).

[43] Bishop Jewel, whose scriptural literalism has been noted, is admittedly a spokesman for Anglicanism; but his scriptural emphasis is not generally characteristic of Anglicans at that period. Cf. Buckle, I, 340.

[44] E. N. S. Thompson, "Richard Hooker Among the Controversialists," *PQ*

one finds intolerance and repression at that time to have become characteristic of some of the Laudians, "mild and peaceful" words to have become characteristic of moderate Puritans like Brooke, and later William Walwyn and Roger Williams.[45]

It is not so strange when one recognizes the importance of the issue of indifferent things. Because the Anglican view of this matter made it impossible for them to see the Puritans eye to eye in regard to reform of church discipline, it is inevitable that eventually the Anglicans should begin to try to meet the Puritans on their own scriptural ground in order finally to confute them and remove the troublesome menace to good order. Such a retrenchment removed the Anglicans further from the plane of relative toleration characteristic of Hooker, whose rationalism revealed in his thought at least the seeds of toleration if not actually the full flower. At the same time, the only course left to the Puritans in their desire to achieve their ends was an appeal to the liberty of conscience of the individual; and liberty of conscience can be justified ultimately only on the ground of the integrity of the individual reason. Hence Puritans came to expound a rationalistic position that even Hooker would not have accepted.

Indifferent things, then, led the Puritans to a full justification of liberty of conscience, and this development operated as a sort of wedge in the controversy that made possible the curious shift away from rationalism and relative toleration on the part of certain Anglicans, toward rationalism and relative toleration on the part of certain Puritans. The importance of Brooke's *Discourse*, in which the most thorough analysis of indifferency is to be found, is thereby heightened, for it may be seen that his argument touched on the very core of the episcopal issue. It is no accident that among the Puritans of that era there are few whose polemics exhibit a greater degree of rationalism or a more inclusive toleration.

20:457 (1941). The Cambridge Platonist to whom he refers is Culverwel (see above, p. 144).

[45] This statement is to be regarded only as a generalization. There were, of course, among the Anglicans tolerant rationalists, like Falkland and Jeremy Taylor, and intolerant scripturalists, like the Smectymnuans, among the Puritans. But it is a generalization that has significance in that it reveals a shift of current in the main stream of the controversy.

XIII

THE ANTI-EPISCOPAL DEBATE

The years between the era of the Hooker-Cartwright debate and the burgeoning of the pamphlet war over episcopacy need not be examined in detail, but several of the historical beacons that flared during that intervening time are portentously illuminating.

At the accession of James I in 1603 there was widespread hope among Puritans that he would be more kindly disposed toward them and their aims than Elizabeth had been, and the conciliatory tone of the Millenary Petition of that year, subscribed to by about a thousand of the conformist Puritan clergy and phrased not in the language of revolt but as a moderate request for comprehension, clearly reflected this attitude. Only from such a point of view would it have been possible for the signers to expect fulfillment of their wishes for moderation in ceremony and rituals and for leniency in the interpretation of the Book of Common Prayer as embodying absolute truth.[1] But their illusions were dashed by the Hampton Court Conference, at which the famous retort by the King to Dr. Reynolds's request that bishops be required to consult the synod of the lower clergy in their dioceses made the hopeful requests in the Millenary Petition appear in perspective to have been little more than wishful thinking. Before that moment James had been pleasant though firm in rejecting Puritan proposals; but there are no polite tones in the curt rejoinder with which he terminated the session:

> If you aim at a Scottish Presbytery, it agreeth as well with a monarchy, as God and the Devil. . . How they used the poor lady, my mother, is not unknown, and how they dealt with me in my minority. I thus apply it . . . no Bishop, no King. . . Well, Doctor, have you anything more to

---

[1] For the text of the Millenary Petition see Fuller, *Church History*, V, 305–309.

say? . . . If this be all your party hath to say, I will make them conform themselves, or else will harry them out of the land.[2]

James clearly saw the danger of Puritanism as a threat to the royal prerogative; but what he did not see was the danger of forcing conformity. Under the rigorous measures of Bancroft, the new Archbishop of Canterbury, whose hostility to the Puritans was certainly manifest in his derisive treatment of them at the Hampton Court Conference, large numbers of Puritan clergy were driven into extreme sectarianism. It is not without significance that Parliament, even at this early stage, indicated its support of Reynolds rather than Bancroft.[3]

Throughout the reign of James the Puritans remained loyal subjects of the Crown; yet James, in spite of the lively interest and even favor he showed toward the decisions of the Synod of Dort of 1618–19, Calvinistic though they were, continued to take steps that could only antagonize the Puritans further. His insistence upon the reading of the Book of Sports (1618) and his advancement in the church of men like Laud who were Arminian in persuasion could scarcely have given the Puritans comfort.[4] The growing distrust of the Crown by the Puritan clergy began to spread to the people at large as James permitted negotiations for the highly unpopular Spanish marriage for his son Charles, allowed insolent favorites like Buckingham to gain in power, and appeared to wink at extravagances in the court and among his bishops and judges. The pride and patriotism of the English people, a force with which any monarch after 1588 surely should have reckoned, helped to arouse them to resentment. "Step by step," as Professor Haller has described it,

the Stuarts and their creatures alienated subjects of all classes. Englishmen were becoming ever more aggressively English. That meant that they hated Spain, despised France, dreaded the Pope and embraced Protestantism with the greater fervor the more these historic enemies seemed to menace England. Consequently the more the church fell under the control of the prelates, the more the prelates identified the church with the crown, and the more royal policy fell into popular disfavor, so much the readier became all elements in the population to listen to the Puritan preachers.[5]

[2] Fuller, V, 296.
[3] Trevelyan, *England Under the Stuarts*, p. 80.
[4] Neal, *History of the Puritans*, I, 251, 263–270.
[5] Haller, *The Rise of Puritanism*, p. 51.

Charles I, whose failure to comprehend the depth or the fervor of the Puritan opposition is remarkable even in the annals of British monarchy, did nothing to reverse these unfortunate tendencies. His marriage to Henrietta Maria seemed no better than the Spanish marriage would have been, and his reliance on Buckingham, until that unhappy favorite's murder in 1628, appeared to stamp him a true image of his father. The first of the Three Resolutions with which Parliament ended its existence in 1629 is a suitable gauge of the religious pressure of that troubled decade:

> Whosoever shall bring in innovation in religion, or by favour seek to extend or introduce Popery or Arminianism, or other opinions disagreeing from the true and orthodox Church, shall be reputed a capital enemy to this kingdom and the commonwealth.[6]

Archbishop Laud, whom Charles elevated to the Primacy in 1633, was undoubtedly a man of sincerity, neither the ogre of whom the Puritans were "adrad as of the deeth," nor the saint that his admiring biographer Peter Heylyn made of him. But Laud, like his royal protector, underestimated his opponents. He may indeed, as Trevelyan suggests, have

> still conceived that all Puritans were like the clerical pedants over whom his first victory had been won [the Puritan clergy at Oxford when Laud was President of St. Johns]. England was to him another Oxford, a place whence Puritanism, at first blustering and assertive, could soon be driven out by methodical application of college discipline.[7]

Laud's measures through the 1630's were, if nothing else, methodical.

First there was the establishment of the Court of High Commission, dominated by bishops, to which the King delegated his ecclesiastical power. There was Laud's rigid supervisory system made possible by his regular metropolitan visitations. The institution of censorship made it difficult for Puritans to appear in print or to "lecture" after the reading of the Anglican service. Ritualism was enforced. The secular use of churches, a time-honored tradition that made possible the pursuit in St. Paul's

---

[6] Trevelyan, p. 155. The other two Resolutions concerned the levying of the subsidies of tonnage and poundage, interesting testimony to the inseparability of civil and ecclesiastical repression in Puritan minds.

[7] Trevelyan, p. 167.

nave of all sorts of enterprise scarcely ecclesiastical, was prohibited. The Church, by claiming jurisdiction over private morals
and taking it upon itself to persecute the conventiclers, stirred
resentment and hastened emigration. The elevation of bishops
to high political position, in conjunction with the improvement
in the status of Roman Catholics at court due to the influence of
the Queen, seemed to Puritans to reek of "popery." Laud could
not justly be held responsible for the effects of the Queen's increasing influence over her husband, but since there was much
that was offensive to the Puritans for which Laud really was
responsible, one can readily see how he became the symbol for
everything that they despised. Besides, Laud's Arminianism
would, at this early stage of Puritan theological development,
before any notable Puritans had themselves espoused the doctrine of free will, have rendered suspect anything he did.[8]

But these activities, troublesome as they were, did not alone
succeed in bringing the cauldron of public indignation to a boil.
The supreme indignity was the treatment accorded to Prynne,
Burton, Bastwick, and later Lilburne. A revealing index to the
temperature of the populace who were victims of the raging fever
of the decade is that Prynne, the master wielder of the scurrilous pen, became a public hero, and that Bastwick's *Letany*,
which in its undignified and vituperative language sank to depths
that would have shocked and saddened Cartwright, became favorite reading for numbers who "[understood] not Latin" — it was
for them, after all, that he wrote it.[9]

The details of Prynne's appearance before the Star Chamber
in 1633, his being pilloried and shorn of part of his ears, to lose

[8] The facts upon which I have drawn for this rapid summary of the repressive
measures under Laud may be found in Trevelyan, pp. 168–180, and any number
of other sources. It should be noted that Trevelyan, in describing the early years
of Charles's reign, makes a statement on Laud's Arminianism that seems over-
drawn: "The doctrine of Free Will promulgated by Arminius was encouraged by
Laud, Charles and Buckingham, because to reject Predestination was to ruin
Calvin's whole logical structure." It is doubtful that Laud adopted Arminianism
out of such pure political calculation. Trevelyan describes the Puritan attitude
toward Arminianism at this time, however, quite accurately: "The victory of Free
Will would establish a coercive and despotic government, a sacramental and
priestly religion; while Predestination implied privilege of Parliament, liberty of
person, Protestant ascendancy, and the agreeable doctrine of exclusive salvation"
(Trevelyan, pp. 153–154).

[9] Haller, *The Rise of Puritanism*, p. 252.

the remainder of them at the time that Burton and Bastwick
lost theirs in 1637, need not be rehearsed here. Professor Haller,
in the seventh chapter of *The Rise of Puritanism,* has traced them
admirably; and a student who wishes to consult original sources
may find a comprehensive anthology of the proceedings against
Prynne, Bastwick, and Burton, written strictly from the Puritan
point of view, of course, in *A New Discovery of the Prelates
Tyranny, in their late prosecutions of Mr. William Pryn, an eminent Lawyer; Dr. Iohn Bastwick, a learned Physitian; and Mr.
Henry Burton, a reverent Divine,* published by Prynne in 1641,
and embodying within it the text of the earlier *A Briefe Relation
of certain Speciall and most Materiall Passages, and speeches in
the Starre-Chamber, occasioned and delivered June the 14th 1637
at the censure of those three worthy Gentlemen, Dr. Bastwick,
Mr. Burton, and Mr. Prynne,* originally published in 1637 and followed by a second edition in 1638.[10] What is worth pointing out,
for this study, is that most of the themes of the more dignified
tracts of the next decade may be found in the writings of these
popular heroes, and that the issues that were to be argued later
on a loftier (though not always exactly elevated) plane were
already before the public. John Cotton, after all, had become a
nonconformist as early as 1633 largely because of his dissatisfaction with the Anglican enforcement of indifferent things.[11] The
writings of Prynne and the others are full of arguments against
the legality of bishops that were to be endlessly echoed. Prynne's
A looking glasse for all lordly prelates, 1636, was a precursor of
A New Discovery of the Prelates Tyranny. He lists abuses of
civil power by the bishops in *A Breviate of the Prelates intolerable
usurpations, both upon the Kings Prerogative Royall, and the
Subjects Liberties,* published probably in Amsterdam in 1637,
and in a prefatory epistle to the King he related the "loytering"
of the bishops to the Puritan dissatisfaction with the decline of
preaching:

[10] Of comparable interest is *The Severall Humble Petitions of D. Bastwicke,
M. Burton, M. Prynne, and of Nath. Wickins, Servant to the said Mr. Prynne. To
the Honourable house of Parliament* (1641).

[11] Neal, I, 317; see also Neal, I, 76; "Upon this fatal rock of uniformity in
things merely indifferent, in the opinion of the imposers, was the peace of the
Church of England split."

But thus much I dare say, that since Lording and loytering hath come up, preaching hath gone down contrary to the Apostles times. For they preached and Lorded not, and now they Lord and preach not. For they that be Lords, will ill goe to the plow. It is no meete office for them. It is not seeming for their estate. Thus came up Lording Loyterers. Thus crept up unpreaching Prelates.[12]

Prynne's *The Unbishoping of Timothy and Titus*, an incredibly voluminous compilation of evidence to support the Puritan claim that there were no bishops in antiquity, may well have been drawn upon by Milton, the Smectymnuans, and Brooke in their arguments against the authenticity of bishops and against the principle of sole ordination.[13] Bastwick's *Letany* propounds, in racy, colloquial language, the argument that the bishops are the King's enemies rather than his supporters, and that their arrogance is not far from blasphemy: "For the Prelates to say, No Bishop no King, is as great impiety, as to say no devill no King, which were damnable to thinke." And yet the devils are, Bastwick continues, more subject to God's commands than the priests and bishops are.[14] Burton's two sermons preached on the occasion of Guy Fawkes' Day, 1636, published under the title *For God, and the King*, rang the by now familiar changes on the theme of papistical prelacy.[15] And "Freeborn John" Lilburne's contributions to the fray, especially *The Christian Man's Triall* and *A Worke of the Beast*, vividly portrayed the indignities that lordly prelacy was responsible for inflicting upon a true wayfaring Christian.[16] The Puritans were more certain than ever that the Pope represented the antichrist and that the bishops were his agents.

[12] *Breviate*, p. 35. This tract presages his 1641 diatribe, *The Antipathie of the English Lordly Prelacie, both to Regall Monarchy, and Civill Unity*, and another of the same year, *A Terrible Outcry against the loytering exalted Prelates*.

[13] See *The Unbishoping*, especially pp. 24, 52, 142, for statements relevant to later stages of the debate. The validity of the orders of Timothy and Titus was still an issue as late as 1648: see Fuller, *Church History*, VI, 335–345.

[14] Bastwick, *Letany*, pp. 2–3.

[15] Haller, *The Rise of Puritanism*, pp. 251–252. Burton also pursued the theme of the subservience of bishops to Rome in *The Protestation Protested*, 1641, replied to in a tract ascribed on the title page (most dubiously) to Bishop Hall entitled *A Survay of that Foolish, Seditious, Scandalous, Prophane Libell, the Protestation Protested*.

[16] See Haller's bibliographical note on Lilburne's writings between 1638 and 1640, *The Rise of Puritanism*, pp. 432–440; and the detailed study of Lilburne in Joseph Frank, *The Levellers* (Cambridge, Mass., 1955).

When the Scots Assembly promulgated its declaration against bishops in 1639, setting off the First Bishops War, Royalists and churchmen realized that matters had taken a serious turn. Bishop Hall was accordingly commissioned to reply to the declaration, which he did in his influential tract, *Episcopacy by Divine Right Asserted*, in 1640. With that publication the antiepiscopal debate can be said to have entered a new and significant phase.

It is difficult to comprehend, from the perspective of such a secular age as ours, the central character of the attitude toward episcopacy in the intellectual ferment that preceded the Civil War. It is already clear that from the time of Elizabeth and the early years of James the bishops had been under fire, and by the time of the Long Parliament there was considerable antipathy to them even on the part of some of the Royalists. As Trevelyan put it, "Episcopacy had defenders in the Long Parliament, but the Bishops themselves had none." [17] As loyal a servant of the King as Sir Edmund Verney, while in the very act of affirming his loyalty, could say, "I have no reverence for Bishops, for whom this quarrel subsists." [18] It was the political activity and civil power of the bishops that aroused antagonism, and it was the absence of scriptural authority for the kind of bishop the English Church had evolved that provided Puritans with their principal ammunition. It was a not unnatural step to move from criticizing the kind of bishop then in power to maintaining the invalidity of the office itself. It was against claims of this sort that Bishop Hall defended his profession.

Hall's "Epistle Dedicatorie" sets the tone of the tract, a lament for the "misguidance" of those of the King's subjects who have been carried away by the "ignorant zeale" of the throng. He is particularly incensed at the recent public renunciation of his office by the Bishop of Orkney. "Good God!" the Bishop explodes on the very first page, "what is this, that I have lived to heare? That a Bishop in a Christian Assembly, should renounce his Episcopal function, and cry mercy for his now abandoned calling?"

---

[17] Trevelyan, p. 203.

[18] Trevelyan, p. 233, quoting Clarendon, *Life*, II, ii, 954. Verney was expressing, however, his lack of regard for the bishops themselves; the Puritan leaders aimed their shafts at the institution of episcopacy, with which Verney and others like himself (cf. Digby and Falkland) had no quarrel.

Even Calvin himself, he asserts, had more respect for the office of
a bishop than the Scottish bishop had, and many divines and
authorities both among the reformers and among other noted
theologians might be cited who not only accepted the validity
of bishops but who felt that "no Church in the world comes so
neare to the Apostolike forme, as the Church of England." Indeed, England is particularly well off; unlike the continent, the
English do not need further reformation, because they have
already had it! [19]

The Bishop sees two main points to be expounded in the
treatise: first, that episcopacy, implying superiority and jurisdiction of the bishop over the priests, is of divine institution; and
second, that presbyterian government has no "footing" either in
Scripture or in church practice through the ages.[20] His method is
to list a series of "grounds" or postulates demonstrating the truth
of these two points, such as scriptural authority, the practice of
the Apostles, the testimony of Tertullian and Augustine, and that
of other church fathers. These "grounds" are the main business
of the first section of the tract.

In the second part Hall defines the meaning of some of the
terms under dispute — "bishop," "presbyter," "Episcopacy," and
so on — and continues with further citation of authority. After
dividing his adversaries into two sorts, those who merely cry
down episcopacy as unlawful, the separatists and "reformers of
the new Cut, which if Calvin and Beza were alive, to see, they
would spit at," and those who recognize the necessity for some
sort of polity but not for bishops, he addresses himself particularly to the second kind.[21] Much time will be saved, he maintains,
if the interminable arguments over the name and title of bishop
and presbyter be ignored and the discussion brought to the point,
namely, the superiority of bishops over the other clergy. A "manifest imparity" has been evident, he argues, in church government
since the time of Christ himself. Was there not an inequality

---

[19] Hall, *Episcopacie by Divine Right*, sigs. A4v–a1, and I, pp. 1, 7, 10, 16–17.
Among the authorities who accepted episcopacy he cites Calvin, Melanchthon,
Bucer, Beza, Zanchius, and others; and the quotation on the "Apostolike forme"
of the Church of England purports to represent the general attitude of Casaubon,
Fregevill, and Saravia.

[20] Hall, I, pp. 27–28.

[21] Hall, II, pp. 5, 7.

among the twelve apostles themselves? [22] He proceeds through evidence involving the institution of the primitive bishops and enters into the controversy over whether Timothy and Titus were truly bishops and what their jurisdiction was, citing ancient canons and the testimony of the early Church Fathers, declaring that he would rather "trust one Ignatius, than ten thousand Cartwrights, Parkers, Ameses, or any other their ignorant and Male-contented followers." [23] He dismisses with scorn the two main criticisms leveled at bishops, namely, the "perpetuity" of the office and the lordliness imputed to the incumbents. After having satisfied himself, if not his Puritan readers, that neither of these cavils carries weight, he goes on to the third part of the tract.

Here he considers the question of lay elders. The core of the discussion involves the absence of authority for lay elders in Scripture or antiquity, and the danger of sectarianism that would arise if lay eldership should come to be condoned. In the final few pages he summarizes the argument of the tract as a whole, reviewing his claim that an episcopacy was erected by the Apostles, that it is the form of government that obtains everywhere in the Church, that all the saints, martyrs, fathers, and doctors have considered this form of church government to be apostolical, that the synods and councils have acknowledged no other system, that no one of importance has ever criticized it except the heretic Arius, that the bishops of the primitive Church, Mark, Timothy, and Titus, "were altogether in substance the same with ours, in the same altitude of fixed superiority, in the same latitude of spirituall jurisdiction," that the laic presbytery simply doesn't exist, and that the new discipline is not only suspect because it is new but that it is full of imperfections as well.[24]

[22] Hall, II, p. 11 and ff.

[23] Hall, II, p. 78, continuing a line of attack developed as early as II, p. 19. In the course of the discussion of Timothy and Titus, by the way, he takes exception frequently to an antagonist to whom he refers as "Tilenomastix," or "Anti-Tilenus." One might imagine that this is Prynne's tract of 1636, *The Unbishoping of Timothy and Titus* (see above, p. 181). But the argument was older than that, and Hall probably refers to David Calderwood, *Altare Damascenum ceu politia ecclesiae, Anglicanae obtrusa ecclesiae Scoticanae* (1623), subtitled *Confutatio Paraeneseos Tileni ad Scotos Genevensis*, of which "lib. 1, cap. 4," to which Hall refers, is entitled "Episcopus et Presbyter sunt eiusdem gradus."

[24] Hall, III, pp. 42–44. Neal, I, 342, supplies a useful summary of the principal propositions advanced in Hall's treatise: "(1) That form of government which

In many ways *Episcopacy by Divine Right* is an impressive reply to the agitators. The tone is at times lofty and controlled, even reminiscent of Hooker, as in his argument that the situation in England is far more favorable than that on the continent, and in his exhortation to the British people to resist excesses of any kind:

> Be wise, my deare Brethren, and suffer not your selves to be cheated of the Truth, by the mis-zealous suggestions of partiall teachers. Reserve your hearts free for the clearer light of Scripture, and right Reason, which shall in this discourse offer to shine into your soules.[25]

His technique in debate is often skillful and sharply pointed, as when he maintains with obvious relish that the only important authority in hundreds of years to raise serious objections to episcopal government was Arius, the heretic, or when he systematically demolishes the testimony of Ambrose, often cited by Puritan spokesmen in favor of lay eldership, by demonstrating that the passage in question from Ambrose is spurious, and that furthermore nothing more is meant by "elder" in that instance than an old and wise person.[26] The formula with which he concludes each of the chapters in the first section, defending the various "grounds" for episcopal government, is always neatly and concisely put. For example, one may note the conclusion to the thirteenth ground, "That true Christian policie requires not any thing absurd or impossible to be done":

> If therefore it shall appeare, that many foule and unavoidable inconveniences, and, if not impossibilities, yet unreasonable consequences will necessarily follow upon the obtrusion of a Presbyterian government upon a Nationall Church otherwise setled, all wise Christians who are members

---

is of apostolical institution ought to be esteemed of Divine right. (2) That form which was practised and recommended by the apostles, though not expressly commanded, is of apostolical institution. (3) The government set up by the apostles was designed for perpetuity. (4) The universal practice of the primitive Church is the best rule to judge of the apostolical practice. (5) We ought not to suppose the primitive fathers would change the form of government they had received from the apostles. (6) The accession of privilege and honourable titles does not affect the substance of the episcopal function. (7) The Presbyterian government, though challenging the glorious title of Christ's kingdom and ordinance, had no foundation in Scripture, or in the practice of the Church for fifteen hundred years, and is altogether incongruous and unjustifiable."

[25] Hall, I, p. 26.
[26] Hall, I, p. 66; II, pp. 118–120; III, p. 19 and ff.

of such Churches will apprehend great and just cause why they should refuse to submit, and yeeld approbation to any such novell Ordinances.[27]

But there are times when the Bishop is not so capable a controversialist. The logic is sometimes murky, as when in the eleventh "ground" he simply begs the question: "That if Christ had left this pretended order of government, it would have ere this time beene agreed upon, what that forme is, and how to be managed." [28] In his first allusion to Arius he indulges in a logical fallacy unhappily too familiar in a later century, namely, the establishment of guilt by association:

If then it shall be made to appeare, that one only branded Hereticke in so many hundred yeares hath opposed the received judgment and practice of the Church concerning Episcopall government, I hope no wise and sober Christian will thinke it safe and fit to side with him. . .[29]

A modern reader may be repelled not only by this sort of argument but also by a tone of social snobbery that occasionally lets itself show. For example, in describing the inconveniences that a lay eldership might bring, Hall offers this unedifying prospect:

Can it . . . be possible in such a kingdome, as our happy England is, where there are thousands of small village-parishes . . . for every Parish, to furnish an Ecclesiastical Consistory, consisting of one, or more Pastors, a Doctor, Elders, Deacons; perhaps there are not so many houses, as offices are required; And whom shall they then be Iudges of? And some of these so farre remote from neighbours, that they cannot participate of theirs, either teaching, or censure: And if this were faisible, what stuffe would there be? Perhaps a young indiscreet giddy Pastour; and for a Doctor, who, and where, and what? Iohn a Nokes, and Iohn a Stiles, the Elders; Smug the Smith, a Deacon; and whom, or what should these rule, but themselves, and their ploughshares? And what censures, trow we, would this grave Consistory inflict? What decisions would they make of the doubts, and controversies of their Parish? What orders of government? [30]

From such a point of view as this passage reveals, it is not surprising that Hall can weep, even if we are not similarly disposed, over the sad fate of the bishop who, thanks to the "greedy Church-

[27] Hall, I, p. 75.
[28] I, p. 71.
[29] I, p. 66.
[30] Hall, III, pp. 31–32.

robbers" of the past few decades, has had his twenty-seven rich manors within the Diocese, not to mention "other forrain," and fourteen houses and parks about them, reduced to "seven of the meanest Mannors left, in full Lease, and one only house, without so much as a stick of wood for the hearth, or an handfull of Hay for the stable, and yet none of the ancient burdens subtracted." [31] It is comments such as these which justify Haller's remark that Bishop Hall and the other Anglican intellectuals failed "to take the measure of the forces with which they had to contend." [32]

This vein in Hall is scarcely attractive, yet one recalls that it is not characteristic of Anglicans alone. Brooke, after all, objected to bishops on the basis of their low breeding, and the correspondence of Brooke and Saye with Cotton in New England hardly reveals what we would today call a democratic temper. But what one finds in abundance in Hall and does not find in Brooke is a general distrust of anything new, a deep-rooted conservatism, which was no doubt responsible in the main for Hall's aversion to the sects and for his intolerance. The fourteenth "ground" for episcopacy in the first section reads as follows: "That new truths never before heard of, especially in maine points, carry just cause of suspicion." [33] Later, in the discussion of lay eldership, Hall offers this argument as climactic and incontrovertible:

But that which is above all other exceptions most undeniable, and not least convictive, and, which I beseech the reader in the bowells of Christ, to lay most seriously to heart, is the most manifestly-spick-and-span-newnesse of this devised Discipline; for all wise and staid Christians, have learned to suspect, if not to hate noveltie, in those things which are pretended to be the matters of God.[34]

It is the novelty of the sects more than any other aspect of their teaching that renders them suspect. Hall is aware of the claim of some of the sectarians that their form of church government, far from being new, is more ancient than episcopacy, being de-

[31] II, p. 107. In the ninth "ground" of his argument, Hall had said "That the accession of honourable titles, and compatible priviledges, makes no difference in the substance of a lawfull and holy calling. . . These things, being merely external and adventitious, can no more alter the nature of the calling, than change of suits, the body. . . The man is the same whether poore or rich" (I, pp. 66-67).

[32] Haller, The Rise of Puritanism, p. 328.

[33] Hall, I, p. 76.

[34] III, p. 36.

scended directly from the primitive Church. His reply to this
reasoning once again begs the question: "What then? If their
pretended forme were bred from thence; where hath it lien hid all
this while till now?" [35] Hall's emphasis on the dangers of novelty
testifies to the central character in his argument of the appeal to
scriptural authority. If episcopacy is of divine institution, it follows that any new departure from episcopacy must of necessity
be not divine. Hall's defense therefore becomes an authoritarian
appeal. The "clearer light of Scripture" of which he had spoken
is given its due weight, but little influence is allowed from the
"right Reason, which shall in this discourse offer to shine into
your soules."

The good Bishop must have been dismayed at the scant effect
that his carefully wrought document had in stemming the rising
tide of Puritan agitation. During the year of its publication he witnessed the humiliating spectacle of Scottish troops crossing onto
English soil and, as it must have seemed to the Royalists, in-
solently refusing to return until their expenses were paid; and he
watched Charles turn in desperation once again to a Parliament
in November to relieve him of his embarrassment, a Parliament
that gave little evidence of wishing to extricate the King except
on their own terms. In December the direction and force of the
advancing gale was partially to be judged by the "root and branch"
petition "For a Reformation in Church-government, as also for
the abolishment of Episcopacie," signed by the hands of fifteen
thousand Londoners. Restraints had been removed by one of
the first acts of the Long Parliament, the lifting of limitations
against preaching. Not only had Puritan preaching become vocif-
erous and widespread, but Laud's power over the press was
broken by the repeal of censorship, and the bookstalls groaned
under the voluminous publications of arguments against episcopacy. The persecuted heroes of a few years before, Prynne, Bastwick, and Burton, returned in triumph to London, and Lilburne
was released from prison by Parliament on the motion of Oliver
Cromwell. The furor must have resounded in the ears of the
Anglican dignitaries like the din of Armageddon itself.

The liberation of the press did, however, ironically make it

[35] III, p. 40.

possible for the harried and beset bishops to defend themselves,[36] and Bishop Hall appeared in print again in January, 1641, with an outwardly modest little pamphlet entitled *An Humble Remonstrance to the High Court of Parliament, by a dutifull Sonne of the Church.* The tone of its rather disproportionate preface is one of nervous anxiety, as if he really had little hope that the "much-longed-for Parliament" would actually "produce something worthy of so high an expectation." [37] His well-founded apprehension of disaster shows through his skillful, measured sentences as he tries disarmingly to agree that the current disorders in the realm require correction:

> Many things there are doubtlesse, which you finde worthy of a seasonable reformation, both in Church and State. Neither can it be otherwise, but that in a pampered full body, diseases will grow through rest. Ponds that are seldome scoured will easily gather mud; metals, rust; and those patients that have inured themselves to a set course of medicinall evacuations, if they intermit their springs and falls, fall into feverous distempers; Not, that supreme, and immediately subordinate Authority hath in the meane time been wanting to its charge; Surely, unlesse wee would suppose Princes to be Gods, we cannot think they can know all things: Of necessity they must look with others eyes, and heare with others eares, and be informed by others tongues, and act by others hands; and when all is done, even the most regular, and carefully-inquisitive State is not like the Sunne, from whose light and heat nothing is hid.[38]

But among the disorders he cites the excesses of the "furious and malignant spirits" who have been bursting everywhere into print with "sclanderous libels, bitter Pasquines, railing Pamphlets," against the sacred government of the Church.[39] From this point onward his style becomes more relaxed and less anxious as he proceeds straightforwardly along already well-worn paths of controversy. His task, as he sees it, is first to defend the liturgy of the Church, then to defend the institution of episcopacy. The liturgy is sacred; if one wishes to ignore it in private worship he may pray as extemporaneously as he likes, but in public the

---

[36] The irony is pointed out by Haller, *Liberty and Reformation in the Puritan Revolution* (New York, 1955), p. 33; and I am indebted to his authoritative account of this period in more instances than can be acknowledged.

[37] Hall, *Humble Remonstrance*, pp. 2–3.

[38] *Ibid.*, pp. 4–5.

[39] *Iibid.*, p. 7.

"sacred Church-Liturgie" must be given its "due honor." [40] As for episcopacy, the institution has endured for fifteen hundred years, and nothing can be more plain than that it is of divine origin. He disclaims the imputation that bishops no longer admit that their tenure comes from the royal authority but instead insist that it comes from God. To be sure, the King has nothing to do with ordination; the "calling" is indeed of God, but the "place and exercise of Jurisdiction" are of the King. It is "the King that gives the Bishoprick, it is God that makes the Bishop." [41] He disclaims also the charge that the English episcopacy condemns the Continental reformed churches solely on the ground that they are not episcopal; they are all valiant soldiers together against the antichrist, and besides, the day may come when the Continental churches, who have expressed no hostility to the institution of episcopacy, may adopt it themselves. There is only one Church after all, and these "frivolous and causeless divisions" only serve to foment dissension and schism, to "rend the seamlesse coat of Christ." [42]

In his *Humble Remonstrance*, then, Bishop Hall does not breathe fire and brimstone, and one might wonder how the pamphlet could have fed the flames anew, stirring into blaze a group of strong-spoken controversialists who up to that time had merely smoldered. Yet it did, for antiprelatical feeling had gathered itself to a head, and there was enough in Hall's new tract, insignificant in scope though it might appear, to draw fire. For example, the weakness of the appeal to scriptural authority in defense of Anglicanism is absurdly evident in the Bishop's affirmation that when Moses prayed, and when Peter and John went up to the temple to pray at the ninth hour, they used prayers of regular prescription rather than expressing themselves in extemporaneous outpourings.[43] Hall exposes a vulnerable naïveté when he remarks that changing the form of church government is more reprehensible than changing the form of civil government; when he begs the question once again by noting matter-of-factly, as if it could not be doubted, that nothing could be more plain

[40] Hall, *Humble Remonstrance*, p. 13.
[41] *Ibid.*, pp. 27–28.
[42] *Ibid.*, pp. 30–42.
[45] *Ibid.*, p. 19.

than the divine origin of episcopacy; when he asks Parliament, toward the end of the tract, in an almost confidential manner, not to tell in Gath nor publish in Ascalon any real scandals that might prove to be true of the "inferior clergy," advising the members that "Your wisedomes well see, under what malignant eyes we are, of opposite Spectators; What a death it is, to think of the sport, and advantage these watchfull enemies will be sure to make of our sins, and shame . . ." [44] The prevailing Anglican distrust of the sects is manifest in his concluding plea for "one Church," and Hall's conservatism is apparent in his argument, conventional among Anglicans since the time of Hooker, on the necessity of complying with indifferent elements in Church worship and polity:

Yea, the wisedome of the ancient Grecians went so farre, as to forbid the removall of a well setled evill; But, if religion teach us better things, and tell us, that nothing morally evill, can be setled well: and being, however, setled, had the more need to be (after too long delay) removed; Yet right reason, and sound experience informe us, that things indifferent, or good, having been by continuance, and generall approbation well rooted in Church, or State; may not upon light grounds be pulled up.[45]

A reply was not long in coming. In February (1641) there was published, under the pseudonym of Smectymnuus, *An Answer to a Booke entituled, An Humble Remonstrance*, written as a collaborative effort by five Puritan preachers of some prominence, headed by Stephen Marshall, whom Haller has called "the most famous and probably the most admired preacher of the Puritan brotherhood." [46] They wrote as spokesmen for the Puritan point of view, and the pamphlet is more interesting and significant because of its semiofficial character than for stylistic quality or polemical eloquence. It is for the most part a dry, point-by-point

[44] *Ibid.*, pp. 37–38.
[45] *Ibid.*, p. 19.
[46] Haller, *Liberty and Reformation*, p. 36. There is in Haller, pp. 35–39, a full and illuminating sketch of the five Smectymnuan controversialists, whose initials made up their rather barbarous pseudonym: Marshall, Edmund Calamy, Thomas Young (Milton's old friend and former tutor), Matthew Newcomen, and William Spurstowe. See also Parker, *Milton's Contemporary Reputation*, pp. 265–266. The Smectymnuan *Answer* was actually not the first reply to Hall, as Haller acknowledges; there was a Scottish pamphlet too, but it is not significant in the development of the English phase of the debate.

refutation in the manner of the times, and it must be admitted that if it has been read in succeeding years it is only as a document of historical importance and for the light that it sheds on the development of the greatest poet of the century. But at the time it was almost in the category of a Party handbook, and there is evidence that it was read widely and avidly.

The body of the tract attempts to answer Hall's two main sections, proving first that the liturgy of the Anglican Church is indeed "popish" and secondly that episcopacy cannot claim the ancient pedigree that the Anglicans assign to it. Bishops are nothing more than presbyters, and the "imparity" that has come to exist between the two degrees has arisen through custom rather than divine institution, and certainly cannot be said to have descended from apostolic hands "unless our Bishops will draw the Line of their Pedigree through the loynes of Antichrist, and joyne issue, and mingle blood with Rome." Indeed, modern bishops differ so utterly from those of antiquity that "Episcopacy may well be likened to the Shippe Argo, that was so often repaired, as there was nothing left of the First Materialls; yet still it challenged the first Name." [47] In methodical fashion the Smectymnuans examine the nature of the bishop's election and the execution of his office, under the familiar headings of his sole jurisdiction, delegation of power, and the exercise of that power, and they inveigh particularly against the episcopal assumption of civil power that characterized Laud's hierarchy. The claims of Timothy and Titus to the title of bishop are once again, inevitably, drawn up for lengthy review, and the argument is advanced that the doctrine of the divine right of bishops is prejudicial to the royal sovereignty. Lay presbytery is given space in the discussion, though here the controversialists are dealing, as they are occasionally elsewhere, with *Episcopacy by Divine Right* rather than the *Humble Remonstrance*,[48] and after some sharp remarks on Hall's describing the dissidents as the "Antiprelaticall" church, the tract closes with a number of "Quaeries about Episcopacie," reviewing some of the ground already covered. A postscript provides an his-

[47] Smectymnuus, *Answer*, pp. 31–33. In attacking episcopacy as well as liturgy it was common for Puritans to condemn the institution because of its necessary dependence, before the Reformation, upon the Roman succession.

[48] Smectymnuus, *Answer*, pp. 71–75.

torical sketch of "those bitter fruits, Pride, Rebellion, Treason, Unthankefulness, etc. which have issued from Episcopacy." [49]

Yet the Smectymnuan *Answer* is not by any means an unmitigated triumph of dullness. Some other Puritan contributions perhaps merit this dubious distinction, but not this one. The style is seldom elevated, but one can at least admire the gusto with which the ardent preachers rush in to attack the Bishop at those points where he inadvertently lowered his guard. Occasionally they score decisively against him. Within the first few pages they comment scornfully on the inordinate length of his preface, which "fils almost a fourth part of the Booke," [50] and on the elaborateness of the style, which "swels with so many passionate Rhetorications, as it is harder for us in the multitude of his words to finde what his argument is, that we have to answer, then to answer it when it is found." [51] They complain justly about Hall's imputation that a word against episcopacy is heresy, and they are quick to seize upon his ill-considered remark that changing the civil government would be a less culpable act than changing the sacred government of the Church:

Had he found but any such passage in any of his Lewd Libellers (as his modesty is always pleased to tearme them) certainly if we may borrow

[49] It is quite possible that Brooke in the *Discourse* drew upon this postscript for his historical account of the abominations of episcopacy (*Discourse*, pp. 41–43 *et passim*). Brooke must have known at first hand a document as important in the controversy as the *Answer*, and there is evidence that he drew upon it elsewhere in his own tract. See the extensive footnote 21 to chapter 4, Barker, *Milton and the Puritan Dilemma*, pp. 350–351. Barker thinks it unlikely that Milton, as Masson thought, supplied much of the material for this postscript; all the Puritans were reading Holinshed and other historical sources for ammunition at this time, and the Smectymnuans were perfectly capable of finding their own (Barker, pp. 341–342).

[50] The Smectymnuan complaint about the length of Hall's preface contains an allusion that may reveal familiarity on their part with Brooke's earlier pamphlet, *The Nature of Truth*. Cf. the following two passages: (1) "It was a constitution of those admired sonnes of Iustice the Areopagi; that such as pleaded before them should pleade without prefacing and without Passion: had your Honours made such a constitution, this Remonstrance must have been banished from the face of your Assembly: for the Preface fils almost a fourth part of the Booke" (*Answer*, pp. 1–2); and (2) in the preface to Brooke's treatise, Sadler writes, "I am now a Pleader, and so am forbid φροιμιάζειν [to prologuize] or ἔξω τι λέγειν [to digress]: Yet, with submission to that Severe Court* [marginal gloss: Areopagus: for such were the orders for all Pleaders there], I hope 'twill be no offence, by breaking their First Injunction, to keepe their Second" (*The Nature of Truth*, sigs. A4–A4v).

[51] Smectymnuus, *Answer*, p. 2.

his owne phrase, the eares of the three Interested Kingdomes, yea, all the
neighbour Churches, and if we may say, the whole Christian world, and
no small part beyond it, had rung with the lowd cryes of no lesse than
Treason, Treason.[52]

They ask, again with some justice, how the Bishop knows what
sort of prayers Peter and John used when they went up to the
temple to pray, especially as it is indisputable that when the
Publican and the Pharisee went up to the temple to pray their
prayers were not of regular prescription.[53] As for Hall's wish
that examples of scandalous behavior among the "inferior clergy"
remain unpublicized, the preachers gleefully oblige him by citing
not only among the lower orders but among the bishops themselves, examples of corruption that are already "told in Gath." [54]
A good instance of their forensic technique at its best may be
seen in the sixteenth section, in which they take up Hall's reply
to one of the possible objections to the authority of episcopacy
that he has anticipated: "that pleading the Divine right of
Episcopacy . . . casts a dangerous imputation upon all those
reformed Churches that want this Government." If Hall maintains that he is not condemning the Continental churches, that
bishops are not essential to the Church but only contribute to
its greater glory, then what, pray, is all the furor about? Does
not this admission undercut all the preceding argument? There
is of course, everyone will admit, a far greater difference between
the Continental churches and the English than what Hall suggests here to be true; "but if it be so little as this Remonstrant
here pretends; then the Alteration and Abrogation of Episcopacie
will be with the lesse difficultie, and occasion the lesse disturbance." [55] Like one of Donne's ladies, the Bishop has unwittingly
demonstrated how false fears be.

The Smectymnuans occasionally reveal a strain of self-right-
eousness characteristic of a good deal of the controversial literature of the times. This holier-than-thou attitude is evident in
their describing themselves as "humble petitioners" in their

[52] Smectymnuus, *Answer*, pp. 2–4.
[53] *Ibid.*, p. 8.
[54] *Ibid.*, pp. 75–79 (misnumbered 89).
[55] *Ibid.*, pp. 66–71.

efforts to achieve reformation at home, while the Anglicans, in their relations with Scotland ("our Neighbour Church"), are "strangers, endevouring violently to obtrude Innovations upon a setled Church and State." [56] They exhibit also a kind of intellectual narrowness and sterility that contrasts sharply with the breadth of vision and humanistic learning that characterizes the more moderate thinkers on both sides. [57]

But they are capable also of rising to a degree of liberalism that Hall, for all his allusion to the light of reason, does not achieve in this series of tracts. In their fourth section they set out to answer the argument that since episcopal church government has been in existence for some fifteen hundred years it should not now be changed. Christ is Truth and not Custom, they argue, citing Cyprian, and "Custom without Truth, is a mouldy errour." Furthermore, alluding to Bishop Hall's appeal to reason to hinder us from violent change:

> As for that supply of Accessory strength, which he begs to this Argument, from the light of nature, and the rules of iust policy, which (saith he) teacheth us not easily to give way to the change of those things, which long use and many Lawes have firmly established, as Necessary and Beneficiall; it is evident, that those things which to former Ages have seemed Necessary and Beneficiall, may to succeeding Generations, prove not Necessary but Noxious, not Beneficiall but Burthensome. And then the same light of nature, and the same iust policy, that did at the first command the establishment of them, may and will perswade their abolishment; if not, either our Parliaments must never Repeale any of their former Acts (which yet they have justly and wisely done) or else in so doing must run Counter to the light of nature, and the Rules of iust policy; which to think were an impiety to be punished by the Iudge. [58]

There is a glimpse in this passage of the concept of the validity of the reason of individuals here and now that was to characterize

---

[56] *Ibid.*, pp. 4–5.

[57] There is a comparatively limited range of allusion in the writings of the Smectymnuans which is conspicuous when they are set beside Brooke and, of course, Milton. They are learned in theology but little else. Note an interesting, though not especially significant, sidelight on their ignorance of the new science in a passage in their third section: they are maintaining that "there is no more Truth" in Hall's assertion that Calvin and Beza admitted the existence of episcopacy in apostolic times "then if he had said . . . with Copernicus, the Earth moves, and the heavens stand still" (*Answer*, p. 16).

[58] Smectymnuus, *Answer*, pp. 20–21.

the plea for liberty of conscience as phrased later by Brooke. The ancients and the Church Fathers had no monopoly on the light of nature, and although it is in the interest of good order to adhere to their precepts and follow their church polity, it is not impossible that the reformers are justified in their desires for change on the perfectly legitimate testimony of their own sovereign reason. Yet, as it will be subsequently shown, this passage is not an expression of liberal rationalism in the full sense. If it were, it would be difficult to reconcile such an attitude with the authoritative and antirational outlook characteristic of the Westminster Assembly, of which all five Smectymnuans were to be members. It would be more typical of them to have made this statement in the perspective of their ultimate distrust of human reason as frail and inconstant. For the moment, however, it does indeed appear that the Smectymnuans are, as Professor Barker has expressed it, "balancing Hall's appeal to Cartwright's principles by a counter-appeal to ideas more characteristic of Hooker." [59] But in this same tract they were shortly to maintain that the form of church government which they favored was exactly specified in Scripture, and the argument was to reduce itself, again in Barker's words, "to the blank opposing of biblical interpretations and the citation of a cloud of patristic witnesses," [60] an untenable thesis that the early antiprelatical tracts of Milton likewise tried to expound. It was not until somewhat later that a genuinely rational argument became characteristic of liberal Puritan thought, and it will be seen that Brooke played a prominent role in this development.

Bishop Hall's *Defence of the Humble Remonstrance, against the frivolous and false exceptions of Smectymnuus* was published in April (1641). At this stage of the debate Milton, it might be noted, was in the midst of composing *Of Reformation,* to be published probably in May, replying to no one in particular but merely entering the lists, and *Of Prelatical Episcopacy,* to be published certainly by summer and perhaps also in May, replying to a tract by Archbishop Ussher (to be discussed shortly). Hall's *Defence* succeeded in arousing Milton to the com-

[59] Barker, *Milton and the Puritan Dilemma,* p. 49.
[60] Barker, p. 22 and n., p. 342.

position of his *Animadversions upon the Remonstrants Defense against Smectymnuus,* an effusion that does him less credit than anything with which he ever appeared in print, to the embarrassment of idolaters of that transcendent genius ever since. But it is difficult to find in Hall's *Defence* much more than reiteration of the wearisome points of controversy that had already been aired. After defending himself on the length of his preface and absolving himself of the charge of treason, Hall proceeds to answer again the two principal complaints of the Smectymnuans, namely, regarding the validity of the liturgy and concerning the divine origin of episcopacy. There are passages that exhibit the skill in debate that he had shown before, such as his disposing of their objection that the liturgy, far from being sacred, had been composed by particular men, by asking with incontrovertible good sense how else it could have been composed.[61] There is further evidence of his essential conservatism, such as his final question as to the legality of opposing institutions established by law and custom:

> Whether since both God hath set such a government in his Church, as Episcopacie, and the Lawes of this Land have firmly established it, it can bee lawfull for you to deny your subjection unto it; and whether it were not most lawfull and just to punish your presumption and disobedience in framing so factious a question.[62]

But the body of the tract consists in the main of endless citing of authority, the pointing out of what Hall insists are merely verbal quibbles on the part of the Smectymnuans, further defense of the argument from antiquity, answering the objections to episcopal elections, sole jurisdiction, and ordination,[63] delegation of authority, and the use of oaths *ex officio,* reviewing once more the claims of Timothy and Titus to episcopal eminence, maintaining stoutly that "Episcopacy is no prejudice of Soveraigntie,"[64]

[61] Hall, *Defence,* p. 12.

[62] *Ibid.,* p. 162.

[63] A sentence in Brooke's *Discourse* reveals that he had read Hall's *Defence* on this point, and that he knew the unsigned author was a bishop. Cf. *Discourse,* p. 72: [on the subject of sole ordination] ". . . of late one of their owne . . . offers to yeeld the Cause, for one example of Lawfull Ordination by Presbyters without a Bishop." Hall, *Defence,* p. 71: ". . . shew us but one instance of a Presbyters regular and practised ordaining, without a Bishop, and carry the cause."

[64] Hall, *Defence,* p. 129.

and demolishing the relevance of the authorities that have been cited in defense of a lay presbytery.

In June (1641) the five Puritans countered with *A Vindication of the Answer to the Humble Remonstrance*. In spite of their lofty intention "not to contend for words, but things," [65] there is the usual proportion of pettiness. In the preface they adopt a tone of injured innocence in protesting the names that they have been called, and in the first section they descend to the level of attacking Hall for addressing his tract to the King (to whom the five preachers claim not to have such easy access), accusing him of ignorance in his use of Latin, indulging in some sport over his having called their verbal quibbling "light froth" that "will sink alone," which they call "a strange piece of Physicks," and so on. [66] The frequent (though by no means consistent) tone of levity is well illustrated by their comment upon a key passage in the *Defence*:

> For your conclusion, that things indifferent or good, having by continuance and generall approbation beene well rooted in Church and State, may not upon light grounds be pulled up, Good Sir, never trouble your selfe about such an indifferent thing, as Episcopacie is. Never feare, but if Episcopacie be rooted up, it will be done by such hands as will not doe it upon light grounds. [67]

But it would be distortion of the pamphlet to imply that the *Vindication* does not embody significant steps in the controversy, or to suggest that the Smectymnuans therein desert the high-minded aims that motivated their composition of the *Answer*. One may doubt, upon reading the following passage, the single-mindedness with which they succeeded in pursuing their aim, but not their sincerity:

> Thus we have vindicated the first part of our answer concerning Liturgie, Wherein we professe, as in the presence of God, that wee have written nothing out of a spirit of contention and faction, but only as lovers of the

---

[65] Smectymnuus, *Vindication*, p. 11. Cf. Brooke's *Discourse*, which opens with a similarly Baconian pronouncement: "I ayme not at Words, but Things" (*Discourse*, p. 1).

[66] Their jibes descend no lower, however, than Milton's in the *Animadversions*. He likewise finds the "light froth" cause for derision (*Works*, III, 114).

[67] Smectymnuus, *Vindication*, p. 60. Hall was in this passage in the *Defence* echoing a statement in the *Humble Remonstrance*, p. 19 (see p. 191 above).

Truth, and the peace of the Church, which is now miserably divided in judgement and affections . . . which rents and distractions, wee are so far from fomenting, that wee would willingly goe over divers Seas (as Calvin once said) to finde out one uniforme way of worshipping of God, in which all Christians might happily agree.[68]

It was in the *Vindication,* too, that the Smectymnuans called attention to Hall's new tactics in attempting to prove the divine right of episcopacy instead of standing firm on the classical Anglican defense of the institution as grounded on the light of reason.[69] But it is no exaggeration to say that this tract makes exceedingly tiresome reading outside the context of the debate, or for that matter within it. For the most part it does little more than cross and recross, with the usual wealth of historical and patristic documentation, ground that is already well trodden.

Hall's reply, *A Short Answer to the Tedious Vindication of Smectymnuus,* appeared during the summer. In his preface Hall explains that he will reply only to the first three sections of the *Vindication,* those that deal with the liturgy, because that subject "is untracked with any frequent pens of others." One is moved almost to applaud his resolution regarding the remainder:

. . . as for that other head of Episcopacie, which hath already filled so many rhemes of waste-paper, for as much as I see they offer nothing, but that which hath passed an hundred ventilations, *Transeat.* I have resolved to bestow my time better, then in drawing this Sawe to and fro, to no purpose.[70]

The Bishop then settles down to defend himself against their various attacks on his position, paragraph by paragraph. He has clearly been bewildered by the assaults upon his "meek and peaceable Remonstrance" and its defense, and he sees his antagonists as a "strange generation of men, unprovoked, unthought of," who have to his astonishment flown in his face from nowhere, and who now "inraged with a moderate opposition . . . heat their furnace seven times more, and break forth into a not more voluminous, then vehement Invective." [71] He

---

[68] Smectymnuus, *Vindication,* pp. 46–47.
[69] *Ibid.,* pp. 113–114. See also Barker, p. 22.
[70] Hall, *Short Answer,* sig. a4v.
[71] *Ibid.,* sigs. A3–A3v.

brings to bear a certain amount of new documentation on points that have already been argued, but the effect is, as in the *Vindication*, largely one of cut-and-dried reiteration. At one stage, interestingly enough, he reverses the logic that led him to condemn the opponents of episcopacy because of their intellectual heritage descended from the heretic Arius; even if Puritan claims that the liturgy "symbolizeth with the Popish Masse" were true, this fact would not disprove its efficacy, for even the devil can speak true.[72] But for the most part the *Short Answer* adds little of historical importance or significance for the debate to what has been amply said before.

On this note the flyting between Bishop Hall and the five Smectymnuans ends. It might conceivably have gone further but for the fact that a far more skillful controversialist than the preachers intruded upon this particular battle.[73] Milton's *Animadversions upon the Remonstrants Defense against Smectymnuus* appeared about the same time as the *Short Answer*, and from the tone of the *Modest Confutation*, written as an answer to Milton late in the year and published early in 1642, whether it was actually composed by Bishop Hall or by his son, as has been conjectured, it is evident that he and his Anglican confreres were stung to fury. This interchange and Milton's succeeding *Apology against a Pamphlet call'd a Modest Confutation of the Animadversions*, published very shortly after the *Modest Confutation* early in 1642, do not, however, form part of the background for Brooke's *Discourse*, and it would be irrelevant to treat them here in detail. It is necessary, rather, to backtrack slightly in time.

A second prominent Anglican had joined battle during the spring of 1641: no less distinguished a personage than James Ussher, the Archbishop of Armagh. A slight tract of his entitled *The Iudgement of Doctor Rainoldes touching the Originall of Episcopacy* was registered for publication on May 21.[74] It

[72] Hall, *Short Answer*, p. 58. Cf. *Episcopacy by Divine Right*, I, p. 66 (see p. 186 above).

[73] It must be admitted that there is little evidence that Milton's antiprelatical tracts were noticed by the public, even by the Smectymnuans themselves. It may be that the debate had merely run itself out. But the *Animadversions* certainly attracted Hall's attention.

[74] Parker, *Milton's Contemporary Reputation*, chronology on pp. 263–265.

deserves attention not so much because it contributed any general statement of importance to the argument (for it did not), but because it was specifically answered both by Milton and by Brooke, and it forms therefore a relevant area of the background for Brooke's *Discourse*. It concerns itself entirely with the citing of authorities to support the antiquity of episcopacy, from the Council of Chalcedon and a certain Leontius, Bishop of Magnesia, on down through Ignatius, Tertullian, Clement of Alexandria, and others. Milton's reply, *Of Prelatical Episcopacy*, appeared almost immediately, refuting step by step Ussher's claims. Brooke in the *Discourse* covers briefly the same ground.[75] It does not seem likely that Brooke is paraphrasing Milton in his refutation, in spite of the provocative parallel quotations cited by Professor Whiting as evidence that he was.[76] The community of Puritan ideas at this time was, as Professor Barker has demonstrated, incredibly complex and interwoven, and it is quite possible that many of the controversialists were reading the same sources to garner facts for the debate.[77] And there is no other evidence, to my knowledge, that Brooke took notice of Milton's tract. What is interesting is that Milton considered the refutation of these authoritarian claims a matter important enough to warrant his attention in an entire pamphlet, and that Brooke should have thought it likewise worth while to meet the Anglicans on that ground in a treatise marked in general by a broader conception of the significance of the quarrel.[78]

[75] Brooke, *Discourse*, pp. 66–68.
[76] Whiting, *Milton's Literary Milieu*, pp. 301–306.
[77] Barker, *Milton and the Puritan Dilemma*, n. 21 to chapter 4, pp. 350–351.
[78] This seems an opportune occasion for clearing up a certain amount of confusion that exists between Ussher's tract as it originally appeared, in the spring of 1641, and as it appeared in a small volume published at Oxford later in the year, perhaps in the fall, entitled *Certain Briefe Treatises, written by Diverse Learned Men*. This collection was without doubt known by Milton, as he alludes specifically to it in *The Reason of Church Government*. It contains the following items: (1) Lancelot Andrewes, "A Summarie View of the Government both of the Old and New Testament: whereby The Episcopall Government of Christs church is vindicated." (2) Richard Hooker, "A Discovery of the Causes of the continuance of these Contentions touching Church-governments," prefixed to the Andrewes fragment. (3) "The Originall of Bishops and Metropolitans, briefely laid downe by Martin Bucer; sometimes Professor of Divinity in the University of Cambridge. Iohn Rainoldes; late Professor of Divinity in the University of Oxford. Iames Ussher; sometime Professor of Divinity in the University of Dublin; afterward Arch-Bishop of Armagh and Primate of all Ireland." (4) Ussher, "A

It has been noted that Milton had published *Of Reformation*, the first of his antiprelatical treatises, earlier even than *Of Prelatical Episcopacy*. Unlike the second pamphlet, *Of Reformation* does not answer any particular person. In fact, in content and in style it stands conspicuously apart from the tracts that surround it in time. One has to read only a little way into it to realize that here one breathes a far different air, heady and bracing:

> But to dwell no longer in characterizing the Depravities of the Church, and how they sprung, and how they tooke increase; when I recall to mind at last, after so many darke Ages, wherein the huge overshadowing traine of Error had almost swept all the Starres out of the Firmament of the Church; how the bright and blissfull Reformation (by Divine Power) strook through the black and settled Night of Ignorance and Antichristian Tyranny, me thinks a soveraigne and reviving joy must needs rush into the bosome of him that reads or heares; and the sweet Odour of the returning Gospell imbath his Soule with the fragrancy of Heaven.[79]

Its content is more directly concerned with the issues in general than with any special facet of them. But even though there is no indisputable evidence that it was directly influential upon any of the controversialists, it will be worth while summarizing

---

Geographicall and Historicall Disquisition, touching the Lydian or Proconsular Asia and the seven Metropoliticall Churches contained in it." (5) Edward Brerewood, "A Declaration of the Patriarchicall Government of the ancient Church." (6) Francis Mason, "The Validity of the Ordination of the Minisers [sic] of the Reformed Churches beyond the seas, maintained against the Romanists." (7) John Dury, "A briefe Declaration premised thereunto, of the severall Formes of Government received in those Churches." The item to which Milton and Brooke were replying is the third listed above. The relationship between the original Ussher tract, *The Iudgement of Doctor Rainoldes*, and this third item, "The Originall of Bishops and Metropolitans," is as follows: (a) the prefatory section of *The Iudgement*, pp. 1–3, appears in *Certain Briefe Treatises* (hereafter referred to in this note as *CBT*) on pp. 49–50, as Reynolds's contribution to "The Originall of Bishops"; (b) in *CBT*, two further paragraphs that had not appeared earlier are added to Reynolds's testimony, pp. 50–51; (c) in *CBT*, Ussher's tract contains several pages of prefatory material (pp. 51–56) that does not appear in *The Iudgement*, mostly concerned with analogies between the Priests and Levites of the Old Testament and the Bishops and Presbyters of the early Christian church; (d) after a suitable transitional passage on p. 56, *CBT* follows *The Iudgement* thereafter with only minor additions (such as one on p. 57 concerning St. Peter) from p. 56 to p. 64; (e) in *CBT*, pp. 64–75 of Ussher's tract are newly added. It is quite clear, aside from the matter of dates of publication, that both Milton and Brooke are replying to *The Iudgement* as it was originally published.

[79] "Of Reformation," *Works*, III, 5–6.

its argument. There are matters within it that are paralleled in Brooke's *Discourse,* whether or not Brooke might have had Milton's treatise in mind. And in order properly to appraise the position and contribution of Brooke, it is necessary to understand where the debate stood, as far as one can judge from the most representative publications, and to estimate the degree to which Brooke moved beyond that stage, as he surely did in at least two important areas.

Milton begins his tract by listing some of the abuses of the Anglican Church, especially those which appear to mistake outward show for inner essence, arising from the error of having "magnifi'd the external signs more then the quickening power of the Spirit." [80] But what particularly concerns him is the causes "that hinder the forwarding of true Discipline," both in the days of their forefathers and in their own time. After a sketch of the rise of "prelatism" during the reigns from Henry VIII to Elizabeth, he lists three kinds of "hinderers" of the reformation, characteristic of his own age, with whom the main part of the treatise will deal: antiquitarians (rather than antiquaries, "whose labours are usefull and laudable"), libertines, and politicians.[81]

In answering the "votarists of antiquity," Milton announces that he will first show what a modern bishop will have to do in order to conform himself to those "purer times" that are so continually cited by the proponents of the divine right of episcopacy from apostolic times. For one thing, bishops then were elected by the whole church rather than appointed by some central authority. The withdrawal of the most vital elements of the church from the people is signalized, for example, by the modern corruption of the communion service.[82] A true reformer, honestly desiring to return the church to the people and to "mould a modern bishop into a primitive," must

[80] *Works,* III, 3.

[81] *Works,* III, 14.

[82] *Works,* III, 19. This claim is argued in rather graphic and not very lofty language, such as: "the Table of Communion now become a Table of separation stands like an exalted platforme upon the brow of the quire, fortifi'd with bulwark, and barricado, to keep off the profane touch of the Laicks, whilst the obscene, and surfeted Priest scruples not to paw, and mammock the sacramentall bread, as familiarly as his Tavern Bisket," etc. (III, 19).

yeeld him to be elected by the popular voyce, undiocest, unrevenu'd, un-lorded, and leave him nothing but brotherly equality, matchles temperance, frequent fasting, incessant prayer, and preaching, continual watchings, and labours in his Ministery.[83]

For another, the times themselves were corrupted, the men of those years, even the best of them, were "foully tainted," and their writings "dangerously adulterated." Heresies were rife and impurity had infected the Church itself, as Ignatius and Eusebius testify, and even Constantine, "the Load-starre of Reformation as some men clatter," was a heretical libertine who might justly have laid at his door the responsibility for the lordliness and worldly pomp of prelates ever since.[84] And finally, the antiqui-tarian should realize that these Fathers and authorities of those "purer times," which have been shown not to have been so pure after all, did not claim that their works were sufficient in them-selves for the ordering of church polity, but "sent all commers to the Scriptures, as all sufficient."[85] Custom without truth, Milton avers, echoing the Smectymnuans and quoting Cyprian, and anticipating the dedicatory epistle to the first Divorce tract, is but "agednesse of Error";[86] and Ignatius, Cyprian, and others are agreed that the Scriptures, the embodiment of truth, are the ultimate and final authority. What is so difficult in the Scriptures? Their "sober, plain, and unaffected" style is far clearer than the "crabbed" writings of the Fathers, with their "fantastick, and declamatory flashes; the cross-jingling periods which cannot but disturb, and come athwart a stil'd devotion worse then the din of bells, and rattles."[87] Indeed, writes Milton in one of the great passages of his prose,

The very essence of Truth is plainnesse, and brightnes; the darknes and crookednesse is our own. The wisedome of God created understanding, fit and proportionable to Truth the object, and end of it, as the eye to the thing visible. If our understanding have a film of ignorance over it, or be blear with gazing on other false glisterings, what is that to Truth? If we will but purge with sovrain eyesalve that intellectual ray which God hath

[83] *Works*, III, 19.
[84] *Works*, III, 23–25. Milton quotes Dante, Petrarch, and Ariosto to support his low opinion of Constantine, pp. 26–27.
[85] *Works*, III, 28.
[86] *Works*, III, 29. Cf. Smectymnuus, *Answer*, p. 19 (see p. 195 above).
[87] *Works*, III, 34.

planted in us, then we would beleeve the Scriptures protesting their own plainnes, and perspicuity . . . and as the Scriptures themselvs pronounce their own plainnes, so doe the Fathers testifie of them.[88]

Milton anticipates his eulogy of the "true wayfaring Christian" of the *Areopagitica* as he praises the "plain upright man that all his dayes hath bin diligently reading the holy Scriptures" as one who has come closer to truth than the "admirers of Antiquity" who have been "beating their brains." [89]

In a word or two Milton disposes of his second category of hinderer, the libertines, those who would be unable to bear the discipline that reformation would bring, who fear that such a polity would spawn "a pope in every parish." [90] No discipline exists under which such people could live, he observes, as he passes to the second book of the treatise and the third category of hinderer, the politicians.

In the first place, no art has been more "soyl'd, and slubber'd with aphorisming pedantry" than the art of government ("policie"). Foreshadowing the ideal of education, so striking a combination of the humanist's broad vision and the Puritan's practicality, to be expressed in the tractate *Of Education* a few years later, Milton complains that writers on the science of government no longer teach "that to govern well is to train up a Nation in true wisdom and vertue, and that which springs from thence magnanimity . . . and that which is our beginning, regeneration, and happiest end, likenes to God." [91] The modern politician rather is more concerned with trying to "mould the sufferance and subjection of the people to the length of that foot

[88] *Works*, III, 33. Milton's affinity on the subject of truth with Brooke's earlier treatise has been noted (see pp. 132–133 above). Cf. Brooke: ". . . what is the Understanding other than a Ray of the Divine Nature, warming and enlivening the Creature, conforming it to the likenesse of the Creator? And is not Truth the same?" (*The Nature of Truth*, pp. 3–4).

[89] *Works*, III, 34.

[90] *Works*, III, 36. The phrase was probably originated by Lord Digby in *The Third Speech of the Lord George Digby, To the House of Commons, Concerning Bishops* (February, 1641). Professor Whiting thinks that Milton had the speech before him as he wrote, and that "the refutation in *Of Reformation* is directed chiefly, if not solely, at Digby's *Speech*" (Whiting, *Milton's Literary Milieu*, p. 283 and elsewhere in chapter 10).

[91] *Works*, III, 37.

that is to tread on their necks," [92] and it is these descendants of Machiavelli who claim that reformation is against the interests of the state. Their arguments come under two main headings: first, that church government must conform to the civil government; second, that no form of church government except episcopacy is agreeable to monarchy. As for the first, there is no reason why church discipline must be "minted and modell'd out to secular pretences." Church and state must on no account be linked together, for the Church is established and governed by divine precept, not by human. Seeing that

the Churchmans office is only to teach men the Christian Faith, to exhort all, to incourage the good, to admonish the bad, privately the lesse offender, publickly the scandalous and stubborn; to censure, and separate from the communion of Christs flock, the contagious, and incorrigible, to receive with joy, and fatherly compassion the penitent, all this must be don, and more then this is beyond any Church autority.[93]

As for the second claim, it would be more just to say that the kind of episcopacy that exists in England, far from being "agreeable" to monarchy, actually tends to its destruction. History abounds in examples of spiritual leaders whose ambition for worldly power has been fired by the acquisition of temporal dignity. After providing a catalogue of sobering examples, Milton assures his readers that "the fall of Prelacy . . . cannot shake the least fringe that borders the royal canopy: but . . . their standing doth continually oppose, and lay battery to regal safety." [94] Think, Milton particularizes, how the monarchy has of late been weakened by prelacy. The love and respect of the people has been wrested away, their "multitude and valor" diminished, the coffers of the kingdom reduced by ostentatious ceremonies. The enduring health of a monarchy must depend both upon the liberty of the subjects and upon the supremacy of the king. Both are threatened by the menacing ambition of priests and prelates. Far from being the only church government agreeable to the English monarchy, it is apparent that prelacy is a "noysom and diseased tumor," and it is high time that it be cut away

[92] *Works,* III, 36.
[93] *Works,* III, 40–41.
[94] *Works,* III, 49.

from the public body.[95] England is blessed with an enlightened civil government in which the people have a controlling influence on policy. How absurd that in the Church of England the people have no say!

Wee therfore having already a kind of Apostolicall, and ancient Church Election in our State, what a perversnesse would it be in us of all others to retain forcibly a kind of imperious, and stately Election in our Church? [96]

The body of the treatise ends here, though Milton goes on for a number of pages further to reply to some "Objections, which I have heard commonly flying about," one of the most notable of which is that "the government of Episcopacy, is now so weav'd into the common Law" that the establishment of a new discipline would be disruptive: "In Gods name," Milton exclaims, "let it weave out again; let not humain quillets keep back divine authority." [97] The tract concludes with a ringing prayer for national regeneration.[98]

The story of the antiepiscopal debate is now sufficiently told. It is not, of course, the whole story, perhaps no more than a fraction. There were published from as early as the 1620's on up through that summer of 1641 countless other pamphlets and tracts that bore on the issue and that might be relevantly cited. But because of their semiofficial status as spokesmen for the Puritan cause, the writings of the Smectymnuans in their forensic contest with Bishop Hall may be taken as representative. And because of the author's preëminent position in the later Commonwealth, as well as because of his unmatched style and his power of generalization, Milton's *Of Reformation* is uniquely significant as part of the story.[99] With these reservations in mind, one may say in at least a qualified sense that the stage is now set for the proper entrance of Brooke's *Discourse*.

[95] *Works*, III, 62.
[96] *Works*, III, 64.
[97] *Works*, III, 69. Whiting argues that these "Objections" refer without question to Digby's *Speech* (Whiting, p. 286 and ff.).
[98] *Works*, III, 76–79.
[99] *Of Prelatical Episcopacy* and *Animadversions* are so specifically directed in answer to Ussher and Hall, contributing little that is new (aside from undisputed originality and vigor of expression) to the main current of the debate, that it does not seem necessary to treat either in detail.

XIV

INDIFFERENCY AND TOLERATION

It is evident from even a cursory perusal of Brooke's *Discourse* that he is dependent upon his predecessors in the anti-episcopal debate for many of the steps in his argument and much of his documentation. A modern student of the period may well wonder how this treatise can be distinguished in usefulness from the numerous and voluminous publications of other contributors to the controversy. Yet there are unique elements in Brooke's tract, areas in which he transcends his predecessors and significantly advances the debate. In an evaluation of Brooke's stature as an antiprelatical pamphleteer these areas must be brought fully into focus and scrutinized with some care.

Before analyzing these unique contributions, however, it will be helpful to review parts of the treatise briefly to see in what respects the argument is dependent upon some of the tracts that have already been considered. In this discussion I do not feel that establishing the "sources" of Brooke's ideas and premises would be either possible or, if it were, of particular importance, as such a procedure proved to be in the earlier critical treatment of *The Nature of Truth*. A good many of the issues are not important enough to the literary historian to warrant the effort that would be involved, even if it were possible to unravel the threads of the unnumbered pamphlets that touched on this contentious matter during the decade or two preceding the outbreak of the Civil War. Nor would such minute documentation lead a student to a fuller understanding of the Puritan mind. It is instructive to learn that among the Puritans a representative intellectual like Brooke was dependent upon Platonic, medieval, and Renaissance sources for the background of his philosophical position on so crucial a matter as the nature of truth, with its repercussions for the future development of empirical and idealistic philosophy. But it does not help one to understand the Puritans more clearly to distinguish among the Smectymnuans, Prynne, or Cartwright as sources of Brooke's scriptural and patristic arguments as to whether bishops truly existed in ancient time. My intention, then, is not to identify "sources," but to indicate the degree to which Brooke was indebted to pamphlets in the antiepiscopal debate already published.

In propounding the opening thesis, that the institution of episcopacy is repugnant to "state-policy," Brooke might be said to be following the well-known Party line. When in the first chapter he describes the bishop, endowed with civil as well as spiritual power, as "too officious, two-headed," entrusted with the supervision of a diocese instead of a single congregation — a notion that he identifies as having crept into the Church a century or so after the apostolic establishment of the primitive polity — his readers would recognize the argument that runs through the Smectymnuan *Answer* on the original identity of bishops and presbyters. When he observes that the civil power of the episcopate was a corruption that appeared while the world was "busie," looking at the "new Beast, successour to the Dragon," he is doubtless reflecting his reading in the eschatological tomes with which *The Nature of Truth* demonstrated his familiarity, as well perhaps as his acquaintance with the less learned but far more widely read efforts of John Lilburne, the fiery young man who was later to enlist in Brooke's own regiment. When Brooke says that a bishop should be only "a true faithful Overseer, that, over one single Congregation, hath a joynt care with the Elders, Deacons, and rest of the Assembly," [1] he is repeating a notion too often expressed to need authority, for it is a cornerstone of the antiepiscopal argument.

The unedifying complaint in the second chapter against the low birth of the bishops is probably largely Brooke's own, as it was for this particular utterance that Fuller singled him out for special opprobrium. Yet one recalls Milton's remark on the corruptions of the Church occasioned by Constantine, who showered such a wealth of riches upon the bishops that

[1] *Discourse,* p. 2.

in this manner the Prelates both then and ever since coming from a meane, and Plebeyan Life on a sudden to be Lords of stately Palaces, rich furniture, delicious fare, and Princely attendance, thought the plaine and homespun verity of Christs Gospell unfit any longer to hold their Lordships acquaintance, unlesse the poore thredbare Matron were put into better clothes.[2]

The idea can hardly have been a new one; but it probably did seem more reprehensible to Fuller when voiced by a peer of the realm.

In the third chapter Brooke disposes of the often cited analogies between the Jewish priests of the Old Testament and modern bishops, fairly common elements in the Anglican arguments both for the antiquity of episcopacy and for the precedent of investing ecclesiastical officials with civil power.[3] His succeeding passage on the duties of a modern minister is reminiscent of Milton's definition of the "Churchman's office," not so much because their arguments are similar but as evidence of their mutual concern for reëstablishing the clergy in their true status. The implication is clear that when a minister properly carries out his clerical duties, there is neither the time nor the appropriate opportunity for civil duties.[4]

Other arguments in the *Discourse* that adhere to the usual Puritan line of attack are numerous, and little is to be gained by ferreting them out of the treatise as a whole, as I have done illustratively for the first three chapters. But among some of the suggestive parallels at least worth noting are the following: the idea in the eighth chapter that bishops are actually enemies of monarchy, which reminds one strikingly of Milton once again;[5] the similar idea in the seventh chapter that temporal honors are destructive to spiritual men;[6] the refutations, in the first four chapters of the second part of the tract, of the various claims

[2] "Of Reformation," *Works*, III, 25.

[3] Cf. Ussher's additions to *The Iudgement of Doctor Rainoldes* in *Certain Briefe Treatises* (see n. 78 to Chapter XIII, pp. 201–202 above).

[4] Cf. "Of Reformation," *Works*, 40–41. I need not reiterate that such a parallel does not imply an indebtedness to Milton for the idea; it is simply that here Brooke is touching upon a matter that has been suggested earlier and often.

[5] *Discourse*, pp. 38–41; "Of Reformation," *Works*, III, 41. Brooke's catalogue of grisly examples of treasonous bishops (*Discourse*, pp. 41–43) may be drawn in part from the Postscript to the Smectymnuan *Answer* (which, as has been noted, Masson thought had been compiled by Milton).

[6] *Discourse*, p. 37; "Of Reformation," *Works*, III, 44.

of episcopacy to apostolic origin based on "antiquity and scripture"; [7] the argument that the most suitable form of church government as far as the authority of Scripture is concerned is "Democraticall," with the conclusion that in matters of election, decision in controversies, cases of conscience, and excommunication, the Church as a whole rather than merely the clergy should act, a line of reasoning comparable to Milton's plea to return the Church to the people.[8]

There are a number of instances in which Brooke pushed on beyond the scope usually attained in discussions of those subjects an argument for which he was indebted to earlier critics of episcopacy. In most of these areas, to be sure, no significant or lasting contribution to Puritan thought emerges; but a glance at one or two such instances, even though the issues involved may be intrinsically only of secondary importance, should be helpful in delineating Brooke's position among his contemporaries. One of these is in the ninth chapter of the first part. It has been noted that Brooke paralleled in the eighth chapter Milton's conviction that episcopacy is actually destructive to monarchy. In the ninth he proceeds along the following path of logic. When moderate proponents of episcopacy argue that under a monarchy the best form of church government is likewise monarchical, do they mean that any other sort of church government would be destructive to monarchy (that is to say, "No bishop, no king"), or that monarchy is destructive to all other forms of church government other than monarchical? Monarchy should in fact be able to subsist comfortably with any sort of church government, or none at all, for the civil power receives no essential support from the Church. A heathen emperor is just as lawful a monarch as a Christian prince, and

---

[7] The reply to Ussher (*Discourse*, pp. 66–68) covers the material similarly refuted by Milton in *Of Prelatical Episcopacy*, as has been noted. The lengthy discussion of the bishops' election, ordination, jurisdiction, and delegation of authority to lesser functionaries (*Discourse*, pp. 69–74), is parallel to and may be indebted to Sections VII–X of the Smectymnuan *Answer* (pp. 34–43). These subjects had, however, attracted Puritan scrutiny since the time of Cartwright. The raking over of the claims of Timothy and Titus to episcopal rank (*Discourse*, pp. 76–79) had been repeated *ad nauseam*, as any investigator of the writings of Prynne and the Smectymnuans well knows.

[8] *Discourse*, pp. 81–83; "Of Reformation," *Works*, III, 19–20, 63–64.

to maintain that monarchy cannot stand without monarchical church discipline is to weaken civil power. What these apologists really must mean is that monarchical church government cannot endure *except* under a civil monarchy, for only princes can uphold a discipline "which hath no footing in Scripture," and must be held up parasitically like ivy, in time to destroy its prop. The bishops have foreseen this danger and hence, as propaganda for the public, have reversed the proposition, asserting that the civil monarchy cannot stand without church monarchy, whereas in truth, as Milton was shortly to argue in *The Reason of Church Government*, the "prelatical razor" would deprive the King of his "wonted might" as Samson was bereft of his by the Philistines.[9]

Another instance may be found in the tenth chapter. Here again Brooke pursues his point beyond the usual stage, so far as I can recognize it at least, though the issue, even more than the preceding one, has become a dead one in the succeeding years and is no longer of significance or even of interest except to the specialist in religious history. The idea that the Pope was the antichrist of the Book of Revelation was an old one already in Brooke's time, stemming perhaps from Foxe's *Actes and Monuments* of the preceding century, and probably from the writings of Continental reformers before that. Brooke begins with this original premise, defines the nature of "popery" on grounds of both doctrine and discipline, and in an elaborate and detailed "proof" satisfies himself that the bishops of the English Church, whether they owe allegiance to the Pope or not, are strictly in the tradition of the antichrist, encroaching upon the office of Christ himself and destroying true religion.[10]

These are matters of only peripheral importance, however, either in regard to religious history or as evidence of Brooke's achievement. Two of the areas in which he advanced the argument conspicuously demand closer attention, for in these instances Brooke signalized a broadening of Puritan thought beyond the strict and narrow bounds to which it was generally confined by the scriptural authoritarians in the tradition of

[9] "The Reason of Church Government," *Works*, III, 276.
[10] *Discourse*, pp. 49–63.

Cartwright. Here he did transcend his predecessors and contemporaries. One of these areas is his discussion of indifferency, the other his conclusions regarding toleration of the sects.

Brooke's conviction as to the unhappy effects of the power of the bishops to enforce indifferent matters as necessary has been described in an earlier chapter.[11] In the fifth and sixth chapters of the *Discourse* Brooke undertakes a full examination of the nature of indifferency, first to ascertain whether it has actual existence or only apparent existence, then to determine where the power of decreeing the proper course of action in an indifferent matter lies. His argument is closely reasoned, and his conclusion is sufficiently far-reaching in its importance to warrant one's following him through to it in detail. There is nothing else quite like it in the pamphlet literature of that era.

In the first place, says Brooke, the exact meaning of the word "indifferent" must be clarified. The prefix "in" does not have a wholly negative sense. The word "imprudent," for example, does not mean "without prudence," for this would imply an irrationality impossible in a human being; the prefix is negative only in a particular sense. "Indifferent" does not mean *"non differens,"* but rather, "in such, or such a respect, it Differeth not."[12] In natural science there can be an indifference between two extremes: lukewarm as "warm" does not differ from "hot," but as "cool" it does; as "cool" it does not differ from "cold," but as "warm" it does; therefore it is indifferent to both extremes.

It would be convenient to be able to apply this criterion to moral matters as well as natural science, to say that a certain action could be indifferent to two extremes, such as "good" and "bad." Unfortunately, however, in moral matters the two extremes are not positive: evil is merely the privation of good,[13] and passions cannot be described as *wholly* good or bad. The same individual action (or passion) cannot be both good and bad in the same respects (as lukewarm can be both hot and cold); for if in any one respect it is bad it cannot be said to be

[11] See Chapter XI above, pp. 155–156.
[12] *Discourse,* p. 18.
[13] It will be remembered that Brooke demonstrated his adherence to this Augustinian principle in *The Nature of Truth* (see pp. 109–110 above).

truly good. A small sin is as much a sin as a great one, as Cicero and the Stoics understood.[14]

Now, an indifferent thing must in itself be wholly good; for if it has in it anything evil it must be regarded as wholly bad and hence cannot be indifferent. It must be good and therefore lawful. And it must be able to be done or not done, used or not used. Indifferency cannot mean being lawful at one time, unlawful at another, or something that must be done at one time or not done at another. In a pair of contraries, such as doing or not doing, one *must* be better than the other, considering the time and place and circumstances. In such a case, a person must choose the *better*: he cannot be indifferent to both. His choice must be lawful, or it could not be better; it must be expedient, or something else for that time and those circumstances would be better.

If a person follows right reason, he must do what it dictates as the best thing to be done. Right reason must dictate what is best, or at least seems to be best. For if it ever should dictate what is *not* best, then how can one believe that it *ever* dictates what is best? Otherwise it might appear to dictate what is best only by chance, like a corrupt judge who judges by whim rather than principle.

It would be "strange doctrine" indeed to argue that we need not follow the dictates of right reason, or that we need not consult it at all. For if one may even once ignore right reason without sin, all one's acts could then be irrational without sin: a manifest impossibility except in "a distracted man";[15] and simply not consulting right reason is the same as acting against its dictates. This does not mean, of course, that the reason must be consulted in every little unimportant action, but only when a scruple arises.[16]

The next question is this: is there always one *best*? Can two things be so equally good that one is not better than the other, considering time and place and circumstances? Probably not.

---

[14] *Discourse*, p. 19.

[15] *Discourse*, p. 23.

[16] Cf. Hooker's insistence that though we must follow Scripture where it is explicit, the Scriptures need not direct us in the "taking up of a rush or straw" (II, i, 2, cited above, p. 170).

To determine which is better, one must appeal to right reason, which makes its decision on the basis of some good ground. One may take "to marry or not to marry" as a hypothetical illustration.[17] If right reason does not or cannot make a judgment as to which is better, man sins by acting unreasonably, following his humor or his fancy instead. Indeed, it can be said that of any two extremes, such as doing or not doing, marrying or not marrying, not only can they not be equally good, they both cannot even be good. If one is better and therefore necessary to be done, the other cannot be good or even lawful, because there is a better thing to be done. In fact, in choosing between evils, should one be forced to do so, the less-evil is good, the less-good is evil.

There is therefore no one thing that an individual either may or may not do: there is always a best. From this proposition one must inescapably conclude, *nothing is in itself indifferent.* If it is best, it is necessary; if it is less good, and therefore to some degree bad, it is unlawful. What we think of as "indifference" then has no actual existence; indifference simply "lies in our Understandings, and the Darkenesse thereof." Things may *seem* indifferent, but they cannot be indifferent in actuality. They may seem so to our understanding only "for want of Good light." [18]

In the sixth chapter Brooke advances to the second general question that he has posed, namely, wherein lies the power of determining the proper course of action in what is called an indifferent matter. It is clear by now that since all things are either good or bad and there is no such thing as an indifferent thing, it does not lie within the power of the Church to *make* a thing indifferent. It is equally impossible for the Church to determine what is indifferent; for indifference arises from the "Darkness of our Understanding," and no man (or institution made up of men) can tell what is or is not dark to another.

In that case, then, what about the things that *seem* indifferent, which neither Scripture nor the "light within" has made clear? Indifference lies between extremes. When neither extreme is

[17] *Discourse,* p. 24.
[18] *Discourse,* pp. 26–27.

necessary, the Church has no power to determine either extreme; but when one extreme is necessary, the Church determines which is best. Only one of the extremes (such as doing or not doing) *can* be best and lawful; the other will be evil and unlawful, and hence "poyson." To reach its decision the Church must follow right reason, as any human being or body of human beings must do.[19]

The crux of the problem is now revealed: what shall I do if I dissent from the judgment of the Church? Shall I merely secede from the Church, creating a schism or faction? "God forbid, no," says Brooke. I must submit in prayer and humility to the reason of others in an effort to clarify my judgment. And what if, after due season, I remain yet unsatisfied? Then I must "suspend till my judgement be cleared, lest that which to another is Lawfull, become sin to me: Who cannot Act in Faith, while I act against or with Doubts, or Scruples." And in the meantime,

I must quietly deport my selfe without faction, turbulent commotion, or uncharitable censure of those who dissent from mee, both in Judgement and Practice; well knowing that the same thing may be Lawfull and necessary to one that sees it so; which yet to me is unlawfull, while I so doubt.[20]

No power should force my practice any more than my judgment. Unless it is clear that dissent involves danger to the state, there should be imposed no fines or imprisonment on its account. In all things not clearly determined by Scripture, one should not be forced to act or believe against his conscience.

Many matters seem indifferent because they are not clearly dictated by Scripture, such as the time and place of a service or the gestures that we use in worship. Some determination must be made because one of the extremes is necesary: we must have *some* time or place or gesture. The Church may then determine the proper action, not arbitrarily but according to the dictate of right reason. If one doubts the judgment of the Church, how-

[19] By "the Church" Brooke, following a conception like Milton's that the Church belongs to the people, emphasizes that he means "not onely One or Two, or a Few, of what Ranke soever; but All, even every true Member of the whole Church. For I conceive every such Member hath *de jure* a Vote in This Determination" (*Discourse*, p. 29).

[20] *Discourse*, pp. 29–30.

ever, on the basis of one's own reason, it would be a sin to
"yeeld her more than Passive Obedience." And as for the Church,
"if she force one so Doubting, I thinke she sinneth more." [21]

Brooke's quarrel with the bishops is clear. Even if they *were*
the Church (and Brooke hastens to reiterate that they are not)
they would have no power to determine the course of action
in indifferent things arbitrarily, much less to force men to comply
with what they "make" (rather than "find") indifferent and then
declare to be necessary, "on paine of Imprisonment, losse of Eares,
yea life it selfe." It might be tolerable if they assumed this
dictatorial power only in abstruse or doubtful matters; but "they
scruple not, point blanke to contradict our Reason, and force
our consciences, in things extremely manifest," which may indeed
be actually unlawful.

The far-reaching effect of Brooke's clinical dissection of this
fundamental problem may now be discerned. Professor Barker
is perfectly correct when he concludes that "complete freedom
of conscience is the inescapable result." [22] It is well recognized
that this was the issue that caused the irrevocable division among
the Puritans themselves within a very few years, and it is not
too much to say that to Brooke belongs the distinction of having
clarified this issue more cogently than did any of his predecessors
or contemporaries in the antiepiscopal debate. The "Puritan
dilemma" was the irreconcilable choice between complete
national reformation and the achievement of true liberty for
believers. As long as the specific aims of the Puritans remained
indefinite, that is, while they were busily agitating for reformation but without a clear program for carrying it out, they could
demonstrate a forceful unanimity that helped them win their
struggle with episcopacy. But when episcopacy fell, with the
first few weeks of the Long Parliament, the divisive tendencies
within the amorphous Puritan body began to disrupt their uneasy
federation. Could Christian liberty be achieved without opening
the way to sects and schisms? The fears of the extreme conserva-

---

[21] *Discourse*, pp. 30–31.
[22] Barker, p. 57. The notes suggest the magnitude of my indebtedness to
Barker's masterly analysis of Milton's development through these years in *Milton
and the Puritan Dilemma*.

tives, like Thomas Edwards, that the ideal of Christian liberty would lead to full toleration were well founded. When the implications of true freedom of conscience were understood, the minor fault between the Separatists and the Presbyterians widened into a chasm, and the likelihood of its being bridged grew increasingly remote. The Separatists, who leaned toward the ideal of liberty, accepted the implications carried by freedom of conscience and moved to the left; the Presbyterians, who were more concerned with the establishment of national reformation, were reluctant to provide the slightest opening for heretics and schismatics, and swung unhesitatingly to the right. Among the Presbyterians were the Smectymnuan authors, members of and faithful adherents to the principles adopted by the Westminster Assembly. Among the Separatists were the authors of the *Apologeticall Narration* protesting the Assembly, one of whom was Thomas Goodwin, the admirer of Brooke who had dedicated a treatise to him. With the latter Brooke would unquestionably have cast his lot had he lived, as did Puritan liberals like William Walwyn, Roger Williams, and in time, Milton himself. While the Presbyterians adhered to the principle of scriptural authoritarianism, the Separatists moved toward liberal rationalism, for which Brooke's analysis of indifferency had stated the case with incisive clarity.

The development of Milton's thought between his antiprelatical pamphlets and the *Areopagitica* is of considerable interest and pertinence at this point. Although Milton had a high conception of human dignity arising from man's being endowed with reason, the "intellectual ray," his argument in the antiprelatical tracts is almost entirely consonant with the Smectymnuan point of view, based on the conviction that church government is exactly prescribed by the Scriptures.[23] In eulogizing reason at that stage in his own growth, Milton is not really being a rationalist, any more than the Smectymnuans themselves were in the *Answer* when they appealed to reason as justifying change.[24] Ever since the time of Cartwright Puritans had been disposed to see

[23] Barker supplies an impressive number of relevant excerpts from the tracts as documentation for this point, pp. 23–24.

[24] Smectymnuus, *Answer*, pp. 20–21. See above, pp. 195–196.

reason as subject to the corruptions and frailties of the flesh, even though it might be divinely implanted in man just as frail man is divinely created. What emphasis Milton does put upon reason in *Of Reformation* is in the interest of showing its deficiency rather than its power, in contrast to the infallibility of Scripture. As Barker expresses it, in 1641 Milton was "impressed, not by the powers of the human reason, but by the consistent perversity with which throughout its recorded history it has preferred corrupt and antichristian error to divinely revealed and prescribed truth." [25]

As for the matter of indifferency, it appears that Milton did recognize the tyranny of forced compliance with indifferent matters, and that he did see this tyranny in terms of liberty of conscience. One recalls the passage in *Of Reformation* in which he laments the emigration of so many "faithfull and freeborn Englishmen" to the "savage deserts of America,"

because their conscience could not assent to things which the Bishops thought indifferent. What more binding then conscience? what more free then indifferency? cruel then must that indifferency needs be, that shall violate the strict necessity of Conscience, merciles, and inhumane that free choyse, and liberty that shall break asunder the bonds of Religion.[26]

But where Milton does not advance the issue, and where Brooke does, is in making the connection between liberty of conscience and reason. Milton is still more intent upon arguing the divine prescription of church government in Scripture, and he is not concerned enough with demonstrating the strength of the "intellectual ray" to see its relevance in application to the problem of forced conformity.[27]

The Smectymnuans moved from this general position to the rigidly scriptural authoritarianism of the Westminster Assembly, and from Milton's early tracts it might appear that Milton would move in that direction with them. Yet by 1644, in the *Areopagitica*, he had unequivocally taken his stand with rationalism. A literary historian cannot, of course, assign a definite or simple cause for this change in the wind, but he may hypothesize from

[25] Barker, p. 50.
[26] "Of Reformation," *Works*, III, 50.
[27] Cf. Barker, p. 58.

the evidence that is known. For one thing, in between the anti-prelatical tracts and the *Areopagitica* came the divorce tracts. Professor Barker is probably correct once again when he maintains that Milton, facing the issue of divorce more acutely than if he were composing merely another academic prolusion, and realizing that he could not follow the Westminster Assembly on the subject of divorce, came to see divorce as a case of conscience. Here was no divine prescript as to what should be done; rather, it was a matter of the individual's own choice, in an area where the dictate of Scripture is not clear.[28] The privilege of the individual Christian is to choose on the basis of his reason: this is Christian liberty, anticipating the later and fundamental position of the *Areopagitica* and *Paradise Lost*, that "freedom is but choosing." If one substitutes, as Barker suggests, "faith and religion" for "love and marriage," the divorce tracts sound rather like the *Areopagitica* itself.[29]

For another thing, Milton had in the meantime read Brooke's *Discourse*, and was sufficiently impressed with it to cite it specifically later on in the *Areopagitica*. It is not altogether farfetched to imagine that Brooke's hypothetical illustration in his reasoning out of indifferency, "to marry or not to marry," could have come to the surface of Milton's mind when he was debating his own question, "to divorce or not to divorce." Whatever other causes for his change there may have been, it is certainly true that while his thought was undergoing that change he had read Brooke, and his conception of the nature of choice was put to the test by his ruminations on the subject of divorce. He had recognized right reason as the pathway to truth, and his emphasis shifted from the deficiencies of reason to its supreme potentialities.[30] The "one right discipline" that Milton had argued in the antiprelatical tracts seemed to him by 1644 as tyrannical under Presbyterians as it had been under Anglicanism, and the *Areopagitica* expresses a plea for liberty, specifically for liberty in indifferent things.[31] In reaching his own personal solution of

[28] Barker, pp. 69–74.
[29] Barker, p. 74.
[30] Barker, pp. 83–85.
[31] Barker, p. 97.

the Puritan dilemma, Milton moved from emphasis on reformation to insistence on liberty.

Brooke's central position in the shift of emphasis, which I have outlined earlier, that developed between the late sixteenth century and the time of the Long Parliament regarding the positions of Puritans and Anglicans as to scriptural authoritarianism and rationalism is now clear. The appeal to divine authority that formed the keystone of Cartwright's prescription for church government becomes the central argument of the official spokesman of the Anglicans, Bishop Hall. The Bishop here departs from the philosophical rationalism that was characteristic of his great predecessor, Hooker, as has been noted. Hall departs further from Hooker by basing his claims on the authority of the Fathers where the Scriptures are insufficient; for Hooker, who was something of a scripturalist himself in a broad sense, had spoken scornfully of the claims of tradition — "traditions urged by the Church of Rome" are not due "the same obedience and reverence we do to [God's] written law." [32] To Hooker reason was the authority to be followed where Scripture was an insufficient guide. Indeed, reason is necessary to us in elucidating the meaning of Scripture, and traditions, when they are not supported by reason, are to be rejected.[33]

Meanwhile, the rationalism that had been characteristic of Hooker was apparent enough in the writings of certain proponents of Anglicanism who were not, like Hall, its official spokesmen, notably Chillingworth, Hales, Falkland, and Jeremy Taylor. But it was shortly to be embraced by the liberal wing of the Puritans, including Brooke, Milton, Roger Williams, and the authors of the *Apologeticall Narration*. The wedge that forced this ironic turnabout was the issue of indifferent things, the implications of which became clear to the liberal Puritans in view of their concern for liberty of conscience.

One may summarize this development in a general fashion. To the principal antagonists on both sides in the sixteenth century indifferency was not a matter that involved liberty of conscience. To Hooker, indifferent matters are properly determined by rea-

[32] Hooker, *Ecclesiastical Polity*, I, xiii, 2.
[33] I, xiv, 5.

son, and once having been established they should be enforced in the interest of good order.[34] To Cartwright, indifferent matters, like the wearing of vestments, were inconvenient and troublesome but not worth seceding from the Church for, and certainly not involved with one's liberty of conscience.[35] In fact, as Pearson succinctly stated it, Cartwright in all his controversial teaching "aimed at ascendancy for his own beloved system and not liberty of conscience for all." [36] Nor did indifferent things have these broader implications for Bishop Hall or for the Smectymnuans in the 1640's. To Hall, it was perfectly plain that the authority of the Church should be respected in indifferent matters; since Scripture neither prohibited them nor prescribed them, he could not see how anyone could object to them. This view is a natural adjunct to the "divine prescript" theory of church government,[37] and the simplicity of Hall's conception of the issue, uncomplicated by considerations of the sort that Brooke introduced, is exemplified by his plea for the liturgy in the *Defence*: "Tell me, Is this Liturgie good or evill? If it be evill, it is unlawfull to be used; If good, it is not unlawfull to be imposed." [38] It was as easy as that. And the Smectymnuan position as adopted by the Westminster Assembly was comparable to the Anglican position, though in a way in reverse: church polity must be ordained according to divine prescript, and indifferent things, not prescribed in Scripture, may not therefore be enforced.[39] In none of these attitudes was any concern shown for liberty of conscience.

Hall was driven back to argument from Scripture and tradition by the furious and heavily documented Puritan polemics of the 1630's, like those of Prynne. They could not be effectively answered from Hooker's position, the appeal to reason, and in the controversy Hall deserted it. The Smectymnuans were the spiritual heirs of Cartwright and, as later events proved, were like him in desiring the ascendancy of their own system rather

[34] Hooker, III, viii, 18; III, ix, 1. See Jordan, I, 230. This was also Whitgift's position.
[35] Pearson, *Cartwright*, pp. 148–150.
[36] Pearson, p. 406.
[37] Barker, p. 52.
[38] Hall, *Defence*, p. 30.
[39] Barker, p. 53.

than freedom of conscience for all. But the growing awareness on the part of liberal Puritans, imbued as many of them were with a respect for the dignity of man, that liberty of conscience and human dignity were violated by forced conformity led them to embrace rationalism as the only avenue to freedom. Brooke emerged at a critical stage in this development and formulated in his *Discourse*, as he expounded the implications of indifferency, the significant relationship between liberty and reason. That liberal rationalism did not prove incompatible with Puritanism is increasingly clear as one goes on to read the later Milton, the works of such representative Independents as Henry Robinson, John Goodwin, and Roger Williams, and eventually the Cambridge Platonists.

The second area in which Brooke broadened the bounds of Puritan thought arises very naturally from the first. The seeds of toleration are obviously imbedded in the firm subsoil of the argument on indifferency. One recalls Brooke's statement as to what a conscientious person should do who finds himself dissenting from the judgment of the Church and who cannot even with prayer and humility and the help of others reconcile his scruples: "I must quietly deport my selfe without faction, turbulent commotion, or uncharitable censure of those who dissent from mee . . ."[40] One should not be forced in any way against one's conscience. Carried to its logical conclusion, such an attitude could only lead to toleration of the beliefs of others. It is to be expected, too, that such a breadth of view might be more easily achieved by the laity than by the more directly involved and committed clergy.[41] The Smectymnuans were writing with the objective of freedom of the clergy from Anglican restraints — that is only natural, for they were all clergymen. Brooke and, later, Milton, both of whom were devout and theologically well-informed laymen, wrote with the objective of freedom for all the people, for the laity as a whole.[42]

[40] *Discourse*, pp. 29–30 (see p. 216 above).
[41] A suggestive remark of Buckle's is pertinent, that toleration in religious matters has usually been forced upon the clergy by secular pressures (Buckle, I, 337).
[42] Barker relates Milton's concern in this regard to his belief in the "priesthood of all believers" (Barker, p. 41).

The relationship between liberty of conscience and toleration is indeed so fundamental and even obvious that it scarcely requires elucidation. It was apparent even in the sixteenth century, as Professor Jordan has demonstrated,[43] and the ideas of thinkers like Acontius on this relationship may very well have directly influenced Brooke and his contemporaries. "The worst and most damning error," said Acontius, "the prime heresy into which Satan would betray us, is anger and persecution directed at those who think differently from ourselves." [44] But the conservative Puritan reformers who were intent on establishing Presbyterian church government were guilty of a serious inconsistency. They taught that every man should obey his conscience according to his own individual religious experience; but since they were primarily interested in consolidating their own kind of uniformity, they insisted that heresy and schism should be suppressed. Brooke's remarks on toleration at the end of the *Discourse* deal with this inconsistency and provide a way out of it, though it is not one of which the Presbyterians could have approved.

In the argument of the final two chapters of the *Discourse*, the import of which has earlier been summarized,[45] Brooke maintains, in answer to a hypothetical objection that a change in church government would open the way for schisms and heresies which would be worse than anything the existing system might be responsible for, two propositions: first, that schisms and heresies always have arisen under any system and doubtless will continue to; and second, that episcopacy has actually been responsible for many of the divisions of recent times.[46] In the final chapter he essays a third answer, which is worth scrutinizing.

[43] See, for example, Jordan, I, 251–261.

[44] Quoted by Haller, *The Rise of Puritanism*, p. 198. See also Haller's comments on Brooke himself, p. 337; and on such significant figures as John Goodwin, p. 202. The influence of Acontius in England is well known. His particular importance in the thought of William Ames, whose works Brooke knew, has been shown by Jean Jacquot, "Acontius and the Progress of Tolerance in England," *Bibliothèque d'Humanisme et Renaissance* 16:192–206 (1954).

[45] See above, pp. 159–161.

[46] One notes a close parallel with part of Milton's argument in *The Reason of Church Government*, which Milton may have been composing at about the time the *Discourse* appeared: ". . . in stead of finding Prelaty an impeacher of Schisme or faction, the more I search, the more I grow into all perswasion to think rather that faction and she as with a spousall ring are wedded together, never to be divorc't" (*Works*, III, 212).

The dangers and inconveniences that a change in church government might bring to the state have been discussed, says Brooke. It will now be well to examine the possible dangers to the Church itself, for one must admit the possibility that the remedy may be worse than the disease. Prelacy has carried in its train such evils as Arminianism, Socinianism, superstition, idolatry, and popery. If prelacy is eliminated, presumably these evils will be eliminated too. But what new evils might appear under a new system? Principally these: Anabaptism, Brownism (or Separatism), and unlicensed preaching. Each of these may bear examination so that one may know how evil they are.

First, Anabaptism. To be sure, there is among the Anabaptists one branch that adheres to free will, community of all possessions, denial of magistracy, and refusal to baptize children; these people are heretics and atheists whose beliefs cannot be condoned, and repressive measures against them are justified. But there is another branch that merely denies baptism to children until they reach an age of discretion. Is this really so serious an error? Adherents of this view are perhaps to be pitied but not condemned; rather than being simply branded as schismatics, they should be enlightened. Besides, Brooke concedes, Scripture is not very clear on this point anyway.

As for the Brownists, their difference from the established Church lies in discipline rather than doctrine. One of their crimes is that they admit to their assemblies only those who appear to be "Beleeving Saints"; [47] another, that they grant to every congregation its own independence. As for the first offense, is it really so heinous? All churches are made up of a company of "believers," even the Roman Church. The Anglican Church defines a believer as one who "professeth the truth," though he may not live a life appropriate to a believer. The Brownists define a "Beleeving Saint" as one who not only "professeth the truth" but practices it as well.[48] Is it indeed such an error to require both profession and practice for church membership? As for the second, must it necessarily be true that an independent church will also be a "schismaticall" one? Dependence upon another church is not a neces-

[47] *Discourse,* p. 98.
[48] *Discourse,* p. 99.

sary part of being a church. Besides, once such dependence is admitted the difficult question of precedence is raised, and if this spreads out too far one is in danger of returning to the Pope as the supreme earthly head. "Perhaps," Brooke concludes, "all the Inconveniences that can be objected on Independence . . . will not ballance this one inconvenience of Dependence." [49]

Finally, what about unlicensed preaching? Perhaps shoe-makers and cobblers will turn preacher and the Church will be overrun with disorder. Well, order is very important, but is it worth burning people to achieve? What do these preachers say in their own defense? They argue that preaching is one church ordinance that a layman who feels moved to do so should be permitted to perform, especially since under the recent prelatical tyranny there has been so little preaching anyway. If one has the "parts" for preaching, should his humble background or humble trade be a deterrent?

Objections of various kinds, Brooke continues, have been raised against such preachers, a few of which, with the answers that have been given by the proponents of unlicensed preaching, might usefully be cited. It is said that if every man can preach what he will, errors and heresies will spread. One of their answers to this caveat is that they do not desire that just any person may preach, but only those who have the gifts and abilities, as judged by the godly men who hear them. Furthermore, suppose any man *could* preach anything he wanted to: would the inconvenience in fact be so great? All such preachers are either wise men or fools; if they preach wisely they will do good, if foolishly they will do little harm. Fools cannot spread heresy, for the true heretics were men of ability gone wrong. And suppose they did spread heresy: would it spread any more for being unlicensed? A licensed and able preacher who spread heresy could do far more harm, and it would be very difficult to stop him, or to anticipate when licensing him that he would spread heresy.

Another objection that is sometimes raised is this: if such preachers think themselves fit to be ministers, why then do they

[49] *Discourse*, p. 104. Cf. again Milton in *The Reason of Church Government*: ". . . if Prelaty must still rise and rise till it come to a Primat, why should it stay there? . . . all controversie may end in the finall pronounce or canon of one Arch-primat, or Protestant Pope" (*Works*, III, 212–213).

not take orders? Some of them say they do not know whether they are worthy, some object to the manner in which orders are conferred, some object to the power that confers them as an authority that is unlawful or even anti-Christian.

Now, says Brooke, I do not want to defend all of these individuals, but I do not want to condemn them without a hearing. For after all, one cannot tell where truth will appear:

> These whom they so brand, may maintaine some errors, may not carry on the truth in the glory of it; who is so perfect? but oft-times in the midst of thickest ore we finde the purest gold: discover their errors and reject them; but doe not refuse what is good, because they hold it forth but darkly: no truth can shine in its perfect lustre at the first: light is darknesse when it first appeareth.[50]

In his concluding pages Brooke shows himself a true liberal in his willingness to give at least a trial to what is new. One recalls Bishop Hall's distrust of "noveltie" which all "wise and staid Christians have learned to suspect," [51] against which it is revealing to set this passage from the *Discourse*: ". . . it is a strange thing, men call, men long for new things; and yet if any doe hold forth new and quicke actings of the Spirit, they fall under censure, of those who forget that Text; Judge not, lest ye be Judged." [52] Why, Brooke asks, can we not dissent in judgment without also disagreeing in affection?

> So far as Christ is in us, we shall love, praise, honour Christ, and the least particle of his Image in others: For we never prove ourselves true members of Christ more, than when we embrace his members with most enlarged, yet straitest Affections.[53]

He concludes with the familiar prayer that many Puritans were using in pamphlets and sermons, from Ephesians 3:4, which takes on more profound meaning in the context of Brooke's plea for toleration, "to keepe the Unity of the Spirit in the Bond of Peace."

Brooke's desire for broad toleration was not unique, as Jordan's abundant evidence demonstrates. But Brooke carried his

[50] *Discourse*, p. 115.
[51] Hall, *Episcopacy by Divine Right*, III, p. 36.
[52] *Discourse*, p. 116.
[53] *Discourse*, p. 118.

interpretation of the meaning of toleration further than most of his contemporaries did. Milton, for example, did not go so far toward defending the sects until the *Areopagitica*, and even there, as Barker has explained, his principal purpose was not defense of the sects but of learning and learned men.[54] Milton dealt with the sects at some length, of course, in *The Reason of Church Government*. But he is concerned here with the "meere fictions and false alarmes of the Prelates" [55] in crying down schism, which Milton regards as little more than a smokescreen to obscure their tendencies toward "popery." They strain at the petty gnats of schism while swallowing "the Camel heresie of Rome"; in their unwillingness to permit criticism of prelatical ceremonies and the liturgy ("an extract of the Masse book translated") they point to the comparatively harmless schismatics as menaces to true religion.[56] Some of these modern heresies, given pejorative labels such as Familists and Adamites and so on, are little more than reflections and aspects of the primitive Christianity that the prelates have abjured.[57] And those that are truly heretical and dangerous are useful as trials for godly men, "winds and flaws to try the floting vessell of our faith whether it be stanch and sayl well, whether our ballast be just, our anchorage and cable strong." In fact, continues Milton, anticipating one of the central and most eloquent passages in the *Aeropagitica*, "if there were no opposition where were the triall of an unfained goodnesse and magnanimity? vertue that wavers is not vertue, but vice revolted from itselfe, and after a while returning." [58] But Milton does not go so far as to suggest that the sects are justifiable on the ground that some light shines through their darkness. Brooke's final chapter is, to give it the very least its due, a major step in the evolution of full toleration.

It must of course be admitted that Brooke's position is still short of full toleration. His refusal to condone the first sort of Anabaptist that he mentions is a case in point, and he certainly looked upon the adherents of the Family of Love, the Anti-

---

[54] Barker, p. 80.
[55] "The Reason of Church Government," *Works*, III, 222.
[56] *Works*, III, 215–216.
[57] *Works*, III, 217.
[58] *Works*, III, 222–223.

nomians, and the Grindletonians with alarm.[59] He scarcely exhibited a tolerant restraint in contemplating with satisfaction the
probable fate of the bishops at the hands of an "enlightened, en-
flamed Multitude." [60] If Professor Hughes seems a little harsh
in calling the *Discourse* "a far more intolerant plea for toleration"
than the *Areopagitica,* he is admittedly correct in observing that
if "we are looking for religious toleration as the principle has
been understood for the past century, we cannot stop with Lord
Brooke." [61] It is evident enough, for that matter, that Brooke was
not exactly a tolerant person aside from his religious views as
well as within them. It is not only true that he was no more
tolerant of Roman Catholics than he was of bishops or extreme
Anabaptists; beyond that it is clear that he scarcely held what we
would now call democratic views (assuming democracy as one
of the outgrowths of toleration). His remarks on the low birth of
bishops, his evident consciousness of his own rank,[62] his and
Saye's demands to the settlers in New England concerning the
conditions of their removing thence, might be repellent to a
modern reader who would expect something else of a political
and religious liberal. But Puritanism itself was molded of con-
tradictions, as Tawney once observed:

> There was in Puritanism an element which was conservative and tradi-
> tionalist, and an element which was revolutionary; a collectivism which
> grasped at an iron discipline, and an individualism which spurned the
> savorless mess of human ordinances; a sober prudence which would garner
> the fruits of this world, and a divine recklessness which would make all
> things new.[63]

It would be expecting too much of Brooke, a representative
seventeenth-century Puritan in so many ways, to be more consistent than the circumstances of the time allowed.

The important thing to emphasize is that Brooke's defense of

[59] *Discourse,* p. 90.
[60] *Discourse,* p. 95.
[61] Merritt Y. Hughes, *John Milton: Prose Selections* (New York, 1947), introd.,
pp. lxxii–lxxiii.
[62] It is perhaps revealing that Brooke finds an opportunity to use the Greville-
Warwick family motto, *Vix ea nostra voco,* in support of a point (*Discourse,* p. 5).
For a reproduction of the family standard see Thomas Lant, *Sequitur celebritas
et pompa funeris* (London, 1587), Plate 6 (describing the funeral of Sir Philip
Sidney).
[63] Tawney, *Religion and the Rise of Capitalism,* p. 212.

toleration of the sects, while not as unique an utterance as his reasoning out of the implications of indifferency, is unusually broad. Brooke is a distinguished early member of the liberal wing of Puritanism that was later to be more impressively adorned by Walwyn, Williams, and Milton. He is in the company not only of liberal Puritans but also of the Oxford Latitudinarians, the Jeremy Taylor of *The Liberty of Prophesying,* and the Cambridge Platonists. As one of the voices heard in the land, Brooke can be said to have been partly responsible for the growth of that strong tendency in English thought arising from belief in the integrity of the individual which eased the way toward not only complete religious toleration but the beginnings of the democratic tradition.

CONCLUSION

Although Lord Brooke was certainly not one of the geniuses in a century that produced so many, his life and literary achievements are instructive to the student of the seventeenth century on more than one level. Even though his knowledge is sometimes revealed to be merely the smattering of the virtuoso, sometimes he attains a profundity beyond his years. His versatility is that of the Renaissance gentleman.

One is never permitted to lose sight of his aristocratic upbringing and his distinguished family connections, whether one senses the patrician in the tone of the demands to John Cotton, his arrangements for the rental of the Conway estate, his willingness to assume leadership and financial liability in colonization, his marriage into the prominent family of the Earl of Bedford and the rearing of sons and heirs who were "his own pictures," [1] or the haughty bearing of the portrait at Warwick Castle. As designated successor to the title of one of the most courtly of Elizabethans, Brooke traveled abroad and was educated in universities of preëminent stature on the continent and in England. As was fitting for one of his station and talents he cultivated an interest in the new science and in current literature, and developed a prose style of his own which achieved, even though he occasionally became entangled in his own syntax, a stately and measured dignity.

Nor can one forget that Brooke was imbued with a devout piety, perhaps acquired first at Leyden, surely strengthened in the Cambridge of the 1620's, which led him to become not only a Puritan but one of the leaders among the active reformers in a Parliament dominated by Puritans. He prayed in public, befriended victims of prelatical oppression, championed dissident preachers, and supported schemes to provide a haven abroad for the faithful who were persecuted for their beliefs. His per-

[1] *Englands Losse and Lamentation,* sig. A3.

sonal loyalty to the King was a conviction that he often publicly expressed, but it did not keep him from outspoken resistance to the King's demands when he considered them unjust. When the war came he was vigorous in its prosecution until it took his life, and in his military capacity he could be described, in the words of a modern historian, as having "rivalled Essex in political and social position and surpassed him in military daring." [2]

Brooke's writings reveal a contemplative side to his life as well as an active one. He had acquired a background in classical and Renaissance literature, philosophy, and theology which was not inconsiderable, and his familiarity with current controversies over eschatology and church doctrine and discipline is amply witnessed by the range of his reference. His own publications were more than mere reiteration of well-rehearsed themes and arguments, for he succeeded in advancing seventeenth-century thought in more than one way. His conclusion in *The Nature of Truth* that time and place have existence only in the mind marked, with due regard for the Platonic heritage of the notion, an advance in English philosophy toward idealism; his ideas on toleration, while embodying not yet as liberal a position as the century was to achieve, were enough ahead of his time to arrest the attention of Milton; and his elucidation of indifferency, more searching than any of his contemporaries attempted, placed that complex issue for the first time in a clear perspective, illuminating its relevance to liberty of conscience and the integrity of the individual reason. The importance of Brooke's *Discourse* is heightened by the fact that an understanding of the nature of indifferency goes far toward accounting for the strange shift in the positions of representative Anglicans and Puritans over a period of some fifty or sixty years regarding the settlement of problems of ecclesiastical polity in terms of scriptural authoritarianism or rationalism.

Aside from whatever originality there may be in his contributions to seventeenth-century thought, Brooke is an interesting exemplar of tendencies that have been discerned in others. His philosophy manifests the degree to which the Puritan mind, both in England and in America, was infiltrated with the principles of Platonism and scholasticism, and his thought illustrates pre-

[2] Trevelyan, p. 248.

vailing Puritan modes and patterns that have been brought into perspective by the researches of modern scholars like William Haller and Perry Miller. The interdependence of a broad toleration and a conception of all creation as one divine unity, which is later to be discerned in the writings of the Cambridge Platonists, is sharply delineated in Brooke's ambitious synthesis.

Indeed, one could describe the life and works of Brooke as themselves a synthesis, fusing a many-faceted variety into one consistent pattern. A Puritan, striving to carry out the demands of his calling, both spiritual and temporal, Brooke fulfills the Christian mission as it was envisioned by Milton in the tractate *Of Education*, and as it has been defined by one of the distinguished modern students of the Puritan mind: "It is the first duty of the Christian to know and believe in God. . . The second duty of the Christian is to labor in the affairs of practical life." [3] In pursuit of this calling, Brooke, Puritan and Platonist, thoughtful scholar and Renaissance gentleman, labored in his life and in his writings according to his own lights to reconcile the diversities in English political and religious life and to unify the divisive forces in philosophy that seemed to him to dim the beauty of the radiant vision that always shone before his eyes.

[3] Tawney, p. 240.

APPENDIX

APPENDIX

Genealogical chart as follows, compiled from data in Collins:

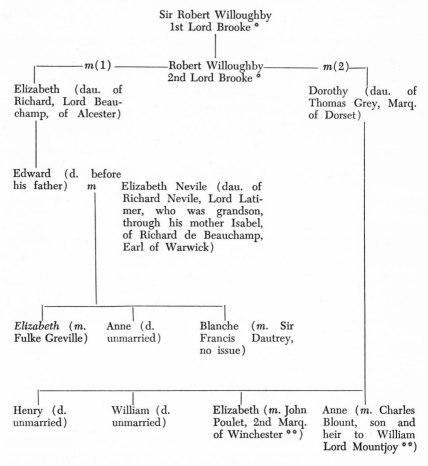

Sir Robert Willoughby
1st Lord Brooke *

————m(1)————Robert Willoughby———— m(2)——
2nd Lord Brooke *

Elizabeth (dau. of
Richard, Lord Beau-
champ, of Alcester)

Dorothy (dau. of
Thomas Grey, Marq.
of Dorset)

Edward (d. before
his father)   *m*   Elizabeth Nevile (dau. of
Richard Nevile, Lord Lati-
mer, who was grandson,
through his mother Isabel,
of Richard de Beauchamp,
Earl of Warwick)

Elizabeth (*m.*
Fulke Greville)

Anne (d.
unmarried)

Blanche (*m.* Sir
Francis Dautrey,
no issue)

Henry (d.
unmarried)

William (d.
unmarried)

Elizabeth (*m.* John
Poulet, 2nd Marq.
of Winchester **)

Anne (*m.* Charles
Blount, son and
heir to William
Lord Mountjoy **)

* The two Lords Brooke of the Willoughby family are not to be confused —
however understandably — with Fulke and Robert, the two Lords Brooke of the
Greville family, whose descent from Elizabeth Willoughby Greville is traced in
the genealogical chart on the following page.

** "The said two noblemen, in right of their wives, after the death of Lord
Brooke, their father, obtained, by order of Henry VIII . . . part of the lands of
this rich family: but the inheritance passed by Edward, his only son, to his three
granddaughters; and he, the said Lord Brooke, died in 1521; leaving them, the
said Elizabeth, Anne, and Blanche, his heirs" (Collins, IV, 340).

Genealogical chart as follows, compiled from data in Collins; Miscellanea Genealogica et Heraldica, ed. A. W. H. Clarke, 5th series, VIII (1932–34), 332 (for "Blaunche ux. Rob. Grevill frater ffulcow," daughter of Robert Whitney of Whitney, Herefordshire, and Sibilla, daughter of James Baskervill); and Lincoln-shire Pedigrees, Harleian Society Publications LI (London, 1903), II, 431, from Harl. MS. 4135 (for baptismal date, December 12, 1575, of Fulke Greville):

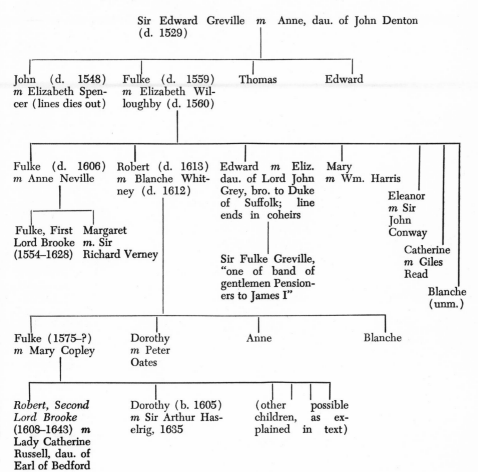

Sir Edward Greville *m* Anne, dau. of John Denton
(d. 1529)

John (d. 1548) *m* Elizabeth Spencer (lines dies out)

Fulke (d. 1559) *m* Elizabeth Willoughby (d. 1560)

Thomas

Edward

Fulke (d. 1606) *m* Anne Neville

Robert (d. 1613) *m* Blanche Whitney (d. 1612)

Edward *m* Eliz. dau. of Lord John Grey, bro. to Duke of Suffolk; line ends in coheirs

Mary *m* Wm. Harris

Eleanor *m* Sir John Conway

Catherine *m* Giles Read

Blanche (unm.)

Fulke, First Lord Brooke (1554–1628)

Margaret *m.* Sir Richard Verney

Sir Fulke Greville, "one of band of gentlemen Pensioners to James I"

Fulke (1575–?) *m* Mary Copley

Dorothy *m* Peter Oates

Anne

Blanche

Robert, Second Lord Brooke (1608–1643) m Lady Catherine Russell, dau. of Earl of Bedford

Dorothy (b. 1605) *m* Sir Arthur Haselrig, 1635

(other possible children, as explained in text)

BIBLIOGRAPHY

The bibliography that follows is a reasonably complete listing of all sources consulted, both primary and secondary, in the preparation of this study. As relatively few of the items included in it have to do directly with Brooke, a prefatory listing toward a Brooke bibliography is in order:

(1) Biographical data:
   (a) The *Dictionary of National Biography* (*DNB*), hitherto the main authoritative source of biographical information.
   (b) Brief notice in various seventeenth-century collections, such as Wood, Baxter, Clarendon, Fuller, Dugdale, several elegies (as noted in the text), and a sketch in Joseph Ricraft, *A Survey of England's Champions* (1647).
   (c) Further notice in subsequent collections, such as: Horace Walpole, *Catalogue of Royal and Noble Authors* (1758); Arthur Collins, *Peerage of England* (1812); John Stoughton, *Spiritual Heroes; or, Sketches of the Puritans* (1848).
   (d) A full but rather uncritical adulatory essay in Frances Evelyn Greville, *Warwick Castle and its Earls* (1903).

(2) Substantial critical comment on *The Nature of Truth*:
   (a) John Wallis, *Truth Tried* (1643).
   (b) Nathanael Culverwel, *A Discourse of the Light of Nature* (1652).
   (c) Charles de Rémusat, *La Philosophie en Angleterre depuis Bacon jusqu'à Locke* (1875).
   (d) J. Freudenthal, "Beiträge zur Geschichte der englischen Philosophie," *Archiv für Geschichte der Philosophie* 6:190–207, 380–399 (1892–93).

(3) Substantial critical comment on the *Discourse*:
   (a) William Haller, ed., *Tracts on Liberty in the Puritan Revolution*, I (1933–34).
   (b) G. W. Whiting, *Milton's Literary Milieu* (1939), superseding Whiting, "Milton and Lord Brooke on the Church," *Modern Language Notes* (*MLN*) 51:161–166 (1936).
   (c) Arthur Barker, *Milton and the Puritan Dilemma* (1942).

(4) Brief critical comment of various kinds:
   (a) W. R. Sorley, *History of English Philosophy* (1920).
   (b) W. K. Jordan, *The Development of Religious Toleration in England*, II (1932–40).
   (c) William Haller, *The Rise of Puritanism* (1938).
   (d) Douglas Bush, *English Literature in the Earlier Seventeenth Century* (1945).

(e) Merritt Hughes, introduction to *John Milton: Prose Selections* (1947).

(f) William Haller, *Liberty and Reformation in the Puritan Revolution* (1955).

(g) Howard Schultz, *Milton and Forbidden Knowledge* (1955).

(5) Editions:

(a) *The Nature of Truth* was issued in only one edition, 1640. There have been no modern editions published, but an edition with extensive annotations may be found in Robert Strider, "Lord Brooke and 'The Nature of Truth'" unpublished Harvard Ph.D. dissertation (1950).

(b) The *Discourse on Episcopacy* appeared in two editions, 1641 and 1642 (the differences between them are noted in n. 1, p. 153, above). A modern facsimile edition with helpful but not extensive annotations appears in William Haller, *Tracts on Liberty in the Puritan Revolution*, II (1933–34).

Primary Sources

Ames, William, *The Marrow of Sacred Divinity* (London, 1638).

An Apologeticall Narration (London, 1645).

Aquinas, Thomas, *Summa theologiae* (Ottawa, 1941).

Aristotle, *De Anima*, tr. W. S. Hett, Loeb Classical Library (London, 1935).

—— *Works*, ed. W. D. Ross (Oxford, 1925–1928).

Articles of Impeachment exhibited in Parliament against Spencer Earle of Northampton, [et al.] (London, 1642).

Augustine, *Confessions*, tr. William Watts, Loeb Classical Library (London, 1931).

Bacon, Francis, *Works*, ed. Spedding, Ellis, and Heath (London, 1862, and Boston, 1860–1863).

Ball, John, *A Treatise of Faith* (London, 1631).

Bastwick, John, *Letany* (London, 1637).

Baxter, Richard, *Reliquiae Baxterianae*, ed. J. M. Lloyd Thomas (London, 1925).

—— *The Saints Everlasting Rest* (London, 1650).

The Bible, Authorized Version.

Bradford, William, *History of the Plymouth Plantation, 1620–1647* (Boston, 1912).

A Briefe Relation of certain Speciall and most Materiall Passages, and speeches in the Starre-Chamber (London, 1637).

Brightman, Thomas, *Works* (London [?], 1644).

Brooke, Robert Greville, Lord, *A Discourse Opening the Nature of that Episcopacie, Which is Exercised in England* (London, 1641); 2nd ed. (London, 1642).

—— *The Nature of Truth* (London, 1640).

Broughton, Hugh, *Works* (London, 1662).

Browne, Sir Thomas, *Works*, ed. Charles Sayle (Edinburgh, 1927).

Burton, Robert, *The Anatomy of Melancholy*, ed. Holbrook Jackson (London, 1932).

Burton, Henry, *The Protestation Protested* (London, 1641).

Calderwood, David, *Altare Damascenum ceu politia ecclesiae* (London [?], 1623).

Calendar of State Papers, Colonial.

Calendar of State Papers, Domestic, Charles I.

Calendar of State Papers, Domestic, James I.

Calvin, John, *Institutes of the Christian Religion*, tr. John Allen (Philadelphia, 1813).

The Cambridge Platonists, ed. E. T. Campagnac (Oxford, 1901).

Camden, William, *Britannia* (London, 1695).

Catalogue of the pamphlets, books, newspapers, and manuscripts relating to the civil war, the commonwealth, and restoration, collected by George Thomason (London, 1908).

Cawdrey, Daniel, *Sabbatum redivivum; or the Christian Sabbath vindicated* (London, 1645).

Certain Briefe Treatises, written by Diverse Learned Men (Oxford, 1641).

Chillingworth, William, *Works* (London, 1820–1838).

Clarendon, Edward Hyde, Earl of, *History of the Rebellion* (Oxford, 1826).

—— *The Life of Edward Earl of Clarendon* (Oxford, 1827).

—— *State Papers* (Oxford, 1767–1786).

Comenius, John Amos, *The Great Didactic*, ed. M. W. Keatinge (London, 1896).

Conway Letters, ed. Marjorie Nicolson (New Haven, 1930).

The Copie of a Letter sent from a special friend in Coventry (London, 1642).

Cotton, John, *The Covenant of Gods Free Grace* (London, 1645).

Culverwel, Nathanael, *A Discourse of the Light of Nature* (London, 1652).

Cusa, Nicholas of, *Opera* (Basle, 1565).

Davies, Sir John, *Nosce Te Ipsum* (London, 1599).

Descartes, René, *Discourse on the Method of Rightly Conducting the Reason* (Chicago, 1927).

D'Ewes, Sir Simonds, *The Journal of Sir Simonds D'Ewes*, ed. Wallace Notestein (New Haven, 1923).

Digby, Lord George, *The Third Speech of the Lord George Digby to the House of Commons, Concerning Bishops* (London, 1641).

Dionysius the Areopagite, *Oeuvres Complètes du Pseudo Denys L'Areopagite*, tr. and ed. Maurice de Gandillac (Paris, 1943).

Donne, John, *Poetical Works*, ed. H. J. C. Grierson (Oxford, 1912).

Dugdale, William, *The Baronage of England* (London, 1675–76).

An Elegie upon the much lamented Death of the Right Honourable the Lord Brooke (London, 1643).

Englands Losse and Lamentation (London, 1643).

Exceeding Joyfull Newes from Warwick-Castle and Banburie (London, 1642).

A Famous Victory obtained by the Right Honorable the Lord Brooks, against the Earle of Northampton, on the third of August, 1642, neere Keintith in Warwick-shire (London, 1642).

Ficino, Marsilio, *Commentary on Plato's Symposium*, tr. Sears Jayne (Columbia, Mo., 1944).

—— *Omnia divini Platonis opera* (Lyons, 1548).

—— *Opera omnia* (Basle, 1576).

Fuller, Thomas, *Church History of Britain*, ed. J. S. Brewer (Oxford, 1845).

Goodwin, John, *Anti-cavalierisme* (London, 1642).

Goodwin, Thomas, *Certain Select Cases Resolved* (London, 1647).

Hakewill, George, *An Apologie or Declaration of the Power and Providence of God*, 2nd ed. (London, 1630).

Hall, Joseph, *A Defence of the Humble Remonstrance, against the frivolous and false exceptions of Smectymnuus* (London, 1641).

—— *Episcopacie by Divine Right Asserted* (London, 1640).

—— *An Humble Remonstrance to the High Court of Parliament* (London, 1641).

—— (?), *A Modest Confutation of a Slanderous and Scurrilous Libell, entituled, Animadversions upon the Remonstrants Defense against Smectymnuus* (London, 1642).

—— *A Short Answer to the Tedious Vindication of Smectymnuus* (London, 1641).

Harington, Henry, *An Elegie upon the Death of the Mirrour of Magnanimity, the right Honourable Robert Lord Brooke* (London, 1643).

Herbert of Cherbury, Lord, *De veritate*, ed. and tr. M. Carré (Bristol, 1937).

Hermetica, ed. Walter Scott (Oxford, 1924).

Heylyn, Peter, *Cyprianus Anglicus* (London, 1668).

His Majesties Proceedings in Northamptonshire (London, 1642).

Historical Manuscripts Commission, 4th to 15th Reports.

Hobbes, Thomas, *Leviathan* (Oxford, 1909).

Hooker, Richard, *The Laws of Ecclesiastical Polity* (London, 1702); and Everyman ed. of first five books (London, 1907).

Horrible Newes from Warwickshire (London, 1642).

Huit, Ephraim, *The Anatomy of Conscience* (London, 1626).

The Humble Petition and Resolution of the Deputy Lieutenants, Captains, Officers, Souldiers and Volunters of the Trained Bands of the County of Warwick (London, 1642).

Journals of the House of Commons.

Journals of the House of Lords.

Lant, Thomas, *Sequitur celebritas et pompa funeris* (London, 1587).

The Last Weeks Proceedings of the Lord Brooke (London, 1643).

Letters of the Lady Brilliana Harley, ed. T. T. Lewis, Camden Society Publications (London, 1854).

Lilburne, John, *The Christian Mans Triall* (London, 1638).

—— *A Worke of the Beast* (London, 1638).

The Manner and Good Successe of the Lord Brookes Forces in pursuing the Cavaliers from Coventry (London, 1642).

Mede, Joseph, *Clavis Apocalyptica*, (London[?], 1632).

Milton, John, *Works*, Columbia ed. (New York, 1931 and ff.).

Plato, *Dialogues*, tr. Benjamin Jowett (New York, 1937).

Plotinus, *Complete Works*, tr. K. S. Guthrie (London, 1918).

Primaudaye, Pierre de la, *The French Academie* (London, 1602).

The Proceedings at Banbury since the Ordnance went down for the Lord Brooke to fortifie Warwick Castle (London, 1642).

Propositions from the Kings most Excellent Majesty . . . To the Lo: Brooks, and the Gentry and Commonalty assembled at Warwick (London, 1642).

Prynne, William, *The Antipathie of the English Lordly Prelacie* (London, 1641).

—— *A Breviate of the Prelates intolerable usurpations* (Amsterdam, 1637).

—— *A looking glasse for all lordly prelates* (London, 1636).

—— *A New Discovery of the Prelates Tyranny* (London, 1641).

—— *A Terrible Outcry against the loytering exalted Prelates* (London, 1641).

—— *The Unbishoping of Timothy and Titus* (London, 1636).

Ricraft, Joseph, *A Survey of Englands Champions* (London, 1647).

Robinson, John, *Works*, ed. Robert Ashton (London, 1851).

Rushworth, John, *Historical Collections* (London, 1703).

Rymer, Thomas, *Foedera* (London, 1735).

"S. P. of Cambridge," "A Brief Account of the New Sect of Latitude-Men," *The Phenix* 2:499–518 (1707–08).

Selections from Medieval Philosophers, ed. Richard McKeon (New York, 1930).

The Severall Humble Petitions of D. Bastwicke, M. Burton, M. Prynne, and of Nath. Wickins, Servant to the said Mr. Prynne (London, 1641).

Smectymnuus, *An Answer to a Booke entituled, An Humble Remonstrance* (London, 1641).

—— *A Vindication of the Answer to the Humble Remonstrance* (London, 1641).

Some Speciall Passages from Warwickshire concerning the proceedings of Lord Brooke (London, 1642).

Suckling, Sir John, *Aglaura* (1638).

A Survay of that Foolish, Seditious, Scandalous, Prophane Libell, the Pro-testation Protested [attributed to Joseph Hall, but unlikely that he wrote it] (London, 1641).

Taylor, Jeremy, *Works* (London, 1847–1854).

Thorius, Raphael, *Hymnus Tabaci*, (Leyden[?], 1625).

Three Speeches Spoken in Guild-Hall, Concerning His Majesties refusall of a Treaty of Peace, and what is to be done thereupon, two by Lord Brooke, and one by Sir Henry Vane (London, 1642).

Tracts on Liberty in the Puritan Revolution, II–III, ed. William Haller (New York, 1933–34).

A True and Exact Relation of the present estate of the City of Norwich (London, 1642).

True and New Newes with an example from Warwick Castle (London, 1642).

A True and Perfect Relation of the First and victorious Skirmish between the Army under the conduct of Lord Brooks . . . and the Army under the command of the Earle of Northampton (London, 1642).

A True Relation of the Lord Brooke's setling of the Militia in Warwickshire (London, 1642).

A True Relation of the manner of taking of the Earl of Northampton (London, 1642).

Twisse, William, *The Doctrine of the Synod of Dort and Arles reduced to the Practice* (Oxford[?], 1651).

Two Speeches Made in the House of Peers, on Munday the 19 of December, For, and Against Accommodation. The One by the Earl of Pembroke, the other by the Lord Brooke [actually composed by Clarendon] (London, 1642).

Ussher, James, *The Iudgement of Doctor Rainoldes touching the Originall of Episcopacy* (London, 1641).

Wallis, John, *A Defence of the Royal Society* (London, 1678).

—— "Dr. Wallis's Account of Some Passages of his own Life," *Peter Langtoft's Chronicle,* ed. Thomas Hearne (Oxford, 1725).

—— *Truth Tried* (London, 1643).

Walwyn, William, *The Power of Love* (London, 1643).

Whitgift, John, *Works* (Cambridge, 1851).

Williams, Roger, *The Bloudy Tenent of Persecution* (London, 1644).

Winthrop, John, *History of New England from 1630 to 1649* (Boston, 1853).

Wood, Anthony, *Athenae Oxonienses,* ed. Philip Bliss (London, 1815).

A Worthy Speech made by the Right Honourable the Lord Brooke, at the election of his Captaines and Commanders at Warwick Castle (London, 1643).

Secondary Sources

Anderson, F. H., *The Philosophy of Francis Bacon* (Chicago, 1948).

Barker, Arthur, *Milton and the Puritan Dilemma* (Toronto, 1942).

Batten, J. Minton, *John Dury, Advocate of Christian Reunion* (Chicago, 1944).

Beesley, Alfred, *History of Banbury* (London, 1841).

Brown, B. Katherine, "A Note on the Puritan Concept of Aristocracy," *Mississippi Valley Historical Review* 41: 105–112 (1954–55).

Buckle, H. T., *History of Civilization in England* (London, 1885).

Bullough, G., "Fulk Greville, First Lord Brooke," *Modern Language Review (MLR)* 28: 1–37 (1933).

Burtt, E. A., *The Metaphysical Foundations of Modern Physical Science* (London, 1925).

Bush, Douglas, *English Literature in the Earlier Seventeenth Century* (Oxford, 1945).

—— *The Renaissance and English Humanism* (Toronto, 1939).

Cassirer, Ernst, *Die Platonische Renaissance in England und die Schule von Cambridge* (Leipzig, 1932).

—— *Individuum und Kosmos in der Philosophie der Renaissance* (Leipzig, 1927).

——, Paul O. Kristeller and J. H. Randall, *The Renaissance Philosophy of Man* (Chicago, 1948).

Clark, G. N., *The Seventeenth Century* (Oxford, 1931).

Cokayne, G. E., *Complete Peerage* (London, 1887).

Coke, Dorothea, *The Last Elizabethan: Sir John Coke* (London, 1937).

Collins, Arthur, *Peerage of England* (London, 1812).

The Court and Times of Charles I, ed. Thomas Birch (London, 1848).

Craig, Hardin, *The Enchanted Glass* (New York, 1936).

Darby, H. C., *The Draining of the Fens* (Cambridge, 1940).

Dawley, Powel M., *John Whitgift and the English Reformation* (New York, 1954).

Dictionary of National Biography (Oxford, 1917 and ff.).

Dyer, George, *History of the University and Colleges of Cambridge* (London, 1914).

Ecclesiae Londino-Batavae archivum (Cambridge, 1897).

Elson, James H., *John Hales of Eton* (New York, 1948).

Firth, C. H., *The House of Lords During the Civil War* (London, 1910).

Frank, Joseph, *The Levellers* (Cambridge, Mass., 1955).

Freudenthal, J., "Beiträge zur Geschichte der englischen Philosophie," *Archiv für Geschichte der Philosophie* 6: 190–207, 380–399 (1892–93).

Gardiner, S. R., *Constitutional Documents of the Puritan Revolution, 1625–1660* (Oxford, 1899).

—— *History of England from the Accession of James I to the Out-break of the Civil War, 1603–1642* (London, 1883–84).

—— *History of the Great Civil War, 1642–1649* (London, 1886–91).

Gray, Arthur, *Jesus College* (London, 1902).

Greville, Frances Evelyn, Countess of Warwick, *Warwick Castle and its Earls* (London, 1903).

Grierson, H. J. C., *Cross Currents in English Literature of the XVII Century* (London, 1929).

Haller, William, *Liberty and Reformation in the Puritan Revolution* (New York, 1955).

—— *The Rise of Puritanism* (New York, 1938).

—— *Tracts on Liberty in the Puritan Revolution*, I (New York, 1933–34).

Hexter, J. H., *The Reign of King Pym* (Cambridge, Mass., 1941).

Houghton, Walter E., "The English Virtuoso in the Seventeenth Century," *Journal of the History of Ideas* 3: 51–73, 190–219 (1942).

Hughes, Merritt Y., introduction to *John Milton: Prose Selections* (New York, 1947).

Hutchinson, Thomas, *History of Massachusetts Bay*, ed. Lawrence Mayo (Cambridge, Mass., 1936).

Inge, W. R., *The Philosophy of Plotinus* (London, 1929).

—— *The Platonic Tradition in English Religious Thought* (New York, 1926).

Jacquot, Jean, "Acontius and the Progress of Tolerance in England," *Bibliothèque d'Humanisme et Renaissance* 16:192–206 (1954).

Johnson, Francis R., *Astronomical Thought in Renaissance England* (Baltimore, 1937).

—— "Gresham College: Precursor of the Royal Society," *Journal of the History of Ideas* 1:413–438 (1940).

Jordan, Wilbur K., *The Development of Religious Toleration in England* (Cambridge, Mass., 1932–40).

Kelley, Maurice, *This Great Argument* (Princeton, 1941).

Kristeller, Paul O., *The Philosophy of Marsilio Ficino*, tr. Virginia Conant (New York, 1943).

Le Neve, John, and T. Duffus Hardy, *Fasti Ecclesiae Anglicanae* (Oxford, 1854).

Lincolnshire Notes and Queries, VIII (1904–05).

Lincolnshire Pedigrees, Harleian Society Publications LI (London, 1903).

Lovejoy, A. O., *The Great Chain of Being* (Cambridge, Mass., 1942).

Massachusetts Historical Society Collections, 5th series, I (1871).

Miller, Perry, *The New England Mind* (New York, 1939).

Miscellanea genealogica et heraldica, ed. A. W. H. Clarke, 5th series, VIII (1932–34).

Mullinger, J. B., *The University of Cambridge* (Cambridge, 1873–1911).

Neal, Daniel, *History of the Puritans* (New York, 1844).

Newton, Arthur P., *The Colonising Activities of the English Puritans* (New Haven, 1914).

Nicolson, Marjorie, "Milton's 'Old Damoetas,'" *MLN* 41:293–300 (1926).

Notes on the Treaty of Ripon, Camden Society Publications (London, 1869).

Parker, William R., *Milton's Contemporary Reputation* (Columbus, 1940).

Peacock, Edward, *Index to English Speaking Students who have graduated at Leyden University* (London, 1883).

Pearson, A. F. S., *Thomas Cartwright and Elizabethan Puritanism* (Cambridge, 1925).

Perry, Ralph Barton, *Puritanism and Democracy* (New York, 1944).

Pinto, V. de Sola, *Peter Sterry, Platonist and Puritan* (Cambridge, 1934).

Powicke, F. J., *The Cambridge Platonists* (Cambridge, Mass., 1926).

Ramsay, M. P., *Les Doctrines Médiévales chez Donne* (Paris, 1917).

Randall, J. H., Jr., *The Making of the Modern Mind* (Boston, 1940).

Rémusat, Charles de, *La Philosophie en Angleterre depuis Bacon jusqu'à Locke* (Paris, 1875).

Schultz, Howard, *Milton and Forbidden Knowledge* (New York, 1955).

Scott, Sir Walter, *Works* (New York, 1833).

Soermans, Martinus, *Academisch Register* (Leyden, 1704).

Sorley, W. R., *History of English Philosophy* (London, 1920).

Spencer, Theodore, *Shakespeare and the Nature of Man* (New York, 1942).

Stimson, Dorothy, "Amateurs of Science in Seventeenth Century England," *Isis* 31:32–47 (1939).

——— "Comenius and the Invisible College," *Isis* 23:373–388 (1935).

——— *Scientists and Amateurs* (New York, 1948).

Stoughton, John, *Spiritual Heroes: or, Sketches of the Puritans* (New York, 1848).

Syfret, R. H., "The Origins of the Royal Society," *Notes and Records of the Royal Society of London* 5:75–137 (1948).

Tawney, R. H., *Religion and the Rise of Capitalism* (New York, 1926).

Taylor, A. E., *Plato, The Man and His Work* (New York, 1936).

Thompson, E. N. S., "Richard Hooker Among the Controversialists," *Philological Quarterly (PQ)* 20:454–464 (1941).

Trevelyan, G. M., *England under the Stuarts* (London, 1926).

Trumbull, Benjamin, *A Complete History of Connecticut* (New Haven, 1818).

Tulloch, John, *Rational Theology and Christian Philosophy in the Seventeenth Century* (Edinburgh, 1872).

Turnbull, G. H., *Samuel Hartlib, a Sketch of his Life and his Relations to J. A. Comenius* (Oxford, 1920).

Ueberweg, Friedrich, *History of Philosophy*, tr. G. S. Morris (New York, 1871).

Venn, J. and J. A., *Alumni Cantabrigienses* (Cambridge, 1922).

Walpole, Horace, *Letters*, ed. Mrs. Paget Toynbee (Oxford, 1903).

—— *Works* (London, 1798).

Weber, Kurt, *Lucius Cary, Second Viscount Falkland* (New York, 1940).

Whiting, G. W., "Milton and Lord Brooke on the Church," *MLN* 51:161–166 (1936).

—— *Milton's Literary Milieu* (Chapel Hill, 1939).

Willan, T. S., *River Navigation in England, 1600–1750* (Oxford, 1936).

Willey, Basil, *The Seventeenth Century Background* (London, 1934).

Wolfe, Don M., *Milton in the Puritan Revolution* (New York, 1941).

Woodhouse, A. S. P., *Puritanism and Liberty* (London, 1938).

Young, R. F., *Comenius in England* (Oxford, 1932).

INDEX

Acontius, Jacobus, 224
Alsted, J. H., 85, 114
Ambrose, 185
Ames, William, 84, 93n, 112n, 118, 121, 184, 224n
Anaxagoras, 98
Andrewes, Lancelot, 201n
Anselm, 114n
Aquinas, Thomas, 84, 112, 113, 114n, 146n
Ariosto, Lodovico, 204n
Aristotle, 84, 86, 91n, 97, 111–113, 119, 127, 146n, 170
Arius, 184, 185, 186, 200
Arminius, Jacobus, 7, 116, 179n
Augustine, 84, 94, 97, 108–110, 118, 183

Bacon, Sir Francis, 8, 9, 16, 17, 81, 83–85, 94n, 95, 121, 122, 128–130, 135, 145, 147, 198n
Ball, John, 116
Bancroft, Richard, Archbishop, 177
Barber, Gabriel, 18
Barclay, John, 85, 98
Bastwick, John, 28, 149, 179–181, 188
Bath, Earl of, 39
Baxter, Richard, 48, 76
Bedford, Earl of, 11, 17, 35, 59, 136n, 231
Bell, Philip, 18
Bellarmine, Robert, Cardinal, 98
Beza, Theodore de, 183, 195n
Boyle, Robert, 81
Brereton, Sir William, 67
Brerewood, Edward, 202n
Brightman, Thomas, 92, 117
Brinckley, Daniel, 10
Bristol, George Digby, Earl of, 77, 182n, 205n, 207n
Brooke, Catherine Russell, Lady, 11, 76–77
Brooke, Fulke Greville, 1st Lord, 4–5, 9–10, 14, 54, 65n, 237
Brooke, Robert Greville, 2nd Lord, ancestry, 1–6, 236–237; education, 6–9; advancement to peerage, 9–10; marriage, 11; support of church uni-

fication, 14–15, 17; efforts at colonization, 17–27; nonmilitary resistance to the King, 28–41; *The Nature of Truth*, 34–35, 81–148; *A Discourse on Episcopacy*, 39–41, 149–230; struggle for the militia and armaments, 43–56; early Civil War encounters, 57–60; Guildhall speeches, 60–62; Clarendon's practical joke, 63–66; the "Worthy Speech" to his troops, 68–69; death at Lichfield, 70–76
Broughton, Hugh, 84
Browne, Sir Thomas, 35, 83, 87, 130–131, 135, 145, 147
Bucer, Martin, 158, 183n, 201n
Buckingham, Duke of, 177–178, 179n
Bunyan, John, 162
Burton, Henry, 28, 179–181, 188
Burton, Robert, 83, 146n
Butler, Samuel, 117
Butts, Henry, 14

Calamy, Edmund, 191n (*see* Smectymnuus)
Calderwood, David, 184n
Calvin, John, 93, 116, 117n, 118, 179n, 183, 195n
Cambridge Platonists, 87, 135–147, 156, 173, 174, 223, 230, 233
Cambridge University, 5, 7–9, 12–14, 165–166, 169, 231
Cartwright, Thomas, 151, 165–169, 170, 172–174, 176, 179, 184, 196, 209, 211n, 213, 218, 221, 222
Casaubon, Isaac, 183n
Cawdrey, Daniel, 35n
Chaderton, William, 165n
Charles I, 19–20, 28–30, 32–33, 36–40, 42–48, 52–53, 55–56, 59, 61–63, 65, 69, 72, 78, 177–179, 188
Charlton, Stephen, 60
Chaucer, Geoffrey, 163
Chesterfield, 1st Earl of, 70
Chillingworth, William, 28, 221
Cicero, 119, 214
Clarendon, Edward Hyde, Earl of, 43, 64–66, 71, 78–79
Clarke, Samuel, 115